THE
MILITARY
SCIENCE
OF
STAR
WARS

GEORGE BEAHM

THE MILITARY SCIENCE

OF

STAR WARS

A TOM DOHERTY ASSOCIATES BOOK · NEW YORK

THE MILITARY SCIENCE OF STAR WARS

Copyright © 2018 by George Beahm

A Tor Book
Published by Tom Doherty Associates
175 Fifth Avenue
New York, NY 10010

www.tor-forge.com

Tor® is a registered trademark of Macmillan Publishing Group, LLC.

The Library of Congress Cataloging-in-Publication Data
is available upon request.

ISBN 978-1-250-12474-6 (hardcover)
ISBN 978-1-250-12475-3 (ebook)

Our books may be purchased in bulk for promotional, educational, or business use. Please contact your local bookseller or the Macmillan Corporate and Premium Sales Department at 1-800-221-7945, extension 5442, or by email at MacmillanSpecialMarkets@macmillan.com.

First Edition: May 2018

Printed in the United States of America

0 9 8 7 6 5 4 3 2 1

For Jay Edwards,
a former Marine who proudly served in Iraq,
in the 4th Amphibious Assault Battalion, Company A.
Semper fidelis.

CONTENTS

A Note to the Reader   19

PREFACE

May the Military Force Be with You   21

     Why Is Military Verisimilitude Important?

     My Perspective

     A Great Adventure Takes Place

INTRODUCTION

The Starstruck Vision of George Lucas's *Star Wars*:

     A Long Time Ago   30

PART I
Personnel

COMMAND CLIMATE: LEADERSHIP IN

     THE GALACTIC EMPIRE   37

     A Perspective on Leadership

     An Outstanding Commander

     An Incompetent Commander

     Morale

     Kylo Ren

     Fear Trumps All: Desperate Despots

ADMIRAL PIETT ON THE BRIDGE OF THE *EXECUTOR*   42

     Tactical Considerations

     Conclusion

ALL-IN: COMBATING STEREOTYPES ABOUT
WOMEN IN WAR 47

JYN ERSO, REBEL WITH A CAUSE: A STUDY IN LEADERSHIP 50
 Background
 Jyn Erso's Leadership Traits
 U.S. Army Rangers

THE RIGHT STUFF: WOMEN IN COMBAT ROLES 55
 Rey: Scavenger and Star Pilot
 The View from the Cockpit
 Female Fighter Pilots
 Infantry
 Infantry Officers
 Today's Female Infantry Officer
 The Rocky Road Ahead for Women
 The Path Is Long and Hard

U.S. ARMY BATTLEDRESS: WHAT TO WEAR IN COMBAT 65
 Stormtroopers
 Stormtrooper Uniform Design
 Tactical Assault Light Operator Suit

THE DANGER OF OVERCONFIDENCE: THE GALACTIC
EMPIRE'S LEADERSHIP 74

GENERAL STANDARDS: DOES JAR JAR BINKS HAVE THE
RIGHT STUFF? 76
 Jar Jar Binks
 General Ingredients
 Bombad General Jar Jar Binks

SO YOU WANT TO BE AN ARMY OFFICER: PATHWAYS TO
A COMMISSION 82

FROM SMUGGLER TO GENERAL: HAN SOLO 85
 Six Traits of Top Military Officers
 May the Force Be with Han Solo

A RISING STAR—FROM PRINCESS TO GENERAL:
CARRIE FISHER'S LEIA ORGANA 97

FROM FARM BOY TO JEDI KNIGHT:
LUKE SKYWALKER 101

PART 2
Weapons

FROM FLINTLOCK TO BLASTERS AND BEYOND: SMALL
ARMS AND ASSAULT RIFLES 109
    A Call to Arms: From Yesterday . . .
    To Today . . . U.S. Army Handguns
    And Tomorrow . . . Blasters
    And Beyond Blasters

WHEN EAST MEETS WEST: THE JEDI KNIGHT 114

THE FLOWER THAT SHATTERS THE STONE 116
    Lightsaber Advantages
    Blast It: Lightsaber Limitations
    The Force
    The Lightsaber
    Science Fiction
    The Way of the Honorable Warrior
    The Katana Sword
    Kendo: The Way of the Sword
    Jedi Knight

SIZE MATTERS NOT: THE AT-AT 126
    Shock and Awe, Historically
    AT-AT Drawbacks
    Assessment

THE DEATH STAR 131
    Today's Superweapons: Bigger Is Better
    The Aircraft Carrier

Death Star
The Element of Surprise
The Death Star's Fatal Flaw

REDESIGNING THE TIE FIGHTER   138
TIE Fighter Capabilities
TIE Pilot Discomfort
Today's Life-Support Systems

A MISFIRE: THE IMPERIAL ARMY'S HOWITZERS   144
Towed M777 Howitzer
Self-Propelled M109A6 Paladin
Imperial Artillery
The Bottom Line

RETHINKING THE X-WING STARFIGHTER   151
Potential Crew Problems: Inexperienced Pilots
Real World

NO PAIN, NO GAIN: TORTURE   155
A Torturous Past
Truth Serum
Psychological Means
The Atomic Bomb
Torturous Information

THE WAR OF THE MACHINES   160
Lucasfilm Research Library
Droids
U.S. Air Force Pilot
Battle Droid

PART 3
Technology

BATTLEDRESS FOR SUCCESS: DRESSED TO KILL   169
Dressing a Galaxy
Lord Vader

Dressing Darth
Stormtrooper

ARTIFICIAL INTELLIGENCE: THE DROIDS WE'RE
LOOKING FOR   174
 United States Military
 The Sticking Point
 Three Laws of Robotics

THE UNITED STATES HAS DEATH STARS   179

FLY THE UNFRIENDLY SKIES: THE FIGHTER PILOT'S VIEW
FROM THE COCKPIT   182
 Incentive Flights
 Fly the Friendly Skies
 Disney

LUKE'S A SKYWALKER: FROM FIGHTER PILOT TO ASTRONAUT   189
 T-16 Skyhopper
 Today's Pilots
 Rocket Man

PICTURE THIS: HOLOGRAMS AND VIRTUAL REALITY ON
THE BATTLEFIELD   197
 We've Come a Long Way
 Holograms in *Star Wars*
 So, What's a Hologram?

PART 4
Tactics and Strategy

FOLLOWING ORDERS: LUKE SKYWALKER, HIS TARGETING
COMPUTER, AND THE FORCE   207
 The Mission
 The Military Dilemma
 Pros and Cons
 Deviating from Orders
 The Decision

ONLY ONE DEAD EWOK   211
    George Lucas Feels a Draft Coming
    Ewoks

THE FINAL SOLUTION: KILL THEM ALL   218

DEATH STAR II   221
    HIJMS *Yamato*
    The Second Death Star
    Leadership Failures
    The Vietnam War

THE IMPORTANCE OF STANDARD OPERATING
   PROCEDURES   227
    For Want of a Nail
    SOP: Standard Operating Procedure

PART 5
Lessons Learned from Key Battles

THE GROUND BATTLE OF NABOO
Reference: *Star Wars I: The Phantom Menace*   237
    Lessons Learned: Gungan Defense
    Lessons Learned: Galactic Empire

THE BATTLE OF YAVIN
Reference: *Star Wars IV: A New Hope*   242
    Death Star 1
    A Superweapon
    The Manhattan Project
    The Death Star as a Superweapon
    Deploy as a Battle Group
    Defense in Depth
    War-Gaming

THE GROUND BATTLE OF HOTH
Reference: *Star Wars V: The Empire Strikes Back*   253

THE BATTLE OF ENDOR
Reference: *Star Wars VI: Return of the Jedi*   256
   Summary
   Strategic Mistakes

A SKIRMISH ON JEDHA
Reference: *Rogue One: A Star Wars Story*   260

BASIC BATTLE ANALYSIS   265
   Study Guide for Battle Analysis
   Annotated Basic Battle Analysis Methodology
   Suggested Format for Basic Battle Analysis Paper or Briefing

CODA: "WE HAVE HOPE."   272

AFTERWORD
It All Started with a Droid: The Film Future of *Star Wars*   275

PART 6
Resources

BIBLIOGRAPHY   283
   Official *Star Wars* Books
   Unofficial Books About George Lucas and *Star Wars*
   Military Books of Interest

MISCELLANEOUS *STAR WARS* RESOURCES   303

LIST OF OPERATIONAL TERMS   306

About the Author   316

The nature of battle has changed so much, yet the nature of man has altered so little.

—Lieutenant General Daniel P. Bolger, U.S. Army

THE
MILITARY
SCIENCE
OF
STAR
WARS

A NOTE TO THE READER

The officially published books covering the *Star Wars* universe are necessarily general in nature. Written by pop culture writers, these books understandably lack the technical expertise that specialists in their respective fields can bring to bear in any discussion. Thus, there is a growing body of unofficial books written by specialists—philosophers, English professors, scientists, and, with this book, a military officer—that add unique insights about the *Star Wars* universe.

As a *Star Wars* fan who owns dozens of books published about the *Star Wars* universe and who happens to be a former major in the U.S. Army's Field Artillery, I see the military aspects of *Star Wars* in a way that a civilian unschooled in the operational arts cannot. I see how to plan, fight, and, afterward, critique battles with a critical eye and to apply those strategic and tactical lessons learned to future combat operations.

In other words, the civilians who have written official books have compiled useful encyclopedic texts and plot summaries, but for lack of specialized knowledge, they have generally been short on analysis.

For those reasons, I am not repeating what the official writers have covered. (Military personnel prefer not to retake the same ground twice.) I assume you are sufficiently familiar with the *Star Wars* movies that I need not cover well-trodden ground. Instead, my transformational use of subject matter from the *Star Wars* universe covers what the generalists hired to write the official books do not offer: analysis, speculation, and recommendations as they pertain to the operational arts. In other words, my seasoned views are candid and critical analyses.

The official writers chronicling the *Star Wars* universe have an important role to play—and so do unofficial writers, who bring fresh, new perspectives to the ongoing exploration of the *Star Wars* universe. Together, all of our books give a rounded and more comprehensive understanding of a fictional world created by filmmaker George Lucas, which has amused, enlightened, and most of all, entertained us since 1977.

Preface

May the Military Force Be with You

> War is a matter of vital importance to the State, the province of
> life and death, the road to survival or ruin. It is therefore manda-
> tory that it be thoroughly studied.
>
> —Sun Tzu, *The Art of War*

I'm in a classroom at Fort Sill, Oklahoma, the home of the U.S.
Army Field Artillery School, with more than one hundred other
men in their midtwenties, mostly from the U.S. Army but also from
allied forces. We are all senior first lieutenants or captains attending
the Field Artillery Officer Advanced Course. The class is Tactics
and Combined Arms Doctrine. The topic under discussion is a military scenario for which there is no definitive answer; its purpose is
to engage our thinking in terms of military doctrine and tactics.
How we arrive at our conclusions is more important than the answer itself, which we share aloud, after which we must vigorously
defend our viewpoint.

This is the tactical situation: You are the commander of a field
artillery battery which has six guns, in direct support of the infantry. Your unit is taking counterbattery fire from incoming artillery. It
also is obvious that your ability to support the infantry unit is rapidly
degrading. Soon, your firing battery will be combat-ineffective and
unable to continue its fire missions because of casualties. Meanwhile,
the infantry unit is making frantic radio calls for immediate return
fire because they're under heavy fire from the enemy, and they're
taking casualties.

As the battery commander, *what is your next order?**

So, you ask, what does this have to do with *Star Wars*?

In a word: everything. First and foremost, as is implicit in the title itself, *Star Wars* is about war; specifically, its basis is military science, defined as:

> a systematized body of knowledge regarding and relating to the theory, application, and employment of military units and weapons in land warfare (i.e., the conduct of war on land) and armed conflict encompassing issues related to the following areas: military leadership; military organization; military training and education; military history; military ethics; military doctrine; military tactics, operations, and strategy; military geography; and military technology and equipment.†

To understand and fully appreciate the *Star Wars* movies, and indeed the ever-expanding *Star Wars* universe, one must have a basic knowledge of the military science that supports it. Armed conflict is at the heart of *Star Wars*, an intergalactic battle that encompasses galaxies. It also explains why director J. J. Abrams hired an ex–British Army noncommissioned officer (NCO) to serve as the military advisor for *Star Wars VII: The Force Awakens*, because movies must have military verisimilitude.

To adequately cover the subject of military science, it took G. Kurt Piehler, editor of *Encyclopedia of Military Science* ($655 retail), a staggering 1,928 pages, divided into four major volumes. Obviously, a thorough discussion of *Star Wars* and its relevance to military science would also run many thousands of pages, which exceeds the scope of this book.

Consider this book a military primer for the *Star Wars* universe—

---

* *Star Trek* fans will recognize this from the Kobayashi Maru simulation (*Star Trek II: The Wrath of Khan*), for which there is no right or wrong answer. Its purpose is to challenge Starfleet Academy cadets, acting as captains of a starship, to make a timely decision under duress, to reveal character.
† G. Kurt Piehler, ed., *Encyclopedia of Military Science* (Sage Reference, 2013).

Military Science 101—an initial foray into a much larger discussion that is as limitless as its expanding universe.*

The purpose of this book is to explore multiple facets of the *Star Wars* universe as viewed, so to speak, through a pair of military binoculars.

This book was written specifically for the lay reader, the millions of fans who have eagerly snapped up the *Star Wars* reference volumes of pseudo history, art books, comic books, and other printed resources that have contributed to the growing body of knowledge about "a long time ago in a galaxy far, far away," when a great adventure took place, as George Lucas told us in the crawl that precedes the original 1977 movie titled *Star Wars* (later retitled *Star Wars IV: A New Hope*).†

My approach, drawing broadly on military science as a whole, is to make the subject accessible and interesting. This book is not a dry recitation of facts but a thought-provoking and deliberately controversial discussion of the various aspects of military science in the *Star Wars* movies.‡

Unlike a Tom Clancy novel that requires a detailed glossary to understand the military abbreviations and terms, this book is deliberately written to be as accessible as possible to the greatest number of readers, including *Star Wars* fans, students of military history, and lay readers who want to dig a little deeper into the military aspects of the film saga.§

Why Is Military Verisimilitude Important?

Star Wars is obviously a space fantasy. Unlike Stanley Kubrick's *2001: A Space Odyssey*, which takes a rigorous approach to science,

* *Star Wars* historians call *Star Wars* an "expanded universe," a term first used by science fiction writer Robert A. Heinlein, which has now become part of the science fiction lexicon.
† To minimize confusion in this book, *Star Wars* refers to the entire fictional universe, unless it's specifically cited as the title to the original movie; in referring to the movie, I typically use the revised title, *A New Hope*. In any case, contextual use should make my references clear.
‡ The *Star Wars* universe is so large that I've largely restricted this book's discussion to what we've seen in the movies.
§ This book covers *Star Wars* through *Rogue One* (2016).

Star Wars does not. For instance, when twin ion engine (TIE) fighters streak across the screen in *Star Wars*, they roar past as if flying in atmosphere, though they are flying in the soundless vacuum of space.

As moviegoers, we willingly suspend our disbelief because we are caught up in the moment, in its storytelling and visual spectacles. Lucas's imaginative worlds are filled with fantastic creatures, exotic places, and mind-boggling technological hardware. We readily accept *all* of that because the computer-generated images look so utterly convincing. But the military science cannot be so easily dismissed.

In other words, when we watch the technologically inferior Ewoks triumph over a garrison of Emperor Palpatine's "best" troops (as he terms them), in *Return of the Jedi*, we all know, deep down, that the Ewoks don't stand a chance; they'd simply be slaughtered. (If George R. R. Martin, author/creator of HBO's *Game of Thrones*, had written the movie, there'd be hundreds of dead Ewoks littering the forest ground, along with members of Han Solo's strike team. That's what war is really like—not just one dead Ewok.)

But when the violent aspects of war are sanitized, the movie becomes less credible, and eventually it becomes a cartoon. As a result, we shake our heads in disbelief because it lacks verisimilitude; in this case, the appearance of military reality.

It reminds me of what Lucasfilm president Kathleen Kennedy observed about Michael Crichton's films:

Michael brought credibility to incredible subject matter. He was a master builder of a scientific logic to keep the science fiction grounded so it could be believed by people all over the world. And I had not met anybody who had ever done that before. And he did it over and over again in a lot of films and books. *I've always believed that the more incredible your stories, the more credible the science has to be* (italics added).*

---

* Sam Kashner, "The Hit Man," *Vanity Fair*, February 2017.

Of course, in the *Star Wars* movies, above all else, the military science must serve the story. For instance, in *Return of the Jedi* and, later, in *The Phantom Menace*, the military science is not rigorous. The result is that those movies pale in military contrast to *Rogue One*, where we are emotionally involved because the risks taken by the rogue warriors are realistic, and so are their fates.

My Perspective

Obviously, what you get out of the military science in any movie depends on your own perspective. If you have never served in the military, your viewpoint is markedly different from mine, because I lived it. I see it through the lens of my experiences in the U.S. Army— on extended active duty, in the National Guard, and in the Army Reserve. (Similarly, an air force officer, who is more accustomed to seeing combat from a bird's-eye view, would likely be more attuned to the air battles.)

Creator George Lucas famously said of the original *Star Wars*, "It's just a movie."* But it went on to become a phenomenon that took on a life of its own and grew exponentially.

To its credit, Lucasfilm encourages fan celebration of all things *Star Wars*. As Mary Franklin, its former Lucasfilm's senior events and fan relations lead pointed out, "One of the things that we love seeing here—and we see it here every day at Lucasfilm—is fan creativity."

From cosplaying to producing their own films, *Star Wars* fans have explored every conceivable nook and cranny of the *Star Wars* universe, from multiple perspectives. This book is my contribution to the constantly expanding field of fan contributions to the *Star Wars* universe.

---

* Lucas, in an interview with the *Hollywood Reporter* (Alex Ben Block, "5 Questions With George Lucas," February 9, 2012), said, "Well, it's not a religious event. I hate to tell people that. It's a movie, just a movie."

A Great Adventure Takes Place

Here's a little-known fact: the movie originally titled *Star Wars* (May 1977) initially opened in thirty-two theaters in America. Lucas had no great expectations for it because, as a rule, science fiction movies performed decently but not spectacularly at the box office. He certainly didn't imagine, nor did anyone else at the time, that it would become a worldwide phenomenon for the next forty years and go on to redefine Hollywood's rules about how to grow a movie franchise and successfully merchandise spin-off products.*

Back then, getting the word out about a new movie was a challenge, especially for a genre film like *Star Wars*. But those of us in the science fiction community got a first look at George Lucas's space fantasy at a World Science Fiction Convention, in September 1976.† Actor Mark Hamill (Luke Skywalker), producer Gary Kurtz, and Charles Lippincott (vice president of publicity, promotion, and merchandising for the Star Wars Corporation) showed up to promote it. They hoped to build word of mouth among the hardcore fans who would talk it up in fanzines and at conventions.‡

In a small room in the convention hotel, life-size costumes of R2-D2, C-3PO, and Darth Vader were on exhibit, along with props (blasters, lightsabers, and a stormtrooper's helmet), color photographs (movie stills), and conceptual artwork by Ralph McQuarrie, whose work Lucas initially used to pitch the movie to the studios,

---

* Lucas is rightly credited as the father of movie merchandising. He realized the clause that allowed merchandising was one he needed to control. Before the 1977 release of *Star Wars*, the merchandising rights clause, as written in standard movie contracts, was considered and was treated as a "garbage clause." As the conventional wisdom went, merchandising was not a moneymaker; it was a way to get publicity for the film. So the rights were given away or sold cheaply. Today, of course, those rights are very valuable, and studios hold on to them tenaciously, for which they can thank George Lucas.

† MidAmeriCon, in Kansas City, Missouri, was held September 2–6, 1976.

‡ Remember, back then there was no such thing as the internet or cell phones. In fact, in 1977, Apple Computer had just released the Apple II, for which the user had to provide the computer's enclosure.

and who went on to define the visual look of the original trilogy (*A New Hope*, *The Empire Strikes Back*, and *Return of the Jedi*).*

I was at that con, and I vividly remember the *Star Wars* exhibit. My first impression was that this movie promised to be like no other science fiction movie. My second impression was that it would especially appeal to those in the military, because the scope of its interplanetary war was immense, encompassing a galaxy. The good guys were starship troopers against the bad guys called stormtroopers, who all looked alike in plastic uniforms and helmets and armed with blaster rifles.

Wouldn't it be great, I thought, to be able to talk to George Lucas about the movie's military aspects?

Years later, when my wife and I were at the Walt Disney World Resort in Orlando, Florida, the opportunity presented itself. We were standing behind a short, bearded man with jeans, sneakers, and a checkerboard shirt. He was with his children, waiting to buy food at a cafeteria in the Disney–MGM Studios theme park (now called Disney's Hollywood Studios).

I turned to my wife and said, "He looks familiar."

She replied, "He should. That's George Lucas."

I stepped out of the line—there was no one behind me—and took a good look. It was, indeed, the Creator, as he's called by *Star Wars* fans. (Yes, his most hard-core fans can get a bit religious at times.)

"What are you going to do?" she asked. "Ask for an autograph?"

I saw Mr. Lucas asking the kids what they wanted to eat, and although I wanted to simply talk to him about the military aspects of *Star Wars*, I refrained, because this wasn't the time or place. This was a private moment for him and his kids, and I didn't want to intrude. I just *couldn't.*

---

* I highly recommend *Star Wars Art: Ralph McQuarrie*, which retails for $250.

I knew Lucas valued his privacy. He hated being perceived as a celebrity and a wealthy businessman instead of a filmmaker, which is how he saw himself.*

When I got home, I called a friend of mine at Imagineering, Disney's research and development department, where the design of the theme parks and resorts is dreamed up by imaginative artists and designers, and asked, "Was George Lucas at Disneyworld this past weekend?"

My friend replied yes. It turned out that Lucas was overseeing continued work on his Star Tours ride in the theme park.

These days, Lucas is no longer heading Lucasfilm Ltd.; instead, his handpicked successor, Kathleen Kennedy, has the helm. In 2012, he sold the *Star Wars* universe to Disney for $4.05 billion in cash and Disney stock. As Lucas told TV journalist Charlie Rose, "It's a very, very, very hard thing to do. You have to say, 'I have to move on,' and everything in your body says, *Don't. You can't. These are my kids.*"

But his kids, like all children, have had to grow up. From that first film in 1977, simply titled *Star Wars*, the franchise has grown in size and scope, becoming a multibillion-dollar franchise. As Chris Taylor states in his book-length study, *How Star Wars Conquered the Universe* (Basic Books, 2014), as of 2013, the franchise had earned an estimated $40 billion.

But 1977 was a long time ago. . . . Like the world, its principal actors have moved on. In *The Last Jedi* (2017), Mark Hamill is a craggy-looking Luke Skywalker who has fulfilled his destiny; Carrie Fisher's Princess Leia Organa is now a general leading the rebellion; and Harrison Ford's Han Solo—spoiler alert—meets an untimely end.

In this book, I've drawn some examples from what I witnessed and experienced in the military, because they illustrate the points I want

---

* Lucas always wanted the attention from the public and media to focus on his films, not on himself. He abhors the cult of celebrity, which has worsened because of the World Wide Web.

to make. I beg your indulgence for these personal intrusions, which I have kept to a minimum.*

As part of my research, I have consulted dozens of books about *Star Wars*, and even more books and publications about the military: biographies of leading military figures (mostly contemporary), army field manuals and technical manuals, and other official Department of the Army publications. All of these have proven invaluable (see Part 6: Resources).

Obviously, this book doesn't reflect the viewpoints of Lucasfilm, the Disney Company, or the US military. It reflects mine alone, tempered with feedback from others in the military community, who have asked to remain anonymous.

The point of this book is not to nitpick but to illuminate established military concepts and doctrine, contrasting the military culture in *Star Wars* with that in the real world by highlighting the US Army, and to do so in a fun and entertaining way.

By looking at Lucas's vision of future warfare, firmly rooted in military history, we get a glimpse of what may lie ahead in our own future.

May the military force be with us.

George Beahm
February 2018

---

* Less is more. If you check out my website (georgebeahm.com), you'll see what I mean.

Introduction

The Starstruck Vision of George Lucas's *Star Wars*:
A Long Time Ago . . .

A long time ago in a galaxy far, far away, the big bang occurred. "At its simplest, [the big bang theory] says the universe as we know it started with a small singularity, then inflated over the next 13.8 billion years to the cosmos that we know today."*

It's the perfect metaphor for what filmmaker George Lucas accomplished when he set out to film a space fantasy, which he originally planned as a reboot of *Flash Gordon* from the 1930s, from which he borrowed the famous opening text crawl that we first saw in *Star Wars* (1977), later retitled *A New Hope*.

A New Hope was, as Lucas himself explained, "built on top of many things that came before. This film is a compilation of all those dreams, using them as a history to create a new dream."† As *Slate* elaborated,

> Ask what *Star Wars* actually *is*, however, and you'll receive as many answers as there are scoundrels at the Mos Eisley Cantina.‡ *Star Wars* is a Western. *Star Wars* is a samurai movie. *Star Wars* is a space opera. *Star Wars* is a war film. *Star Wars* is a fairy tale. . . . The original *Star Wars* seems notable mostly as the foundation upon which an empire has been built—the sequels and prequels, the heavily indebted franchises, indeed the whole blockbuster economy.

---

* Elizabeth Howell, "What Is the Big Bang Theory?," space.com, June 22, 2015.
† Forrest Wickman, "*Star Wars* Is a Postmodern Masterpiece," *Slate*, December 13, 2015.
‡ See the cantina scene at the Mos Eisley spaceport, in *A New Hope*.

But, initially, it didn't look as if a blockbusting franchise was in the making. As Dale Pollock pointed out in *Skywalking: The Life and Films of George Lucas*, after Lucas initially screened *A New Hope* in 1977 to a select few, including his closest friends and fellow filmmakers and a movie critic, he said, "They all thought it was a disaster. . . . They were all my real close friends and they felt sorry for me more than anything else. There were a lot of condolences, which is even worse than saying you don't like the movie."

Lucas had hoped his friends would be the wind beneath his wings, but instead they took it out of his sails. He concluded, "I figured, well, it's just a silly movie. It ain't going to work."

As Pollock pointed out, Lucas soon discovered that most of his friends were off the mark. He got his first inkling of that when he and his wife at the time, Marcia, went to a burger joint in Los Angeles. It was across the street from the famous Grauman's Chinese Theatre, which was jam-packed with people. Like a blaster set to stun, Lucas's "silly movie" was set for fun—and also set to make a fortune for everyone involved. As Pollock wrote:

"Jesus Christ, what's going on here?" Lucas wondered. As they rounded the corner, he and Marcia saw *Star Wars* in giant block letters on the theater marquee. "We just fell on the floor," Lucas remembers. "I said, 'I don't believe this.' So we sat in Hamburger Hamlet and watched the giant crowd out there. . . . It wasn't excitement, it was amazement. I felt it was some kind of aberration."

But it wasn't an aberration. *Star Wars*, an entertaining family film with something for everyone, was a celebration. It was a time when the public badly needed an escapist movie in which to lose themselves, because the Vietnam War had just ended the month before and left a bitter aftertaste.

Star Wars paved the way for another summer blockbuster a month later: Steven Spielberg's *Jaws*. Together, they swallowed the competition whole.

The back-to-back escapist films made it clear that the public had a voracious appetite for popcorn movies that took their minds far, far away from the rice paddies of the Vietnam War, which they had seen unfold and, later, unravel, during the nightly news. We were losing, not winning, the war, no matter what the White House reassuringly said. We learned that our government could no longer be trusted.

Lucas's modest expectations for his "fairy tale in space guise," as he told *Starlog* magazine, exploded in a big bang, spreading out in every direction across the world. As Chris Taylor pointed out, "*Star Wars* is an increasingly global phenomenon, perhaps the first mythos all cultures can get behind without hesitation."

Years later, *Star Wars*, a multibillion-dollar franchise, drew the Walt Disney Company, like a tractor beam, into its orbit. Having previously spent $9 billion for Pixar and $4 billion for Marvel, WDC's $4.05 billion for *Star Wars* was clearly a prudent investment, as *Wired* pointed out: "Just how do those billions stack up, though? While the exact math is fuzzy, the long-term picture is clear. Disney immediately started making money on an investment that will continue to pay off in a huge way—likely for years to come."*

Disney—the most accomplished entertainment company in the world in terms of orchestrating multiple streams of income from diverse sources—found that the *Star Wars* franchise was a cash cow, waiting to be milked right from the beginning.

The worldwide box office gross of Disney's first *Star Wars* film (*The Force Awakens*, 2015) took in more than $2 billion worldwide; a year later, *Rogue One* took in half that. Given that the plan is to release a new *Star Wars* film every year—alternating between its historic plotline and stand-alone stories—the investment was, as *Wired* observed, "the deal of the century."

George Lucas, who ruled with an iron fist as the founder, chairman, and chief executive officer of the *Star Wars* franchise for de-

---

* Jim McLauchlin, "Star Wars' $4 Billion Price Tag Was the Deal of the Century," *Wired*, December 14, 2015.

cades, was now free to get on with the next chapter of his life. He spoke longingly about going back to his roots, making artistic films. But his immediate concern was finding a permanent home for his pop culture museum.

In the end, after finding himself in a frustrating and losing battle with various groups in Chicago, where he initially had planned on building it, Lucas's billion-dollar Museum of Narrative Art finally found a home in Los Angeles's Exposition Park. To be encased in a futuristic-looking building—not unlike those found in the *Star Wars* universe—the museum, stated National Public Radio, "will display his personal collection of fine and popular art, including Norman Rockwell paintings, *Mad* magazine covers, photography, children's art, as well as Hollywood props and visual effects from his famous movie franchise, *Star Wars*." *

Walt Disney himself wryly observed that his eponymous company had humble origins: "It all started with a mouse." Similarly, with Lucas, it all started with a pair of droids: R2-D2 and C-3PO. They escaped from Princess Leia Organa's *Tantive IV* to safety on the nearby planet of Tatooine, putting Lucas's space fantasy into high orbit. The Frodo Baggins of our time, R2-D2 proved that even the smallest of us can change the world.†

Beyond the phenomenon it created and its pop culture roots, *Star Wars* also can be seen in a more serious light, through the lens of multiple social, economic, and military perspectives.‡

In my case, in this book, I see *Star Wars* through the lens of military science, in as broad a way as possible. By now, you'd think that print publishers would have mined every possible nook and cranny

* Mandalit Del Barco, "George Lucas Chooses Los Angeles as Home for His Art Museum," National Public Radio, January 10, 2017.

† Frodo Baggins is a diminutive hobbit who carries Sauron's Ring of Power to Mount Doom, in *The Lord of the Rings*. The One Ring's destruction also means the end of Sauron's reign and his War of the Ring.

‡ Expanding on the existing *Star Wars* rides, Disney's theme parks will feature the *Star Wars* universe in more detail in the years to come.

of the *Star Wars* universe, but that's not so. Disney is continuing to explore new territories and countless new worlds.

The expanding *Star Wars* universe has room for official and unofficial books, for text-only books and massively illustrated books, for merchandising of all kinds, and for fan fiction that ranges from the imaginable to the unimaginable (don't ask). There's room for all of these things and more.

John Lassiter—chief creative officer of Pixar Animation Studios, Walt Disney Animation Studios, and DisneyToon Studios, and principal creative advisor for Walt Disney Imagineering—explained the importance of immersive storytelling:

> Ask yourself why? Why is this here? Does it further the story? Does it support the whole? The world of your story should feel perfectly natural to the audience. As soon as something looks wrong or out of place, your audience will pop out of your story and think about how weird that looked and you've lost them.
>
> The goal is to create a storyline that will suck your audience in and keep them entertained for the length of your film. When a film achieves this goal, the audience will lose track of time and forget about all their worldly cares. For all that any audience truly wants is to be entertained.*

Likewise, that's what this book is all about: to entertain you, to not take things too seriously, to make you smile, and to provide food for thought. But most of all, to have fun.

So strap on your armor, grab your weapon, make sure your helmet's on tight, and step inside my armored multipurpose vehicle, because it's time to roll.

---

* Jim Korkis, "The Art of Disney Theming," www.mouseplanet.com, February 22, 2017.

▪ PART 1 ▪

PERSONNEL

In no other profession are the penalties for employing untrained personnel so appalling and so irrevocable as in the
military.

—General Douglas MacArthur

Command Climate:
Leadership in the Galactic Empire

Although the Galactic Empire is military in organization, with an established chain of command, its leader, Darth Vader, is a Sith lord and, as such, is considered above and beyond the military rank structure. He reports only to Emperor Palpatine, who is also known as Darth Sidious.

In other words, Darth Vader holds no military rank, but he does command troops. His leadership and command at a senior level mean that his subordinates will watch his every move, assessing, gauging his moods, and most of all, being on guard and hoping they haven't upset him, because he is quick to use his signature weapon against them—the infamous Force-choke.

We must ask ourselves: Is Darth Vader an effective leader? And what can we learn about his management style?

A Perspective on Leadership

The U.S. Army defines leadership as "the process of influencing people by providing purpose, direction, and motivation to accomplish the mission and improve the organization. . . . Confident, competent, and informed leadership intensifies the effectiveness of the other elements of combat power. . . . Influencing entails more than simply passing along orders. Through words and personal example, leaders communicate purpose, direction, and motivation." *

---

* ADRP 6-22, *Army Leadership*, Department of the Army, August 2012.

As an officer and unit commander, I've had the good fortune—and misfortune—of serving under officers of varying competence. In the end, it all boils down to this: as Xenophon of Athens observed, in 400 BC, "The true test of a leader is whether his followers will adhere to his cause from their own volition, enduring the most arduous hardships without being forced to do so, and remaining steadfast in the moments of greatest peril."

An Outstanding Commander

I recall one officer who took command of our battalion right before an important evaluation from higher headquarters. Because I previously had served under him, I knew him fairly well. He took over our battalion, took charge, and energized it. As a direct consequence of his leadership, the battalion did well on the evaluation.

Had it had been wartime, I would not have hesitated to follow him to the gates of hell. I would *willingly* have followed him, because he inspired us, believed in us, and would do everything he could to get the mission done and get as many of us as possible back home alive.

An Incompetent Commander

General Schwarzkopf wrote about an incompetent commander in *It Doesn't Take a Hero*:

Instead of executing the flanking attack the situation called for, he ordered a full frontal assault. When it became obvious this tactic was a disaster, the colonel came unglued. He started running up behind troops and shaking their canteens, saying, "Soldier, why don't you have any water?" . . .

I'd have felt sorry for him, except that if we'd been at war, his brand of leadership would have gotten us all killed.

Morale

The acid test: Does the leader inspire leadership, or do his subordinates do his bidding because they fear him? In Darth Vader's case, it's fear. To make a mistake means risking instant death, because he often uses his Force-choke against those who displease him.

Case in point: In *A New Hope*, Darth Vader is on the Death Star, in a meeting with high-ranking military officers overseen by his boss, Grand Moff Tarkin. When Admiral Motti gives Vader the sharp edge of his tongue, belittling him in front of the other high-ranking officers on the Death Star, Motti has apparently forgotten that Vader's "sorcerer's ways" include the infamous Force-choke. Motti would have been well advised to get a grip on himself rather than have Vader do it for him. To his dismay, Motti finds himself being Force-choked by Vader, until Tarkin orders Vader to stop.

In another instance, in *The Empire Strikes Back*, Admiral Ozzel is subjected to a Force-choke, as others look on in horror, wondering which of them would later suffer the same ignominious fate.

The command climate created by Vader is such that no disagreement is allowed, and mistakes are dealt with too harshly. One wrong call on your part, and you're in deep Bantha poo.* Better to hold your tongue than to speak and have your tongue protruding from your mouth as Vader chokes you.

That was the unspoken wisdom among Galactic Empire officers, who lived in perpetual fear when Vader was around.

Vader's officers were not the only ones who came to fear him. No matter where he went, his reputation, like his black flowing cloak, followed him. In *A New Hope*, for instance, Vader interrogated a rebel ship's officer and demanded, "Where are those transmissions you intercepted?" The officer's response displeased Vader, and he

---

* A large, four-legged mammalian creature indigenous to the deserts of Tatooine, Banthas excrete a large amount of dung.

soon felt Vader's strong fingers around his neck, his life slowly squeezed out of him.

The lesson was not lost on Vader's men.

Kylo Ren

In *The Force Awakens*, Kylo Ren, who serves Supreme Leader Snoke, is seen contemplating the smashed and melted helmet of Darth Vader, like Hamlet considering Yorick's skull. Ren reveres Vader, so it's not surprising that he wishes to follow his example. Thus, in one scene, when Ren gets unwelcome news, he goes on a rampage, attacking everything in sight with his lightsaber while a subordinate looks helplessly on, silently thankful that he's not on the receiving end of Kylo Ren's wrath.

Like Darth Vader, Ren cannot control himself. And, like Vader, he holds a unique leadership position, answering only to his master, Supreme Leader Snoke. Both Vader and Ren are in control of legions of troops but often can't control even their own selves.

That goes a long way toward explaining why neither of them got the optimum performance from their subordinates, who feared them.

Fear Trumps All: Desperate Despots

Regardless of how they came to power, despots share one fundamental flaw: they use fear to rule. North Korea's supreme leader Kim Jong-un comes readily to mind, as does Syrian president Bashar al-Assad and the deceased Iraqi president Saddam Hussein.*

The Galactic Empire's strategy of ruling by fear ultimately proves

---

* Think about these despots who ruled by fear, who once held their countries under their dominion: Hitler died by suicide, shooting himself with a pistol in his underground bunker in Berlin; Mussolini was shot by Italian partisans as he tried to escape to Switzerland; Tojo, after a failed suicide attempt, was tried by an international tribunal; and, in recent years, Saddam Hussein was extracted from an underground "spider hole." Both Tojo and Hussein were hanged.

counterproductive. In *Star Wars: A New Hope*, Grand Moff Tarkin told the others in the conference room on the Death Star, "Fear will keep the local systems in line. Fear of this battle station." Instead, the rebels' fear was transmuted into hope, and even before the countless people on planets throughout the system were aware of the existence of the Death Star, the Rebel Alliance destroyed it.

Seven Habits of Spectacularly Unsuccessful People

1. See themselves and their forces as dominating the environment (arrogance/hubris).
2. No clear boundary between leader's personal interest and that of the Organization.
3. Leaders who think they have all the answers.
4. Leader who ensures everyone is 100% behind them, eliminating opposition.
5. Leader who devotes the largest portion of their time to the unit's image.
6. Underestimate major obstacles.
7. Leaders who revert to what worked for them in the past (yesterday's answer).

Source: Dr. Sydney Finkelstein, *Why Smart Executives Fail: And What You Can Learn from Their Mistakes* (Portfolio, 2004).

Admiral Piett on the Bridge
of the *Executor*

Admiral Kendal Ozzel, commanding a fleet during combat operations, is suddenly and unexpectedly relieved by Darth Vader in *The Empire Strikes Back*. Ozzel, in fact, is summarily executed by Vader because of what he perceives to be a tactical blunder on the part of Ozzel: the admiral took the fleet out of light speed too close to the planet Hoth, with the result that the rebels who have a base on its surface were alerted to the fleet's presence.

Vader then turns to Captain Piett, upon whom he bestows an unexpected field promotion. Captain Piett is now Admiral Piett. He is, of course, grateful for the promotion, despite the circumstances, but in the back of his mind he's wondering if and when he might suffer the same fate as his predecessor.

In *Return of the Jedi*, we see Admiral Piett in action. He is now the fleet commander, and he's at the bridge of his flagship, a Super Star Destroyer called the *Executor*. The ship is the pride of the fleet. It's the biggest ship by far, eleven miles in length, and from its bridge Admiral Piett conducts an air battle. He's under attack by the Rebel Alliance and gets a crash course in how quickly things can change during combat operations.

The flagship's command tower, as we're told in *Star Wars: Complete Locations* (DK Publishing, 2016), "is practically a ship in its own right. It houses a profusion of vital components, including shield generators, communications systems, and sensor arrays, as well as officers' quarters, briefing rooms, and escape pods for the vessel's upper-echelon commanders."

Of those components, the shield generator is of paramount importance, because when the shield is down, enemy ships are able to attack the vessel itself.

What subsequently happens is unthinkable. When the command tower is attacked and the shield generator becomes inoperative, the flagship is suddenly vulnerable. Unfortunately, a rebel fighter, spinning out of control, heads directly toward the panoramic viewing window of the bridge as Admiral Piett and the ship's captain look helplessly on.

What they see horrifies them. What they know is that, because the shield generator is down, they have only seconds to live.

The rebel fighter slams into the bridge, killing the ship's two most senior officers. Mayhem results. The Super Star Destroyer, out of control, spears the second Death Star, setting the stage for General Calrissian and his fighters to move in for the kill.

Looking back at the sequence of events, we come to the inescapable conclusion that none of that should have happened. It's instructive to ask ourselves what happened and why, and how things could have been done differently. In short, what lessons can be learned?

1. *Admiral Ozzel*. In fandom, most fans share Darth Vader's low assessment of Ozzel. As I'll discuss elsewhere in this book, I don't believe this was a tactical error on Admiral Ozzel's part. I submit that Admiral Ozzel, with his many years of experience, should instead have been relieved of his duties and reassigned, since Darth Vader is the boss and is unhappy with Ozzel's performance, right or wrong. It's Vader's prerogative to relieve any subordinate commander for any reason.

Keeping all of that in mind, we must ask ourselves, if he had not been relieved and he had lived to command operations during the Battle of Endor, would he have made the same mistakes his successor did?

2. *Admiral Piett*. I submit that Piett was promoted too soon. Of course, as the second-in-command, Piett was the logical choice, but between the time he was promoted and his appearance on the bridge of the *Executor*, three years have elapsed.

During those years, we must assume that he has undergone

additional training to ensure he is capable of commanding the fleet. Ideally, he'd go to an Imperial Navy course for newly minted admirals and then return to the fleet for field duty. Clearly, given his additional rank and responsibilities, Piett would have benefited from additional high-level training.

Tactical Considerations

1. The flagship is the fleet's principal command and control (C & C). As such, it is a high-value target and must be protected *at all costs*. Therefore, Admiral Piett should have positioned the Super Star Destroyer so that no rebel ships could get anywhere near it. In other words, the *Executor* should be sufficiently distanced and protected from any enemy aircraft.

For whatever reason, Admiral Piett positioned his flagship too close to his Star Destroyers, as well as too near the second Death Star. Even if the unthinkable happens and the *Executor* is damaged or destroyed, it should *not* be so close to the Death Star that it will present a hazard.

In the U.S. Air Force (USAF), the issue of overcrowding is carefully monitored during air combat, and available airspace is "deconflicted" to minimize midair collisions. Likewise, the navy maintains similar safe zones to prevent overcrowding that can lead to collisions on and below the surface.

2. The shield generator is too exposed. In the *Star Wars* universe, emphasis is placed on the importance of the field/shield generator: the Gungans used it as their principal defensive weapon (*The Phantom Menace*); the Rebel Alliance used it to protect the base on Hoth (*The Empire Strikes Back*); the Galactic Empire used it to protect the second Death Star (*Return of the Jedi*); and the Empire used it to protect its flagship, the *Executor*, in the air battle near the Endor moon.

In all these cases, though, the shield generators were not adequately protected, and no backup shield generators were available. As a result, the Gungans were forced to retreat in sudden panic, the Rebel Alliance had to evacuate its base, the Galactic Empire's second Death Star was destroyed, and Admiral Piett's flagship was destroyed and collided with the Death Star.

With all pieces of critical hardware, such as a shield generator, redundancy management is indispensable. In Piett's case, he had no backup, and as the fighter aircraft, spinning out of control, headed directly toward the window of the bridge, he ordered "Intensify forward firepower," but it was too late. The fighter slammed into the bridge's window.

3. The defensive system on the Super Star Destroyer was inadequate. We're told it's twelve times the size of a Star Destroyer; moreover, it "bristles with thousands of turbolasers and ion cannons, and carries starfighter wings and ground troops sufficient for a planetary invasion." In other words, it has extensive offensive and defensive capabilities. So how could a single disabled fighter aircraft possibly take it out?

The enemy fighter should (1) never have gotten that close to the fleet, (2) never have gotten that close to the flagship, and (3) have been blown up by close-in weapons systems—onboard guns, antiaircraft guns, or missiles.*

Conclusion

Admiral Ozzel's sudden relief opened a vacancy filled by Captain Piett, who was not sufficiently trained in combat fleet operations. Whether it was due to lack of adequate training at the appropriate service school or for other reasons, the fact remains that Admiral Piett's fleet lacked defense in depth. The fleet was not properly positioned. Consequently, a disabled, errant rebel fighter breached the flagship's airspace and destroyed it, setting off a chain reaction: the second Death Star becomes disabled and is subsequently destroyed.

* A U.S. Navy flagship has no fighter aircraft because they're on the aircraft carriers. Because the flagship's mission is command and control, it has helicopters to shuttle command staff to the other ships. But it must defend itself; thus, it has 25 millimeter guns, .50-caliber machine guns, and two 20 millimeter Phalanx close-in weapons systems designed to fire up to 4,500 rounds per minute against incoming aircraft or missiles.

The Chain of Command

In the U.S. Army, the chain of command is long and composed of many links. It starts from the person in charge at the top and goes all the way down to the lowest-ranking individual in the unit. It is an unbroken chain that ensures that the mission, which comes first, will not be lost for lack of leadership. The chain of command is as follows:

1. Commander in Chief (the president of the United States)
2. Secretary of Defense
3. Secretary of the Army
4. Chief of Staff, U.S. Army
5. Commanding general, US Continental Army Command
6. Theater commander
7. Army group commander
8. Army commander
9. Corps commander
10. Division commander
11. Brigade commander
12. Battalion/squadron commander
13. Company/battery/troop commander
14. Platoon leader
15. Section leader
16. Squad leader
17. Fire team leader

All-In: Combating Stereotypes About Women in War

Give Rey a hand . . . or not. In a scene from *The Force Awakens*, the scrappy Rey, played by British actress Daisy Ridley, is running like hell when the First Order stormtroopers show up. She's with Finn, a stormtrooper who's defected to the rebel side, and when he tries to grab her hand, she yells out, "I know how to run without you holding my hand!"

She can run like the wind, fight like a demon, and fly the *Millennium Falcon* like a bat out of hell. She can take care of herself, just as she's done for years as a scavenger. She's clearly a survivor type, and just as clearly doesn't *need* to have a male protector around.

Finn finally gets the idea, after he tries again to grab her hand and she yells at him, "Stop taking my hand!"*

I suspect Rey would get along splendidly with Jyn Erso (played by another British actress, Felicity Jones), who is every bit as feisty, smart, and badass as Rey. In *Rogue One*, Jyn is an inspirational figure, stepping up to take on the Galactic Empire when the leadership of the Rebel Alliance backs down.

"Lead me, follow me, or get out of my way."† That, in a nutshell, is the order of the day for both Rey‡ and Jyn Erso.

---

* Aside: he's also curious about whether she's got a boyfriend, though they've just met. And who can blame him? Because male stormtroopers outnumber female stormtroopers by an overwhelming margin, he probably didn't date much.

† Source: General George S. Patton, though often misattributed to Thomas Paine.

‡ Rey is her first name. We aren't told her last name, which is a major plot point to be revealed in a future *Star Wars* film.

That's also the marching orders for Captain Phasma, played by British actress Gwendoline Christie, who, in *The Force Awakens*, commands eighty stormtroopers who land on the planet Jakku to find a Jedi harboring a secret.

Rey, Jyn, and Captain Phasma share much in common with resistance leader General Leia Organa, who is a princess in *A New Hope*. That, though, was a long time ago, in a galaxy far, far away. . . .

In the U.S. military, the glass ceiling was shattered on January 24, 2013, when Defense Secretary Leon Panetta lifted the ban against women serving in direct (i.e., frontline) combat positions, which the Pentagon defines as "engaging an enemy on the ground with individual or crew-served weapons, while being exposed to hostile fire and to a high probability of direct physical contact with hostile personnel."

As P.J. Tobia of PBS Newshour reported (December 3, 2015), "The services were ordered to study the issue and develop an implementation plan. They were given until January 2016 to either implement the policy or ask for special exemptions. At the time, women had been serving in war zones in Iraq and Afghanistan for more than a decade."

All of the U.S. military services fell under that order, and on that date it opened up for women 230,000 slots for jobs that traditionally were excluded from the combat arms, and in elite units such as the army's Delta Force (1st Special Forces Operational Detachment-Delta, based in Fort Bragg, North Carolina) and the navy's SEAL teams (U.S. Naval Special Warfare Development Group), based in Coronado, California, Little Creek, Virginia, and Pearl Harbor, Hawaii.

For men used to serving in all-male units—especially those in the combat arms—the inclusion of women, who cite better assignments and promotions as motivating factors, fundamentally changes the face of combat, from male only to male *and* female. As Second

Lieutenant Virginia Brodie,* a "redleg,"† explained, being in the field artillery meant she wouldn't get stuck in an administrative job. She wanted to be where the action was, out in the field, commanding troops, and not behind a desk, shuffling papers.

In today's military, women fly fighter planes and combat helicopters; they serve on submarines and surface ships (including aircraft carriers). And now they get down and dirty in the army's combat arms.

I suspect that Rey and Jyn—from another time and another place—would heartily approve of being counted among the Band of Sisters, standing side by side with the Band of Brothers.

---

* A Marine who graduated from the U.S. Naval Academy, Second Lieutenant Brodie went on to become a distinguished honor graduate of the Basic Officer Leader Course at Fort Sill, the home of the U.S. Army Field Artillery School.

† Field artillerymen, and now women, are called "redlegs," a term that dates back to the Civil War.

Jyn Erso, Rebel with a Cause: A Study in Leadership

> She has been detained and is being given an opportunity to be useful. And by being useful, it may commute her sentence. She's got a checkered past, and has pretty much been on her own since she was 15. She's a real survivor. She becomes a kind of Joan of Arc in the story.
>
> —Lucasfilm president Kathleen Kennedy, on Jyn Erso
> *Entertainment Weekly* (July 1, 2016)

Background

Like Rey (*The Force Awakens*), Jyn Erso (*Rogue One*) is no shrinking violet. She's feisty, street-smart, and resourceful. She finds herself being recruited by the Alliance to Restore the Republic (aka the Rebel Alliance) because of a family connection—her father, Galen. Like Joan of Arc, who had no military training and went on to lead a French army to victory, Jyn went on to become an inspirational figure to all in the Rebel Alliance, disproving her critics, who never recognized her considerable potential.*

Jyn Erso's Leadership Traits

Jyn never had the advantage of formal military training; moreover, she wouldn't be a likely candidate. Rules, regimentation, and working in a

---

* For a closer look at Jyn Erso, check out "Jyn: The Rebel," part of the supplementary material on the *Rogue One* Blu-ray/DVD disc (April 4, 2017).

structured environment would not have suited her nature. But she was ideally suited for the role she was forced to reluctantly take on.

She was a born rebel. She rebelled against the established order, after being forced to live on the street, surviving on her wits. She rebelled against the Galactic Empire even before she was recruited by the Rebel Alliance, as a child soldier on the side of the insurgents. She questioned the leadership of the Rebel Alliance, rebelling against their decision to sanction a mission to steal the data tapes necessary for the destruction of the Death Star. She showed great courage and leadership, taking on a risky but necessary mission when the Rebel Alliance leadership backed down.

The following are some of the leadership principles, drawn from the US Army playbook, that Jyn Erso exhibited in *Rogue One*, successfully accomplishing her stated mission.

I. Be tactically and technically proficient.

At a very early age, Jyn Erso lived the life of a child soldier. Seeing the world at its worst—violent, bloody, and dangerous—and knowing she had to learn how to rely on herself, she became proficient in street fighting, in hand-to-hand combat, and with weapons.

The street training paid off. On the planet Jedha, in what *Star Wars* historians refer to as the Battle of Jedha, she finds herself in the thick of things, in a street fight between Saw Gerrera's insurgents and a well-equipped and well-armed Galactic Empire. Armed with only a blaster pistol, she holds her own as the battle erupts.

Rather than run for cover and hide, like the civilians caught in the cross fire, she stands and fights, and even rescues a stray child caught in the cross fire.

2. Set the example.

When all others fail to take a stand, someone has to. *Has* to. Such is the nature of command, of leadership.

En route to the rebel base, Yavin 4, Jyn had already made up her mind regarding the Death Star. She's got to get its secret plans at any cost.

But Jyn soon found out that although she had the courage of her convictions, they were not shared by the Rebel Alliance leadership. Not surprisingly, Jyn found herself at odds with the leadership, who not only dismissed her but also dismissed her plan out of hand. Defeated even before a mission is set into motion, Senator Pamlo, at the council meeting, threw up her hands and asked, "What chance do we have?"

Jyn set the example. She held to her convictions and passionately argued her position. She's an army of one, though, and walks away. She stands alone, until Captain Cassian and other insurgent soldiers step forward to help.

3. Make sound and timely decisions.

Leaders sometimes err on the side of caution, resulting in paralysis by analysis. As General George S. Patton reminded us, "A good plan violently executed right now is far better than a perfect plan executed next week."

That is what happened after the Rebel Alliance council meeting. Citing doom and gloom, the high-ranking members—both military and civilian—refused to make a timely decision, though time was of the essence. In the end, they decided not to do anything. But Jyn and her fellow rogue warriors decided to act, and in doing so, they made a courageous decision that, later, the council backed up with much-needed air support.

4. Seek responsibility and take responsibility for your actions.

From the beginning, Jyn took responsibility for the proposed mission by strenuously advocating it to the senior members of the Rebel Alliance at the council meeting. She then decided to go it alone, if necessary, but she was aided by others who shared her view and volunteered to assist. She became the leader and decided what had to be done and by whom, and as the team was en route to Scarif, she laid out the mission.

5. Ensure the task is understood, supervised, and accomplished.

Because Jyn Erso lacked rank, and because a chain of command had to be established for the mission, Lieutenant Taidu Sefla, who volunteered for *Rogue One*'s mission, gave her a field promotion to sergeant.

Though Sefla outranked her, as did Captain Cassian, Jyn was operationally the commander of the strike team. She was the one who decided that she and Captain Cassian would be the ones to steal the data tape and that the others would serve as a diversionary force, drawing the attention of the stormtroopers stationed on Scarif. She made sure everyone understood the overall mission and understood their roles in its execution.

6. Employ your unit in accordance with its capabilities.

Jyn correctly decided that she was the best person to retrieve the data tape. Though some of the other team members might have gotten to the data banks, they would have been stymied at the prospect of identifying, especially under duress, the *correct* data tape out of the many thousands available. They had no way of knowing which one it was, but she would. In fact, *only* she would have recognized it by name.

Jyn and Captain Cassian worked well as a team. They learned that when they joined forces to fight Lieutenant Colonel Krennic and his stormtroopers on Eadu. The others had also worked well before as a team; moreover, they were outfitted with the requisite firepower to create havoc among the garrison of troops on Scarif.

U.S. Army Rangers

The contemporary counterpart to *Rogue One*'s commando team would be the U.S. Army Rangers.

Each Ranger battalion is capable of deploying anywhere in the world with only 18 hours' notice. Rangers are part of a highly trained and rapidly deployable light infantry force with specialized skills that enable it to engage a variety of conventional and Special Operations targets.

The Rangers' primary mission is to engage the enemy in close combat and direct-fire battles. This mission includes direct action operations, raids, personnel and special equipment recovery, in addition to conventional or special light-infantry operations.*

As their motto goes: Rangers Lead the Way.

The same could be said for Jyn Erso and her team of commandos, whose special mission resulted in acquiring invaluable information that led to the first major victory by the Rebel Alliance against the Galactic Empire.

* "The Army Rangers: Missions and History," www.military.com.

The Right Stuff:
Women in Combat Roles

Long before Rey burst on the scene, a princess broke the mold. Princess Leia Organa (*A New Hope*) was the template for heroines in the *Star Wars* universe and, years later, for countless others in pop culture books and movies. Princess Leia Organa is no Cinderella or Snow White, waiting patiently for a charming prince to come and sweep her off her feet and into his arms.

Today's Disney heroines, cut from different cloth than those of yesteryear, take charge of their own destinies: Belle (*Beauty and the Beast*) accepts the Beast but only on her terms; Jasmine (*Aladdin*) refuses to marry whomever her father chooses; and Merida (*Brave*) outshoots her suitors to win her own hand.

Feisty and feminine, steely and cerebral, in *The Force Awakens* Princess Leia abandons her regal white gown to don more practical attire. Hers is a paramilitary look (boots, vest, olive drab shirt, brown slacks) that suits her well.

It's a far cry from the days when, enslaved by Jabba the Hutt, Leia wore a metal bikini that left little to the imagination. From model to role model, the reluctant princess becomes a world-weary and battle-wise warrior, so that others may follow in her footsteps.

Without Leia, there would have been no Rey.*

---

* I necessarily exclude Jyn Erso only because her story is set chronologically just before Princess Leia's in *A New Hope*.

Rey: Scavenger and Star Pilot

A scavenger on the planet Jakku, Rey is self-sufficient and ekes out a living selling what she finds on abandoned starships in the desert, a graveyard of fallen imperial spacecraft, including a Star Destroyer sunk in the ground. Selling bits and pieces of it to survive, Rey reminds us of another child of destiny, Luke Skywalker.

They share much in common. Both are orphaned. Both have adapted well to their desert worlds. Both are born pilots. And both have the Force.*

Female pilots in the *Star Wars* saga are nothing new. In fact, we see footage of female pilots engaging the Death Star II, in a supplementary disc released in 1980 to accompany *The Empire Strikes Back*.

These winged furies don't have matrimonial engagements on their minds; they are interested only in engagements that take place in fighter aircraft, against the enemy.

The View from the Cockpit

When stormtroopers who have landed on Jakku go after Rey because of her BB-8 droid, she goes on the run with former stormtrooper Finn. We know little about her background, but when Finn tells her that they're going to need a pilot, she surprises him by saying that she's a pilot.

She's able to sit in the pilot's seat of the *Millennium Falcon* and, after telling Finn that "this ship hasn't flown in years," she gets it airborne, after a few bumps and bruises. She's soon hotly pursued by TIE fighters.

We wonder what Rey's flight background is, particularly given her expertise in maneuvering around obstacles—natural terrain and abandoned military spacecraft—with consummate skill. She certainly knows her way around Han Solo's legendary starship. In

---

* We don't know Rey's full name.

fact, she almost makes it look easy. But, in truth, piloting a jet of any kind in the real world takes skill and a lot of training. If you don't know what you're doing, or even if you do know but are momentarily inattentive, you can get killed. Flying a high-performance aircraft requires heightened situational awareness.

Unlike Rey, most people will never sit in a jet cockpit. In fact, unless they're at an air show, most will never even get near a military fighter jet: an F-16 Fighting Falcon, an F-15 Eagle, an F-22 Raptor, or an F-35 Lightning II.

If you're not an air force or navy fighter pilot—or a television journalist who can wrangle a media flight—your view of the cockpit is limited to what you'll see on TV or in *Top Gun*, neither of which are realistic representations of the culture of military pilots.

In my capacity as a ground liaison officer, I was privileged to spend two weeks working with a fighter squadron in New Mexico. After classroom instruction at Langley Air Force Base in Hampton, Virginia, I found myself, a month later, in a Fighting Falcon ("Viper," to the pilots), model F-16B (two-seat), piloted by a young captain who also flies the A-10 Warthog (a flying Gatling gun).

I came away with a deep appreciation for the pilots' world of quiet professionalism, in which there's no high-fiving, fist-bumping, or chest-bumping, either on or off the flight line. When these pilots strap on their jets in combat, they're deadly serious, because they have to be in order to survive. It ain't *Top Gun* and, boy, it ain't dusting crops.

Before the USAF entrusts you with an expensive aircraft (a Fighting Falcon can cost up to $19 million), they have a time-tested, by-the-numbers plan for training to ensure you know what you're doing before you join the ranks of a fighter wing: fifty-five weeks at Sheppard Air Force Base in Texas, where you learn the ways of the Force—the U.S. Air Force—at the Euro-NATO Joint Jet Pilot Training program.

In phase one, the emphasis is on the word "student," not "pilot."

You hit the books and get a solid grounding in the world of military flight, with classes on aerospace physiology, "rides" in the altitude chamber, and training in using the ejection seat and landing by parachute.

In phase two, the emphasis is now on "pilot." While you fly in a trainer jet with a seasoned pilot instructor, this twenty-six-week course teaches "basic flying skills," involving 125 hours of flight time.

In phase three, all pilots undergo training in the T-38, a two-seat supersonic trainer.* This involves 135 hours of flight instruction over a twenty-six-week period, to "prepare graduates for fighter/bomber assignments."

Based on pilot performance, evaluations, and written exams, pilots are placed in a designated "track" to fly fighters, bombers, tankers, transports, or special operations aircraft. Upon graduation, they receive the coveted silver wings and go on to specific training on the aircraft they will be flying during their air force career. From there, the sky's the limit.

Female Fighter Pilots

Though women were flying X-wing fighters in *The Empire Strikes Back* (1980), it took longer for the USAF to catch up. But when the forty-five-year flight ban ended, in 1993, female pilots who wanted the same vocational challenges and promotion paths as their male counterparts understandably flocked to combat aircraft.

The first was Martha McSally, who went from flying T-37 trainers to the A-10 Warthog, logging three hundred combat flying hours and retiring as a full colonel.

As the *Washington Times* pointed out, women weren't initially welcomed with open arms in the fighter pilot community, which traditionally was an all-male world. As a retired USAF lieutenant

---

* This is the jet NASA astronauts flew when headed to the Kennedy Space Center in Florida for a space shuttle mission.

general explained, "During a major air combat training exercise, one of the opposing force flight leaders was a lieutenant colonel squadron commander who was very vocal that he did not like the idea of women fighter pilots. Subsequently in the exercise, he was 'shot down' by a young female lieutenant who was in my group." The same general concluded, "Combat skills are blind to rank, gender, race, color, or creed. They are based on performance, pure and simple."

We, of course, have no idea what training the pilots—male or female—in the Rebel Alliance have undergone, but the results do speak for themselves. On three separate missions, the Death Star I, Death Star II, and Starkiller Base's superweapon were all successfully destroyed by Rebel Alliance pilots.

Infantry

Likewise, we don't know exactly what training Jyn Erso had before she went on her commando mission, but she was clearly straight-leg infantry, the toughest and most demanding job in the army. She headed a special reconnaissance mission, defined as "reconnaissance and surveillance actions normally conducted in a clandestine or covert manner to collect or verify information of strategic or operational significance, employing military capabilities not normally found in CF [conventional forces]" (*Special Operations*, Joint Publication 3-05, 2014).

Infantry Officers

In the army, the holy trinity is infantry, armor, and field artillery. But of the three, it's the infantryman who is the most exposed and must master a host of skills in order to survive and accomplish the mission.

Let's look at what US officers go through in order to be able to proudly wear the crossed rifles—the branch insignia worn by infantry officers.

The most important thing to remember is that ground combat is principally about the infantry, because in order to win a war, it takes "boots on the ground" to fight the battle, hold the terrain, and, in cities, be the occupying force.

The night the bombing campaign began over Baghdad, on January 17, 1991, I remember an air force general explaining on CNN that it was a calculated campaign of "shock and awe." It was indeed impressive, but it didn't end the war; it merely *began* it. The real challenge lay ahead: the land battle that followed, fast and furious, like a German blitzkrieg during World War II. It took the late General H. Norman Schwarzkopf, who stormed across Iraq, to take it, hold it, and occupy it.

Back then, optimism was high in the White House. Defense Secretary Donald Rumsfeld told the media that Iraq wasn't going to be a quagmire like Vietnam. He dismissed "the idea that it's going to be a long, long, long battle of some kind" and explained, "Five days or five weeks or five months, but it certainly isn't going to last longer than that. It won't be a World War III." *

Well, it wasn't World War III, but it certainly proved him to be militarily clueless. When I heard him on the news, I burst out laughing. I told my wife, "Trust me, it's going to be a decade." It turned out to be nearly nine years . . . and now we're headed back to the Middle East:

> The U.S. military has drawn up early plans that would deploy up to 1,000 more troops into northern Syria in the coming weeks, expanding the American presence in the country. . . . The deployment, if approved by Defense Secretary Jim Mattis and President Trump, would potentially double the number of U.S. forces in Syria and increase the potential for direct U.S. combat involvement in a conflict that has been characterized by confusion and competing priorities among disparate forces.[†]

* John Esterbrook, "Rumsfeld: It Would Be a Short War," *CBS News*, November 15, 2002.
† Thomas Gibbons-Neff, "U.S. Military Likely to Send as Many as 1,000 More Ground Troops into Syria," *Washington Post*, March 15, 2017.

We owned Iraq, we broke it, and we are continuing to pay for it. The late Saddam Hussein ruled with an iron fist, keeping the various sectarian factions in line and at arm's length as he clamped down on terrorists. But what did the United States know about occupying and controlling a country that was still fighting its own civil war? As it turned out: nothing.

Current public sentiment among Americans is that we never should have invaded the country in the first place, because we destabilized the region, paving the way for al-Qaeda and ISIS to fill the power vacuum, first in Iraq and then throughout the region. But we're deeply entrenched there and can never get out. It's a quagmire. It's Vietnam all over again, but much worse.

Iraq has been ravaged in recent years by cycles of warfare, a growing refugee crisis, crippling sectarianism, and the violent spread of the self-styled Islamic State extremist movement (also known as ISIS, ISIL or by its Arabic acronym, Daesh)." [Despite progress,] "governing institutions remain weak, and corruption and poverty endemic. . . . The continued weakness of governance in Iraq—along with ISIS' seizure of much of northwestern Iraq and adjacent parts of Syria, and its recruitment of young Muslims worldwide—poses a long-term challenge to stability in the region and globally." *

Today's Female Infantry Officer

As I have mentioned, the combat arms of the army were closed to women until very recently. But Leon Panetta's lifting of the ban against women serving in frontline positions was finally implemented in January 2016, when then-Defense Secretary Ash Carter

---

* United States Institute of Peace, "The Current Situation in Iraq." In rt.com ("U.S. Preparing Public Opinion for Greater Military Involvement in Iraq, Syria," February 24, 2017), Lieutenant Colonel Karen Kwiatkowski (retired, U.S. Air Force) put things into proper perspective: "The long occupation and wars in the Middle East that the U.S. has been involved in for over 15 years now are very, very unpopular in the U.S. So the term 'advise-and-assist'—that is the mellow, friendly language that's used for the Americans. . . . I think in most cases it is not true, as we found out."

made all combat jobs open service-wide. In making the announcement, Carter said, "They'll be able to serve as Army Rangers and Green Berets, Navy SEALs, Marine Corps infantry, Air Force parajumpers, and everything else that was previously open only to men." That's *if* they can pass all the physical requirements the jobs entail, which are formidable, especially in the Marines.*

But the guys aren't going to make it easy for the gals. You can legislate integration but you can't change the mind-set of a military culture in which old habits die hard and women aren't necessarily welcomed with opened arms.†

The Rocky Road Ahead for Women

Just as female air force pilots shattered the glass ceiling, female army officers stirred up the dust on the battlefield by breaking new ground. In August 2015, two female officers graduated from the US Army Ranger School, which stresses and assesses leadership skills by providing "a small-unit tactics course for dismounted infantry." Specifically, they're tested on "squad and platoon tactics, the use of weapons, fieldcraft, and other tactical and technical skills," according to Major John Spencer, a former Ranger instructor.‡

The two were later joined by Major Lisa A. Jaster, who graduated two months later from Ranger School, now gender-integrated.

Rangers—in this case, female Rangers—led the way.

Following in their footsteps, "Ten female lieutenants completed

* On September 25, 2017, for the first time in its 242-year history, a female graduated from its infantry officer course. Because of her notoriety surrounding her singular achievement, she prefers to keep a low profile and has turned down multiple media interviews.
† It's one thing to fight the enemy, but too many women in the military have also had to fight off their male counterparts, including their leaders. The issue of sexual harassment is one that has yet to be adequately addressed. According to a 2014 RAND National Defense Research Institute study, "Sexual Assault and Sexual Harassment in the U.S. Military" (Volume 2), "The results of the 2012 survey suggested that more than 26,000 service members in the active component had experienced *unwanted sexual contacts* in the prior year, an estimate that received widespread public attention and concern."
‡ Quoted in Modern War Institute at West Point (nwi.usma.edu).

the first step in becoming U.S. Army infantry platoon leaders . . . by graduating from the first gender-integrated class of Infantry Officer Basic Leader Course." As Sergeant Major Joe Davis at Infantry Officer Basic Leader Course Command pointed out, "There has been no change in the standards. There is no change in the course . . . we are in the business of producing leaders. It doesn't matter if they are males or females."*

The Path Is Long and Hard

All army officers start their military training with an in-depth exposure and indoctrination in infantry tactics at small-unit level, to give them perspective.

Between the junior and senior years of the Reserve Officers' Training Course (ROTC), officers attend the Cadet Leaders Course at Fort Knox, Kentucky, which runs twenty-nine days. The hands-on, field exercise–based training includes a wide variety of subjects, including land navigation, fieldcraft, confidence training, a field leader's reaction course, maneuver training, weapons familiarization, cultural awareness, and tactics.

On graduation day, cadets are commissioned as second lieutenants and then go to a basic branch course; infantry and armor officers go to Fort Benning, artillery officers go to Fort Sill, and so on.

After completing the basic course, they may go on to specialized training, such as Airborne School, Ranger School, and others. Later in the course of their career, they go on to their respective school's advanced course, by which time they're senior first lieutenants or young captains. The military schooling, of course, is ongoing and never-ending.

In Jyn Erso's case, if she had been in the enlisted ranks, her career path would start at basic combat training, which runs ten weeks.

* Matthew Cox, "First 10 Women Graduate from Infantry Officer Course," military.com, October 26, 2016.

After Reception Week, she'd go through three phases, regardless of which specific school she'd attend afterward. The phases are as follows:

Red: General orientation, military-style haircuts, issuance of uniforms, basic tactical training, army heritage, the Seven Core Army Values, and the Army Physical Fitness Test.

White: Tactical foot march, basic rifle marksmanship, engagement skills and situational training exercises, field training exercises, and confidence obstacle course.

Blue: Weapons training with individual and crew-served weapons, a field training exercise, and a 10- or 15-kilometer tactical foot march.

After graduation, she'd move on to advanced individual training at one of the various branch schools, at which point permanent change of station orders are cut to let her know where she'll go for her first duty station.

The rank structure starts at private (E-1), then a private 2nd class (E-2), a private first class (E-3), a corporal/specialist (E-4), and then the NCO ranks starting at sergeant (E-5), up to sergeant major (E-9).

The other option is to go to Officer Candidate School, which has several requirements, chief among them a four-year college degree and no more than six years of active federal service.

Jyn Erso would also have made a fine student at Officer Candidate School, given what we saw in *Rogue One*. She had a bright future ahead of her, but her life was cut short: All give some, and some, like Jyn, gave all.

U.S. Army Battledress:
What to Wear in Combat

'm at Fort Sill, Oklahoma, home of the U.S. Army Field Artillery School, at its advanced course. Our class is gathered in an auditorium. We are here to get a preview of what's being cooked up by the U.S. Army Natick Soldier Systems Center, which is, as its website states, "responsible for researching, developing, fielding, and managing food, clothing, shelters, airdrop systems, and Soldier support items. NSSC's goal is simple: Provide America's Soldiers with the best equipment in the world."

We are all dressed in the standard fatigue uniform from back in the day, which is olive drab with brown T-shirts, shined black boots, and baseball-style fatigue caps. So when a young captain took the stage, wearing fatigues, fatigue cap, and matching boots all in desert tan, he got our attention.

He explained that the folks at Natick, Massachusetts, where they develop gear for troops, realized the need for a uniform that was more appropriate for the desert environment, because wearing olive drab green in the desert makes you stand out.

It got me thinking about the utility of combat uniforms, and that got me thinking about army troops wearing black berets, the brainchild of now-retired General Shinseki, then army chief of staff, who felt that adopting it army-wide would improve morale and enhance esprit de corps. It was, he said, about "our excellence as soldiers, our unity as a force, and our values as an institution." So, on June 14,

2001, U.S. Army troops begrudgingly began wearing the ill-fitting black beret.*

The troops *hated* them. They were useless in protecting you from the sun and rain, and they had no practical value in the field. As Shinseki discovered, you can fool yourself but you can't fool the troops, who have to live with bad decisions made by perfumed princes at the Pentagon who command large oak desks.

In 2011, the black beret became a thing of the past, to the infinite relief of the troops. As reported in *USA Today*:†

> The changes were prompted by feedback from thousands of soldiers through post-deployment surveys, social media and discussions with soldiers during base visits. . . . Soldiers complained that the beret takes two hands to put on and can't be carried in a pocket. Unlike the patrol cap, which has ventilated sun protection, the beret isn't included on the deployment packing list. . . . When the *Army Times* asked soldiers . . . for their feelings about the beret, more than 300 of all ranks and specialties chimed in: "Dump it."
>
> "It was time to dump it 10 years ago," wrote CWO3 [Chief Warrant Officer] Mark Vino of Joint Base Lewis-McChord, Washington. "I hate wearing a wet sock on my head. Plus it makes my head/skin break out."

What Shinseki, sitting in the Pentagon, apparently forgot was that fatigues are work uniforms. It's not about show, ceremony, or spectacle; it's about rolling up your sleeves and getting to work, often in dirty, dusty, and wet environments.

Shinseki could have learned a thing or two from how the Marines do things. When faced with a similar proposition—the issue being how to roll up fatigue sleeves—the sensible Marines figured out that it was best to simply roll them up with the inside of the

---

* Previously, the only berets allowed were green (Special Forces), maroon (Airborne), and tan (75th Ranger Regiment). Part of unit pride was knowing that, when one wore the beret, it meant something; it meant you were in an elite unit.

† Lance M. Brown, originally from *Army Times*, June 27, 2011.

sleeve showing. Their commonsense method is fast and easy to roll and unroll, comfortable, and the sleeves stay in place and don't unfurl.

The army way, though, is impractical, uncomfortable, and stresses appearance over functionality. They double-folded the sleeves to show the camo pattern. It also causes the slipping sleeves to bind uncomfortably, requiring frequent adjustments. Again, troops *hate* it, and rightly so, because they're the ones in the field, doing hard work.

That, too, was a decision made at the Pentagon, whose high-ranking officers figured that if the sleeves were double-rolled up, it looked good—or, in army slang, it looked "stract."*

It's a dumb policy, and the troops in the field rightly laugh at the senior officers at the Pentagon who have, for too long, been removed from the field and what it's like, as they sit in an air-conditioned building and wear comfortable office attire. Sadly, they are far removed from the unforgiving field environment where utility must trump appearance.[†]

All of which supports my contention that combat uniforms should be designed for maximum utility; they should be a combination of protection and comfort. There's a fine art to designing combat clothing, and it's important, too, because if you're in the army, you'll be wearing it night and day, in good weather and foul, on sunny or rainy days. In short, you'll have to live and fight wearing that uniform.

As with everything else in the U.S. Army, wait long enough and things will change. In my time, we wore the olive drab fatigues, which were replaced by battledress uniforms and then by today's Army Combat Uniform. The current uniforms are comfortable and practical, unlike the standard stormtrooper uniform in *Star Wars*.

---

* Army slang for a squared-away-looking trooper, especially in terms of dress.
† The dress code changed in June 2016, allowing troopers to roll sleeves up, cuffed inward, in what's called a Delta roll or SF (Special Forces) roll, in field environments, at the discretion of the commander. In garrison, however, the "sleeves up, camo (pattern) out" is still the order of the day.

Stormtroopers

When film visionary George Lucas populated his militarized universe, he drew heavily from World War I and II weapons, clothing, and equipment for inspiration. In most (but not all) instances, we accept Lucas's overall vision because it's consistent with past military history. We recognize their look and "feel."

Such is the case with the inspiration for the stormtroopers, which derives from Germany in the wake of World War I. These were specialized troops whose mission was to infiltrate enemy lines. Called *Sturmmann* (which literally translates to "storm man" but is most often translated loosely, to "stormtrooper"), a company of Sturmmann formed *Sturmtruppen* ("assault troops"), which loosely translates to "storm troops."

Historically, these were not general infantry but in fact specialized infantry troops.

In Lucas's *Star Wars* universe, the stormtrooper is a basic infantryman who, depending on his or her mission, wears a modified uniform.*

Stormtrooper Uniform Design

It makes sense that, in the future, the design of uniforms would take advantage of technology to provide maximum protection, especially since future weapons will be more lethal than today's.

Certainly, the collective effect of seeing an attacking force comprising six-foot-tall troopers in white armor and wearing menacing headgear provides a psychological edge. It dehumanizes the soldiers and gives them the appearance of relentless, attacking, robotic killing machines.†

---

* In Lucas's future, women are firmly entrenched in combat roles; notably, Captain Phasma commands the First Order's stormtrooper soldiers, as seen in *The Force Awakens*. Ordering troops to open fire on captured villagers, she proves that women can be badasses, too.

† Not surprisingly, the stormtrooper helmet and body armor are available for sale, but the best replicas don't come cheap: the helmet and armor, sold as a set, cost £1,449.97 (just over $2,000).

The white armor, we're told, includes eighteen pieces over a "two-piece, temperature-controlled bodysuit." The stormtrooper's utility belt carries "power packs, energy rations, and a compact tool kit. The belt also could tote additional gear, including a grappling hook, comlink, macrobinoculars, handcuff binders, or other items, such as a combat de-ionizer" (*The Complete Star Wars Encyclopedia*, vol. 3).

In other words, the integrated design follows the classic dictum that form follows function. Unfortunately, it's not an easy uniform to wear or fight in.

In *A New Hope*, there's a scene in which a stormtrooper on board the Death Star rushes into a room and bonks his head on the top-down door, suggesting that the helmet's view is restrictive. More-over, imagine how difficult it would be to remove part of or all of the uniform in order to sleep, or to put it on in a hurry when there's a call to battle stations—not to mention dealing with nature's calls.

Stormtroopers never speak out of class, but an actor named Ralph Morse has done so. He donned the one-size-fits-all storm-trooper uniform in *The Empire Strikes Back* and *Return of the Jedi* and pointed out some of its drawbacks. As CBS8.com reported in 2015, the costumes were "unbearable," difficult to get in and out of, impossible to sit down in, and formidable when nature called; moreover, the treadless soles made traction impossible, with re-stricted helmet visibility.

No doubt the Empire will learn from its design mistakes and make the necessary changes, but the height requirement of prospective stormtroopers (six feet tall)* is also central to the idea that they need to mass produce form-fitting suits in large numbers, so they're likely

---

The helmet alone can be had for £499.99 (about $675). These are available from British de-signer Andrew Ainsworth, who originally designed them for the *Star Wars* movie in 1977, after the U.K. Supreme Court "ruled that Mr. Ainsworth has the right to sell the *Star Wars* memora-bilia in England" (Susan Krashinsky, "The Lucasfilm empire strikes out," beta.globeandmail.com, July 27, 2011).

* This explains why, when she first sees Luke Skywalker on the Death Star in *A New Hope*, Princess Leia Organa takes one look at him and says, "Aren't you a little short to be a storm-trooper?" Mark Hamill is five feet nine inches—three inches too short to be a stormtrooper.

available in no more than three sizes, to keep costs and manufacturing issues to a minimum. (Imagine how difficult and expensive it would be to tailor individual suits to every stormtrooper.)

Of course, the actors wearing the uniform for the films aren't the only ones who have had to endure the hassles of wearing them. Fans who construct them have discovered that they don't exactly fit like a tailored Brooks Brothers suit. As one member of the 501st Legion, the *Star Wars* fan group that suits up in stormtrooper uniforms, put it:

> I'm not a stormtrooper myself, but comfort, visibility, and heating/cooling issues are sometimes issues that people forget to keep in mind when they're first starting to build their costume. They're usually reminded of it swiftly as soon as they do their first troop and they can't quite see where they're going, they overheat from lack of helmet fans, and their armor pinches every time they move their arms and legs. But our veteran members have learned over the years (and try to teach the recruits) how to combat lens fogging with helmet fans, trim their armor in specific ways to avoid joint pinching, take frequent breaks and hydrate in hot weather, and wear extra Under Armour in cold weather.

I've never donned the uniform myself, but online research and close observation of photos showing all aspects of the stormtrooper armor convinces me that simply putting on and taking off the body armor is a major pain in the butt, and in some cases, very problematic in actual use. The rear bottom plate and codpiece, for instance, would both need to be removed in order to take care of toilet needs.*

Bottom line: the functionality of combat uniforms is a serious business, especially because there are always compromises to address before battledressing.

For instance, U.S. Army troops are trained to fight in a nuclear,

---

* Here's an idea: Why not hinge the back piece and the front codpiece so they flip up and out of the way?

biological, chemical (NBC) environment. To do so, they must assume the appropriate mission-oriented protective posture (MOPP) level and be prepared to fight with the clothing and NBC protective gear on.*

Today's troops wear the Joint Service Lightweight Integrated Suit Technology, which is designed to be worn up to twenty-four hours in a contaminated environment. It's a two-piece garment (coat and trousers) that is worn *over* the battledress uniform. In addition, the trooper must wear the M40 mask or NBC M50 mask, a helmet cover, and gloves, and must carry NBC equipment: a detection kit, an individual decontamination kit, and antidotes for chemical hazard events. If you are getting the idea that it'd be difficult to suit up like that, you're right. But that's before the mask is worn, which severely restricts peripheral vision, like a stormtrooper's helmet.

There are five levels of MOPP, with MOPP 4 being the highest. That's when the trooper is wearing the full complement of NBC gear, regardless of the weather, for extended periods. (Imagine wearing that in desert, hundred-plus-degree weather, even for a short duration.)

You live, sleep, eat, and sleep with the protective gear on. It must become a part of you. It will also take a toll.

I recall on several occasions having to wear the M17 gas mask for several hours at a time during "mask confidence exercises." What's it like? Imagine having an octopus attached to your face, or a face-hugger from the movie *Alien*, and you get the idea. Not fun, not comfortable, and claustrophobic. That's why, during the drills, which were usually held at night, troops sometimes took them off and used them as pillows. (Not a good idea. That can crush the plastic eye goggles and the dual filters on both sides of the mask.)

Obviously, if you suffer from claustrophobia, these masks are a challenge to wear, because you feel as if you're suffocating.

No question, there's an art to designing effective, efficient, and comfortable combat clothing and gear, especially for today's increasingly

---

* See George Beahm, *Straight Talk About Terrorism: Protecting Your Home and Family from Nuclear, Biological, and Chemical Attacks* (Potomac Books, 2003).

lethal battlefield, which is why the army has decided it's necessary to provide more protection to soldiers in the field than what is currently available.

Tactical Assault Light Operator Suit

As Admiral Bill McRaven tells it, one of his special ops soldiers died during a raid for lack of a battle-worthy uniform. "One of our [Navy SEAL] folks going through the door was killed by the Taliban on the other side in an attempt to rescue a hostage," he told National Public Radio. He was simply shot in the chest with a small-caliber round.

That led to research into a reactive suit composed of liquid armor "that can solidify when it's hit by a bullet." A battery-operated robotic exoskeleton, the tactical assault light operator suit (TALOS) looks uncannily like a stormtrooper's outfit, with segmented, articulated pieces and an enhanced helmet. National Public Radio reported, "Just like [Tony] Stark's [Ironman] suit, TALOS is fitted with built-in sensors that monitor the wearer's health, checking conditions from heart rate to body temperature."

It's a far cry from what our soldiers wore during Vietnam, which offered scant protection: a lightweight olive drab uniform, a steel "pot" for a helmet (with web strapping that always came loose), a web harness with gear attached and ammo secured in pouches, and a pair of black combat boots that offered no protection against the punji sticks tipped with dung and hidden in rice paddies, which went up through a rubber boot's soles.

The infantry also was armed with a toy-like plastic M16 firing a 5.56 round. The rifle often jammed when it became wet or muddy, unlike the enemy's durable wood-and-metal AK-47, which fired a larger 7.62 round with greater stopping power. If you dropped your AK-47 in the mud, you could pick it up and resume firing immediately. Try doing that with the M16 and see what happens.*

---

* For a comparison of the two assault rifles, see "M16 vs. AK-47: Which One Is Better?," http://www.military-today.com/firearms/m16_vs_ak47.htm.

In other words, army troops were outgunned by the inexpensively produced, Russian-made rifle, which is still the assault weapon of choice for today's terrorists worldwide.

The army has upgraded the M16, but what's needed is a new assault rifle with better reliability and durability, fewer maintenance issues, and more penetrating power. (In each of these areas, the AK-47 is demonstrably better.)

Vader's Fist: The 501st Legion

Known and referred to as "Vader's Fist," the 501st Legion is much more than fans cosplaying. Its website tells us that they have a "Sith sense of humor," which is obvious, as we're also told that one member of the organization showed up for a job interview by "delivering his personal résumé to a prospective employer" while "wearing full sandtrooper gear. He left such an impression that he was eventually awarded the job."

As with any military organization, there's a mission—three, in fact. First, "to promote interest in *Star Wars*"; second, "to facilitate the use of costumes"; and third, and most importantly, "to contribute: . . . The 501st is proud to put its resources to good use through fundraising, charity work, and volunteerism."

I contacted three members of the 501st to discuss comfort issues with the uniform, but none responded. (Did they take an oath of silence? Your mileage may vary.) In any event, if you're interested in signing up, they're always looking to add to the ranks—if you can fill their boots. Membership information is available at databank.501st.com/databank/Membership:JoinUs.

The Danger of Overconfidence:
The Galactic Empire's Leadership

In *Return of the Jedi*, Emperor Palpatine, aka Darth Sidious, is on the bridge of his flagship, a Super Star Destroyer, surrounded by Star Destroyers. As Sidious knows, the rebel fleet has assembled at Sullust to make the jump to light speed and confront the Empire head-on in a space battle they hope to win. (The rebels think they have the element of surprise, but they don't.)

Darth Sidious knows all about the "imminent" attack and confidently tells Luke Skywalker that his forces are safe from the rebel forces.

Luke's response: "Your overconfidence is your weakness."

But is he right in thinking so?

Darth Sidious knows that, in terms of raw power, he's got the upper hand. Even without an operational Death Star with even more firepower than the first one, the Empire has a formidable army and navy. He also knows of the impending attack. The stakes are high: if the rebels win, the Death Star will be destroyed, and it will likely be the end of the Empire.

As German military strategist Helmuth von Moltke observed, "No battle plan survives contact with the enemy." Or as Scottish poet Robert Burns observed, the best-laid plans of mice and men often go awry.

Because of the Empire's foreknowledge of the attack, they planned accordingly. The rebel fleet would be met with a prepared force using overwhelming firepower, including a functional Death Star that, among other capabilities, can target ships and destroy them with a single superlaser blast.

So what, from the Empire's perspective, could possibly go wrong? Unfortunately for the Empire, everything. Murphy's Law always applies.*

Darth Sidious felt that a company-size unit of his "best troops" was sufficient to maintain a force on the Endor moon.† They were housed in a standard imperial garrison. So the equation, from the Empire's point of view, looks like this: Best troops+Impregnable garrison=Invincible force.

But their force had not reckoned with the indigenous population, a race called Ewoks, which they viewed as an insignificant military threat. When teamed with General Solo's strike force, however, the Ewoks' significantly smaller, less equipped military force proves instrumental in assisting the commandos on their raid against the imperial garrison.

Dismissing altogether the Ewoks' presence, the Imperial troops, like Darth Sidious, were overconfident. The result was that the Empire lost both the ground *and* the air battle. It was the difference between confidence and overconfidence: the former is a proven asset, the latter a known liability. As Sun Tzu explained, "Master Sun talks often about deception and therefore against being deceived by the enemy and underestimating their ability. 'He who exercises no forethought but makes light of his opponents is sure to be captured by them.' It is important to properly assess your opponent without prejudice or assumption."

---

* What can go wrong, will go wrong.

† No precise figures about manning strength are stated. I'm making an educated guess based on what we see in *Return of the Jedi*.

General Standards: Does Jar Jar Binks Have the Right Stuff?

In *The Phantom Menace*, Jar Jar Binks attains the rank of bombad general (probably equivalent to a one-star, brigadier general). But questions arise: What exactly qualified him to become a one-star general? And, in real-world terms, what's actually involved in becoming a general?

For the moment, let's all give Jar Jar Binks the benefit of the doubt. I think we can all agree that his creation was not George Lucas's finest moment.* I'm not going to add to the catcalls. Instead, let's take a sober look at Binks's leadership potential.

Jar Jar Binks

Binks, who makes his first appearance in *The Phantom Menace*, lives on the planet Naboo. More specifically, he lives in an underwater city named Otoh Gunga, more commonly known as Gunga City, on the floor of Lake Paonga.

When we first meet Jar Jar Binks, he's an outcast from Otoh Gunga. Foraging in a nearby forest for food after being banned by Rugor "Boss" Nass, the leader of Gunga City, Binks is on his own. But because of Binks's role as an unofficial ambassador working with Queen Amidala, bringing the Gungans together with the neigh-

---

* From Den of Geek UK (denofgeek.com/uk): At D23 Expo, an official Disney convention, George Lucas told the audience that "I will say one secret that nobody knows . . . Goofy was the inspiration for Jar Jar Binks. I know you'll look [at him] a little differently now." (Meesa don't think so.)

boring Naboo citizens during the Trade Federation invasion of Naboo, Binks receives an unexpected field promotion. Boss Nass tells him, "Wesa make you bombad general."

Binks, upon hearing the news, promptly passes out.

Shortly thereafter, we see him in action at the Battle of Naboo. It's a classic force-on-force frontal engagement, with the Gungan Grand Army on the field of battle. The Trade Federation Army is clearly larger, stronger, and better equipped. It has heavy transports and heavy weapons, including state-of-the-art tanks using repulsor lifts to float above the ground.

We don't know, but we can speculate that the rank of bombad general is equivalent to that of a brigadier general, who typically serves as a deputy commander in the U.S. Army and is subordinate to a major general (two stars), who commands a division.*

By all rights, Binks is more qualified for an ambassadorial position than a military position. Nonetheless, he plays an important role in the Battle of Naboo, because his actions—both deliberate and accidental—prove useful in defeating the Trade Federation Army.

But his sudden and unexpected battlefield promotion is worrisome. I suspect the Gungan troops (not an active duty force but a citizen militia) were quite surprised when they heard that Binks would be issuing orders in the field during a combat operation. I'm sure a number of them rolled their big eyes when they got the news.

That may be how things work in the Gungan Army, but in the real world, what does it take to make a general?

General Ingredients

As a four-star general, the late General Schwarzkopf enjoyed a stellar career. He worked himself up the ladder, which army-portal.com

---

* My old unit, the 1st Infantry Division at Fort Riley, Kansas, currently consists of the 1st Armored Brigade Combat Team, the 2nd Armored Brigade Combat Team, the 1st Combat Aviation Brigade, 1ID Divarty (Division Artillery), 1ID Sustainment Brigade, Division HQ, and HQ Battalion. The manning of a division varies, and can range from ten thousand to fifteen thousand.

succinctly spells out. The officer rank structure resembles an inverted pyramid: second lieutenants (pay grade 0–1) form its broad base; and at the top are generals, like Schwarzkopf, wearing four stars (pay grade 0–10).*

Army officers get their commissions through the Officer Candidate School program, ROTC (college and universities), or West Point (service school).

The following will give you an idea of the responsibilities an officer assumes at each rank, and how long it normally takes to achieve that rank.

Obviously, time in grade is a key consideration. Officers aren't promoted until they've spent the requisite time at specific levels—unlike Jar Jar Binks, who had spent no time in the military and thus has no idea what his duties and responsibilities are in his current rank.

In the army, the rank structure, scope of responsibility, and time in grade (O for "officer") is as follows:

- **Second lieutenant** (pay grade 0–1): a platoon leader with sixteen to forty-four soldiers. Zero years in uniform; rank is assigned upon commissioning.
- **First lieutenant** (pay grade 0–2): specialized weapons platoons or executive officer; second-in-command of a company-level unit. Time in grade is 1.5 years of military service.
- **Captain** (pay grade 0–3): commands a company-level unit (62 to 190 soldiers, depending on the kind of unit) or serves as a staff officer at battalion level. Time in grade is four years of military service.
- **Major** (pay grade 0–4): normally a staff officer at brigade and task force commands. Time in grade is ten years of military service.

* The General of the Army wears five stars, but it's "awarded only in times of war when the commanding officer must be equal or higher in rank than the commanding armies of other participating nations. Last use was during and shortly after World War II" ("Army Officer Ranks and Promotions," army-portal.com).

- **Lieutenant colonel** (pay grade O–5): commands a battalion (three hundred to one thousand soldiers, depending on the kind of unit) or serves as executive officer for a brigade or task force. Time in grade is sixteen years of military service.
- **Colonel** (pay grade O–6): commands a brigade (three thousand to five thousand soldiers) or serves as chief of division-level staff agencies. Time in grade is twenty-two years. (Only half of lieutenant colonels are selected for promotion to this rank, which is why they're nervous when the promotion board meets to cull the herd. If an officer is passed over for promotion on the first go-around, it's almost certain that the same will happen on the second go-around, and he'll be forced to retire, if he has his twenty years in. If not, he's simply discharged with no retirement benefits.)
- **Brigadier general** (pay grade O–7): deputy commander for the commanding general of an army division. This rank is limited to only 150 officers army-wide.
- **Major general** (pay grade O–8): commands a division (ten thousand to fifteen thousand soldiers). This rank is limited to ninety-nine officers army-wide.
- **Lieutenant general** (pay grade O–9): commands a corps (twenty thousand to twenty-five thousand soldiers). This rank is limited to forty-three officers army-wide.
- **General** (pay grade O–10): commands a large geographic area, such as U.S. Central Command, a theater-level command responsible for the Middle East, North Africa, and Central Asia. Also can serve as the Army chief of staff, or chairman of the Joint Chiefs of Staff. General Schwarzkopf, for example, commanded Central Command and reported to General Colin Powell (chairman, Joint Chiefs of Staff). After Operation Desert Storm, Schwarzkopf was earmarked to be the next Army chief of staff, but he declined. (As he explained in his autobiography, his principal duty would have been to oversee downsizing the army after the war, and "I'd rather retire with a great victory than suffer a

thousand defeats at the hands of Congress." In other words, he preferred to retire as a warrior, not as a bureaucrat in a military uniform.)

Bombad General Jar Jar Binks

Given that an army officer who reaches the rank of colonel has twenty-two years' time in grade, Jar Jar Binks's leapfrogging over all his fellow Gungans was unprecedented. Moreover, such a promotion deflates the morale of fellow officers, who naturally ask themselves, *Why wasn't I promoted instead?* It smacks of a political, not military, appointment. It's not well-deserved rank based on previous military history with a record of accomplishment.

The most important consideration is what kind of leadership Binks will provide on the battlefield.

As it turned out, Binks did play a role, but it's clear that he didn't display the kind of military leadership that Captain Roos Tarpals exhibited. (Later, during the Clone Wars, Tarpals was promoted to general, and rightly so. He *earned* it, unlike Binks.)

In all fairness, we cannot expect Binks to go from being an ordinary citizen to assuming the responsibilities of a general and do so with the requisite skill and knowledge drawn from years of experience. Frankly, instead of being flattered and accepting the promotion, Binks should have respectfully declined.

Though Binks did prove tactically useful on the field of battle—who knew his clumsiness would be an asset?—the fact remains that Gungan leader Boss Nass should not have promoted Binks to high rank at all. As we've seen, premature promotion of an officer can lead to devastating consequences. I term this the Piett Postulate.*

This is why, if I were a Gungan, I would not willingly follow Jar Jar Binks into battle. That's what *mesa* is thinking. *Yousa* are entitled to your own opinion.

---

* Captain Piett was promoted on the spot after Darth Vader relieved his predecessor, Admiral Ossel, in *Return of the Jedi*.

Colored Pauldrons

A pauldron is the large, colored piece of plastic on the right shoulder of the stormtrooper uniform.

If you see stormtroopers advancing on your position and some are wearing distinctively colored pauldrons, target the one with an orange pauldron.

Why?

Because the pauldron indicates rank and/or mission specialization, and an orange one identifies the commander.

According to Wookieepedia, the pauldron colors are thus identified:

1. Stormtrooper commanders wear orange, red, or white.
2. Stormtroopers from the enlisted ranks wear black.
3. Stormtroopers from the NCO ranks wear white. (See number 1. Confusing.)
4. Stormtroopers who are snipers wear blue.
5. Stormtroopers who are grenadiers wear red. (See number 1. Confusing.)

So you'd first want to take out the enemy's command and control, targeting those wearing orange pauldrons—commanders. After that, you'd target the NCOs who wear white, since they lead the enlisted personnel.

What I don't understand is why the pauldrons, part of the body armor, are so highly visible. You can't miss them . . . nor can enemy snipers.

So You Want to Be an Army Officer: Pathways to a Commission

The US Army draws from multiple sources to fill its officer ranks. The one thing all officers have in common is that *it doesn't matter where they came from*. What matters is where they're going, which is based entirely on what they accomplish *after* being commissioned as a second lieutenant in the U.S. Army.

By far, the bulk of the officers who get commissioned are from the Reserve Officers' Training Corps program. Seventy percent of newly minted second lieutenants, nicknamed "butterbars" because of the gold bar designating their rank, come from colleges and universities nationwide, ensuring maximum diversity; after all, the troops also come from diverse backgrounds.

West Point, one of four service academies in the U.S. military, is stereotypically presumed to be the fast track to success for army officers, and, in truth, being part of "the long gray line"* does command attention, but in the end it's job performance that counts. That will determine an officer's assignments, command slots, and how fast they move up the ladder of success.

The army has a vested interest in recognizing and promoting the best leaders to top positions. It's not simply a matter of "punching

---

* That phrase "in its simplest definition is the continuum of all graduates and cadets of the United States Military Academy at West Point, in New York. Uttered affectionately by West Point graduates, the phrase refers to the unique ties which bind every West Point graduate to all the others who have come before, and all those who will come after. . . . 'The Long Gray Line' reflects the gray cadet uniforms and the bright young individuals who endure its itchy wool fabric and stiff collars because that too is part of West Point's tradition and pageantry" ("The Long Gray Line," goarmywestpoint.com).

the right tickets" (Airborne, Ranger, Expert Infantryman Badge, etc.), of having gone to the "right" school, or of wearing the "right" branch insignia (one of the combat arms). It's about hustling your butt off and showing that you've got the right stuff, even for the many ROTC graduates who rise to high rank.

As cadetcommand.army.mil points out, "More than 40 percent of current active duty Army General Officers were commissioned through ROTC," including four-star general Colin Powell, who graduated from City College of New York.

Enlisted personnel with leadership potential can apply for Officer Candidate School. After graduation, they obtain a commission. These "sixty-day wonders"—so called because the course runs approximately two months—make excellent officers. Moreover, because they have a unique perspective—they know what it's like to be in the enlisted ranks—they have a leg up over recently commissioned butterbars who lack that interaction.

For those with professional training in the legal, medical, or religious fields, a direct commission is possible, bypassing the traditional routes. The advantage is that it doesn't require four years of classroom/field ROTC. Moreover, the branch itself, not the Department of the Army, determines your entry rank, which may start at first lieutenant but most likely will start at captain. These fields include the Judge Advocate General's Corps, for attorneys; the Medical Corps, for health professionals (usually nurses and doctors); and the Chaplain Corps.

To be honest, the army life is not for everyone. If your heart's not in it, it's not the place for you. If you can't be a leader and a follower at the same time—for there will always be someone above you and also below you in rank—it's not for you. And if you're a clock-watcher or concerned about how much money you're going to make, it's *definitely* not for you.*

---

* When I was with the 1st Infantry Division, I was sent to the main post to get more tactical maps for our unit. I waited patiently while a civil servant, yakking on the phone, took his sweet time while I fumed and stared at the large clock on the wall. Ten minutes passed slowly. When he finally acknowledged my presence, he looked at the clock and said, "Sorry, lieutenant, but

But if you want to be a part of an organization that's bigger than just yourself—that is, if you want your worldview expanded and your work to be challenging—and you want to test your personal limits by assuming greater leadership roles, with demanding command slots that put you front and center before the troops who stand at attention, awaiting your orders, then it might be the life for you.

---

it's quitting time. It's four thirty." I protested but it did no good. He had decided to close down shop, not caring why he had a job in the first place: to support the field units. Lesson to be learned: don't go into the military if you are a clock-watcher, because the hours won't suit you. (I like to think he was the exception, because I know at least one outstanding civil servant who more than earns his pay. He shows up for work at six in the morning, and sometimes earlier. He's not getting paid to show up that early; he just feels comfortable putting in additional time to get the job done right. As we say in the army: outstanding!)

From Smuggler to General: Han Solo

Han Solo led a charmed life. He escaped death at the hands of the Galactic Empire and others numerous times, including being frozen in carbonite, tortured, chased by TIE fighters and Star Destroyers, and nearly being barbecued by diminutive Ewoks. He had seen and done it all, and in *The Force Awakens* we saw his life come full circle. He went back to his roots, transporting cargo across the galaxy while fending off creditors.

It was a long, strange journey for Han Solo, whom we first met in *A New Hope*, forty years ago. Then a smuggler who was in over his head with considerable debt, Han Solo was gruff stuff and his own boss, which is just the way he and his first mate on the *Millennium Falcon*, Chewbacca, liked it.

Most people in his profession likely come to a bad end—smuggling is a hazardous profession. Instead, Han Solo suffered the slings and arrows of outrageous fortune and eventually became a respected general in the Rebel Alliance.

In looking back at the original trilogy (now titled *Star Wars IV, V,* and *VI*), we see that Han Solo was a man of action from the beginning. He was a born leader who inspired confidence from those under his command. In a just world, Han Solo and his wife, Leia Organa, would see themselves growing old together, sitting on a porch at night, looking up at the twinkling stars, with all the wars behind them. Instead, Han dies an ignominious death and

Leia is now on her own, to her infinite regret and our collective sorrow.

What made Han Solo such an effective leader? Let me count the ways.

Six Traits of Top Military Officers

In "6 Traits of Top Military Officers," Lieutenant Colonel Greg McMahan, who heads the University of North Georgia's Department of Military Science, explains that the old standards in selecting and matching young officers "used to be 'Are you smart? Are you strong? And do you know your tactics?' Now, [the U.S. Army is] looking a little bit deeper into the intellectual and physical attributes and characteristics."

He points out six key traits: character, presence, intellect, leader, developer, and achiever. Let's see how Han Solo measures up.

I. Character: "Aspects of character include showing Army values, empathy, warrior ethos/service ethos, and discipline."

In *A New Hope*, we first see Han Solo commanding a spaceship, the *Millennium Falcon*. We can infer that he's a cut above the rest, since piloting it requires consummate skill.

Moreover, as a smuggler, he plied his illicit trade at considerable risk to himself and his first mate, Chewbacca, because he was often up against the Galactic Empire, other smugglers, and bounty hunters. As he well knew, it was always best to avoid imperial "entanglements," as he told Ben Kenobi and Luke Skywalker at the Mos Eisley spaceport. Han Solo has what every smuggler must possess: courage.

Though Han was known to dump his cargo when he got boarded by imperial troops, he understood that came with the territory. But we assume that, more often than not, Han managed to get his illicit cargo to its intended destination. He made a living, albeit a precarious one, and despite running into Jabba the Hutt or one of his minions no matter where he went, Han always managed to shoot or talk his way out of it.

Han was essentially an army of one, aided by Chewbacca. Han often handled "hot" cargo and blew past imperial blockades, which required a lot of skill and courage.

Unlike other smugglers, who were unreliable and unscrupulous, Han Solo's word was his bond. He was respected, even by his enemies. One of them, an alien named Greedo, showed up with a blaster at the Mos Eisley spaceport to kill him. Instead, it was Greedo who got blasted, because he tried to live up to his name.

Han also had scruples. He was an honorable man. After all, he could have taken Ben Kenobi's cash and left him and Luke Skywalker stranded at the spaceport; they couldn't have stopped him. But Han was true to his word and got them off the planet. In fact, not even the Empire could stop him: he blasted past the Empire's planetary blockade by going to light speed.

There's no doubt that Han Solo was a man of character with an unshakable, inner core of strength.

But, being a smuggler, Han Solo was beholden only to himself and not to any cause. He certainly was not initially sympathetic to the Rebel Alliance's cause. As Han angrily told Princess Leia, who gave him the sharp edge of her tongue at the end of *A New Hope*, "I'm in it for the money!"

That's the smuggler's ethos, and who can blame Han Solo for taking care of Number One? You say you want a revolution? Well, as far as Han's concerned, it can start without him.

Han Solo had the right stuff. As Tom Wolfe described it in his book about the early astronauts:

As to just what this ineffable quality was . . . well, it obviously involved bravery. . . . There was . . . a seemingly infinite series of tests . . . a dizzy progression of steps and ledges, a ziggurat, a pyramid extraordinarily high and steep; and the idea was to prove at every foot of the way up that pyramid that you were one of the elected and anointed ones who had *the right stuff* and could move higher and higher and even—ultimately, God willing, one day—that you might be able to join that special few at the very top, that elite who had the capacity to bring tears to men's eyes, the very Brotherhood of the Right Stuff itself.*

By the end of *A New Hope* we see Han Solo showing his true colors, when other smugglers in his situation would have packed up and left as soon as possible, especially when the Galactic Empire showed up in full force.

2. Presence: "For Army officers, presence means military and professional bearing, fitness, confidence, and resilience."

Boiled down to its essentials, this is all about substance, not appearance. One's presence can best be gauged through the eyes of one's subordinates, peers, and superior officers. It's about being a quiet professional and just doing the job right, every time, without fanfare or applause.

Case in point: On a rainy, cold night in Fort Bragg, North Carolina, we were on our last field problem as ROTC students, huddled beneath our rubberized ponchos and illuminating our maps with red-filtered flashlights.† It was past midnight and all hundred-plus of us were totally exhausted.

We received an information briefing from our evaluator, a young captain. We were expected to listen, take notes, and, when called upon, give a detailed five-paragraph order covering the situation, mission, execution, administrative/logistical information, and command and signal. Someone was going to have to stand up and deliver it.

---

* The book *The Right Stuff* was adapted into a movie in 1983, directed by Philip Kaufman. I highly recommend both the book and the movie.
† In between the junior and senior year of college, ROTC students attend what's informally called "summer camp." But it's no fun under the sun; it's hard work, and designed to give you a realistic taste of what you can expect when, a year later, you are commissioned as a junior officer.

The evaluator knew that whomever he called on would have to be able to condense a lot of material and put it in the right format for an oral briefing, and so he didn't randomly choose one of us. He knew exactly whom to call on—a quiet young man sitting next to me.

My friend stood up in the rain, covered by his poncho, and as I held my flashlight on his notes, he calmly read the mission briefing. It was letter-perfect and outstanding. Had it not been a tactical field problem, we all would have clapped. As it was, we could see the evaluator's face break into a thin smile. That young infantry captain was clearly impressed. It was an example of quiet professionalism at its best. No grandstanding, no ego, no show. Just getting the job done the right way.

We all knew that young cadet would be going places. Not surprisingly, he was the smartest cadet in the class.*

The young Han Solo displayed that kind of confidence and bearing. He believed and trusted in himself and his capabilities, and others sensed it. Men looked up to him. It's no surprise, then, that by the time we saw him in *The Empire Strikes Back*, he was already a proven asset.†

In *The Empire Strikes Back*, when Han told General Rieekan, commander of the rebel base on the ice planet Hoth, that he was leaving to take care of a long-standing and pressing obligation with Jabba the Hutt, the general expressed his regrets.

A good man is always hard to find, and Han Solo was a good man. Everyone could see that—especially Princess Leia, who came to respect him and, though she wouldn't admit it, had a sweet spot in her heart for him as well, which grew in the years to come.

The men at the rebel base looked up to Commander Solo because he earned their respect. They knew of his maneuver in the Battle of Yavin and, afterward, got to see and know him on a professional

---

* He subsequently served in the army as a doctor and went on to become a neurosurgeon as a civilian.

† Presumably, he held the rank of commander, just like Luke Skywalker. In the U.S. Navy, a commander's pay grade is 0–5. The equivalent U.S. Army rank would be lieutenant colonel. After that, full colonel and brigadier general.

and personal level. In short, he lived up to his reputation. Han Solo didn't demand respect; he earned everyone's respect. That's what leadership and presence is all about.

The military profession, as Robert A. Heinlein* pointed out, has many disadvantages, so why would anyone *want* to put on the uniform? He then takes the time to explain the drawbacks of military service (and, believe me, there are many). But his point was that, despite its numerous drawbacks, military service is a high calling only for those who see themselves as part of:

> A tradition of service. Your most important classroom is Memorial Hall. Your most important lesson is the way you feel inside when you walk up those steps and see that shot-torn flag framed in the arch of the door: "Don't Give Up the Ship."
>
> If you feel nothing, you don't belong here. But if it gives you goose flesh just to see that old battle flag, then you are going to find that feeling increases every time you return [to the Academy] over the years . . . until it reaches a crescendo the day you return and read the list of your own honored dead—classmates, shipmates, friends—read them with grief and pride while you try to keep your tears silent.†

3. Intellect: "Critical thinking, innovation, and problem-solving skills are vital . . ."

The stupidest thing I've ever heard a military officer utter was a statement that he didn't need to make decisions because everything was already spelled out in doctrinal Army publications: the field manuals, the technical manuals, and, most important, the Uniform Code of Military Justice.

Wrong. Dead wrong. I was glad, as a junior officer, that I wasn't under his command.

---

* The Dean of Science Fiction writers, Heinlein was an Annapolis graduate (U.S. Naval Academy), served on the destroyer *USS Roper* in 1933–34, and was forced into early retirement for medical reasons.

† "The Forrestal Lecture" given to the Brigade of Midshipmen at the U.S. Naval Academy on April 5, 1973.

It's a truism in the military that you can write the most detailed tactical plan before a battle but, once the bullets fly, you can toss whatever you wrote out the window, because everything is going to drastically change.

Life doesn't follow your written plan, especially on the battlefield, which is fluid and constantly changing. In short, you can't simply look up the answers to life in any book or manual; you have to think through things and think on your feet as well.

Han Solo in *The Empire Strikes Back* was a changed man. He was a little older, a little wiser, and more commanding. When Luke Skywalker was unaccounted for, only Han was concerned about his absence; no one else seemed to be. They just assumed Luke was on the premises, when in fact he wasn't.

On Dagobah or Tatooine, that wouldn't be a pressing concern. But on Hoth, an ice planet, where hypothermia can set in very quickly, it's a grave concern.

Han made a decision to go on a one-man search to find Luke, despite the personal risk to his own safety. The odds, as C-3PO told him, were not in his favor. Thinking his way through the situation, however, Han felt confident that it was the right call to go out and find Luke, which he did. He made a timely, correct decision.

Smart officers like Han never presume or assume; they make it a point to *know*.

There are many other examples from the *Star Wars* saga that show how Han Solo handled himself with distinction, but my favorite is from *The Empire Strikes Back*, when he was on the *Falcon*, pursued by TIE fighters, and he eluded them by deliberately flying into an asteroid field.

Han just went for it. (Just never tell him the odds.)

4. Leader: "The ability to lead under pressure . . ."

As Lieutenant Colonel McMahan observed, "I think what we look for most is interpersonal skills—the ability to manage and lead other people, especially through tough situations. If they can't relate with people and manage them when it's low stress, when it starts to get more difficult, it will be even harder for them."

The army is *all* about people. You can have the best equipment—the fastest tanks, the biggest guns, the fastest helicopters—but it means nothing if you don't have the right people to drive, fire, and fly them.

An officer's leadership skill has everything to do with the ability to manage, lead, and inspire the troops.

Look at how an officer handles the small problems, which foreshadows what he will do when larger problems manifest themselves. In short, if you can't handle a low-stress situation in garrison, how can you expect to handle the high-stress situations in the field?

In *Return of the Jedi*, Han Solo was tasked with his most difficult mission yet. He had to lead a strike team of commandos to the surface of Endor and disable a force field generator protecting the second Death Star. What made it more challenging was that the generator, situated on top of a prefabricated imperial structure, was manned by a garrison of crack stormtroopers. (Or so we were told by Palpatine. They didn't strike me as being tactically or technically proficient.)

Upon arrival, Han apparently didn't know that the indigenous population would view him and his colleagues as intruders. But the small-sized, big-hearted Ewoks are soon won over by them. (It helps to offer them rations, as Leia did.) They joined up with the rebels and took on the stormtroopers, who had All Terrain Armored Transports (AT-ATs) and All Terrain Scout Transports (AT-STs) at their disposal.

Han could not have had more pressure applied to him. If he failed in his mission, his counterpart—General Lando Calrissian—would inevitably fail, with catastrophic consequences. Now *that's* pressure. But in the end Han prevailed.

5. Developer: "It's important for an officer to create a positive environment, develop others, and steward the profession."

Army of One. That is a slogan the U.S. Army used for five years, but nobody really understood what it meant, and the image it presented was confusing. It seemed to imply that each soldier was on his or her own, or maybe not. Whatever. It was a conflicting slogan that never caught on with the brass. In fact, it had replaced a much better slogan, Be All You Can Be, which was used for nearly twenty-one years.

In truth, there's no such thing as an army of one; there's an army of many, millions strong. The grunt in the field is not alone. He's got a long logistics tail behind him to make sure he's got what he needs to sustain combat operations.*

This means that officers must constantly be developing their subordinates, because in combat, if the commanding officer becomes a casualty, the next in line needs to step up and be ready to take charge. In the field artillery, for instance, if the battery commander is killed, the executive officer steps up. And if he's killed, then the fire direction officer steps up. And they'd better be ready.

The command climate, the environment created by the presence and policies of the commander, is also paramount. If you produce an atmosphere of distrust and fear, your officers and troops will mirror your values, because they take their cue from you. Fear breeds fear, just as confidence breeds confidence.

More than anyone else in the *Star Wars* saga, Darth Vader, who misused and abused his position and power, established an environment of fear that had a predictably corrosive effect on his subordinates. He ruled in a zero-tolerance environment, he didn't develop others, and he trusted no one. As Darth Sidious's executive officer, Vader wore the mantle of command poorly. He considered his subordinates expendable and, instead of mentoring them, he simply killed them when they displeased him.

---

* As Lieutenant General Franks, commander of the 7th Corps in Desert Storm put it, "Forget logistics, you lose."

This explains why his subordinates were scared spitless.

The end result of his management style was that when he and his "master" (as Vader termed Palpatine) died by their own hands, in *Return of the Jedi*, the remaining military leaders, divided in their loyalties, broke up into different factions, which weakened them sufficiently that the Rebel Alliance was able to fill the power void and take control of the reins of power.

It would have been far better for Palpatine and Darth Vader to develop their subordinates to take over, in the event one or both of them were killed, ensuring that the chain of command would not be broken. As it was, the debilitating effect of a poisoned command climate that didn't foster individual initiative or personal growth set the stage for the chaos that ensued as the Empire imploded.

6. Achiever: "All Army officers are expected to get results in their specific jobs . . ."

The purpose of the U.S. Army is simply stated: "to fight and win our Nation's wars by providing prompt, sustained dominance across the full range of military operations and spectrum of conflict in support of combatant commanders."*

Put in context: there's a reason the army is the largest force in our military, in terms of the number of personnel. It's because we need the sheer numbers in order to fight the land battle, which cannot be won without boots on the ground.

The navy and air force work in tandem to support the army's ground operations. The navy moves troops and equipment to the battlefield, and the air force provides preemptive air strikes against key installations and massing personnel, and provides close air support for the infantry.

Combat is an interservice team effort, with the principal military forces† working together as a cohesive unit to bring the full strength

---

* "U.S. Army: Organization, Who We Are," army.mil.
† The Coast Guard does not answer to the Department of Defense but to the Department of Homeland Security.

and firepower of a combat arms team to bear at a designated place and at a predetermined time to ultimately achieve victory.

None of this comes cheaply, either. The military budget of any developed country is necessarily enormous, and it's either money well spent or poorly spent. As Robert A. Heinlein noted: "The most expensive thing in the world is a second-best military establishment, good but not good enough to win."[*]

In 2015, the U.S. military had a budget of approximately $598 billion. For that kind of money, Americans expect value for their dollar; they expect victory.[†]

According to Credit Suisse's ranking of the world's top twenty militaries, the United States holds the number one position. (Number two is Russia and number three is China.) As the report states, the US military budget pays for 1.4 million active frontline personnel; 8,848 tanks; 13,892 aircraft; seventy-two submarines; and a fleet of ten aircraft carriers.[‡]

You don't spend that kind of money to fight battles and lose. You spend it because you expect your military to win every time, and decisively so.

But money isn't enough. If you don't have outstanding leadership at every level, you can spend a fortune and still lose, as Saddam Hussein's military found out the hard way.

Han Solo, as a smuggler and then a general in the Rebel Alliance, gave it his all. He was instrumental in the destruction of not one but two Death Stars. Without his actions, the Galactic Empire would have gone on to tighten its grip throughout the galaxy until resistance was futile. That would have been the end of the Rebel Alliance and the beginning of a long reign of terror.

---

[*] From "The Happy Days Ahead" in *Expanded Universe* (1980).
[†] President Trump plans to dramatically increase the budget for the military, raising it by $54 billion, according to the *New York Times* (February 27, 2017).
[‡] A full explanation can be found in Jeremy Bender, "Ranked: The World's 20 Strongest Militaries," businessinsider.com, October 3, 2015.

May the Force Be with Han Solo

For a warrior who survived so much, it seems anticlimactic that Han Solo, in the end, died such a sudden death. Echoing my feelings, and those of many others, Stephanie Zacharek, writing in *Time* magazine ("The Problem With That Major *Force Awakens* Scene," December 20, 2015), is right in saying that "Han Solo's death in *The Force Awakens* isn't operatic at all, and I can't help feeling that this character deserves better."

Han should have died a warrior's death. He should have died gloriously. He should have—

Aw, hell. Let's face it: he died a stupid death because he let his guard down. *He didn't have to die.*

I remember when the commander of the rebel base on Hoth, General Rieekan, said, "You're a good fighter, Solo. I hate to lose you."

I suspect there are millions more Han Solo fans who feel that way. Originally an army of one, as a smuggler, Han Solo eventually lived up to the motto Be All You Can Be. And largely because of him, untold billions no longer had to fear the Galactic Empire.

As Robert A. Heinlein wrote about another fearless and selfless man, in a statement which also applies in Han Solo's case, "That is how a man dies. That is how a man—lives!"

A Rising Star—From Princess to General: Carrie Fisher's Leia Organa

The princess is no more. On a return flight from the United Kingdom to the United States, actress Carrie Fisher, best known for her roles as Princess and General Leia Organa, died of a heart attack, on December 27, 2016. She was only sixty years old.*

In *The Last Jedi*, we will see Carrie Fisher one last time. Because principal photography for *Star Wars: The Last Jedi* (2017) was completed before her death, it will show her as General Organa, in the role that made her famous, from a princess to a general, forever linking her to the *Star Wars* universe.

Though we now take for granted the überfemale model, now a staple in popular culture, that certainly wasn't the case back in 1977, when Fisher, in the role of Princess Leia, was wrapped up in a full-length, shapeless white gown, under which, as she told it, she couldn't wear a bra because, Lucas told her, "There's no underwear in space."† (Six years later, she went from modest to revealing: she wore a metal bikini as a captive dancer for Jabba the Hutt in *Return of the Jedi*.)

Back in 1977, princesses were seen and not heard. But Princess Leia was certainly one who was heard, and loudly. As Mary Pflum Peterson wrote in the *Huffington Post* ("Mourning Princess Leia, the Original Feminist Princess," December 27, 2016):

---

* Sadly, Carrie Fisher's mother, Debbie Reynolds, died only one day after her daughter, from what could best be described as a broken heart.
† Nigel G. Mitchell, "Why Princess Leia Went Commando in *Star Wars*," www.thegeektwins .com, August 16, 2010.

Leia was a princess unlike any other. Thanks to Carrie Fisher's spirited portrayal, she wasn't demure. She was strong. She wasn't quiet. Instead, she had a razor-sharp tongue. She didn't stand back and let life and the men in her life determine her fate. Instead, she sprang into action, wielding weapons, barking orders, making her opinion known. . . .

Leia was the princess who broke the mold. . . .

Leia was the first to demonstrate that a princess could be gutsy and vulnerable. Leia was the first to break the previously impenetrable princess glass ceiling and show she could lead the battle and rescue the prince that had previously worked to rescue her. She was a woman in a man's world, but never seemed to find the need to make that role feel like a struggle that would—or should—define her.

We do not get the impression that Leia wore her princess tiara with any fondness, because it was too tight a fit. Moreover, instead of wearing a shapeless garment like a flowing white robe, she was more comfortable in working clothes, as seen in *Return of the Jedi*, as she walked through the forest on an Endor moon.

In *The Force Awakens*, we see how the passage of the years and the stress of a lifetime of fighting—first against the Galactic Empire and then against the First Order—have taken an inevitable toll on her. She's put her princess past far behind her and taken on the grave responsibility of not only being a general in the Rebel Alliance but also assuming command as its leader.

Also, although she is deeply troubled by her wayward son, who has adopted the name Kylo Ren after defecting to the dark side of the Force, General Leia soldiers on. She feels the weight of the world on her shoulders, and everything about her—her demeanor, the lines etched on her face, her practical, no-nonsense hairstyle—suggests that she's long since given up her personal life, such as it was, for a greater cause.

Leia had wanted to spend her last years growing old with the "stuck-up, half-witted, scruffy-looking nerf herder," as she termed her future husband, Han Solo, in *The Empire Strikes Back*. Obviously, she has a thing for nerf herders, because he grew on her. In time, they realized they were lovestruck. And in the end, they were torn apart by their strained relationship with their son.

As Han Solo told her, in the *Force Awakens* novelization, "We both had to deal with it in our own way. . . . I went back to the only thing I was ever good at."

Leia responds, "We both did."

Han Solo reverted to being a smuggler and Leia Organa returned to her deep roots in the Rebel Alliance. Fate or destiny?

Throughout the *Star Wars* saga, we saw Leia as a feisty fighter. Significantly, we never saw Leia in her princess mode, except at the end of *A New Hope*, when, in a ceremony on a rebel base, she gives medals to Han Solo, Luke Skywalker, and Chewbacca. We saw her beauty, her regal stature, her benevolence, and the gratitude she bestowed when presenting the honors.

For Leia, it's been a long road from that happy day to a more somber day years later, when she again sees her husband, Han Solo, only to lose him forever. They wouldn't be growing old together, as she had hoped. They didn't know it, but they were doomed from the start, because they were star-crossed lovers.

In *A New Hope*, we saw Leia successfully take on armed stormtroopers, resist interrogation, and help Luke escape from the Death Star.

In *Return of the Jedi*, she is similarly resolute, walking into Jabba's hut (a palace), disguised as a bounty hunter and armed with a thermal detonator, to demand the release of Han Solo, now frozen in carbonite and on display on the Hutt's wall. Such boldness earned the respect of Jabba, who remarked, "This bounty hunter is my kind of scum, fearless and inventive."

Princess Leia Organa certainly proved fearless and inventive when imprisoned on Jabba's Sail Barge. Chained on a leash and forced to wear an uncomfortable and revealing metal bikini, she uses the very chain that confines her to free herself: she wraps it around Jabba's neck and chokes him to death.

She subsequently volunteered to be on General Solo's strike team, tasked with destroying a critical field generator protecting the second Death Star. It was Leia, not Han Solo, who initially forged a quick friendship and alliance with the indigenous population, the Ewoks, just as it was Leia who later handily kept stormtroopers at bay with her blaster while Han Solo attempted to hot-wire the controls to the back door of the garrison to get to the field generator.

A pampered princess living the royal life? Hardly. Though battle worn and battle scarred, Leia was never battle scared. She screwed her courage to the sticking place, kept a cool head, and prevailed, time and again.

Though it was clearly not her choice to spend a lifetime fighting against oppression, the princess-turned-general repudiated the life of privilege and luxury to take up a more noble cause, and, in doing so, she didn't change just a world but also the galaxy.

Carrie on.

From Farm Boy to Jedi Knight:
Luke Skywalker

After all these long years, we see Luke Skywalker again. The last time we saw him, thirty-four years ago, in *Return of the Jedi*, he was a young man, boyish in nature, and growing up fast. Now, in *The Force Awakens*, we see that he's not a kid anymore. He's in his early sixties, and his eyes reflect the long wars he's fought with the Galactic Empire and the dark side of the Force. He looks tired, world weary. He's traveled down a long, dark road and is now on a remote world, living by himself, seeing no one, until a young woman named Rey shows up.

He's on distant soil, a planet far, far away from Rey's home planet of Jakku. She has traveled far to see him, to return his lightsaber.

As we're told in the novelization of *The Force Awakens*, "He did not speak, nor did she. Remembering, Rey reached into her pack and removed his lightsaber. Taking several steps forward, she held it out to him. An offer. A plea. The galaxy's only hope."*

That sounds so familiar, doesn't it? It sounds like what Princess Leia Organa, in *A New Hope*, said to General Ben Kenobi so many years ago, in the 3-D hologram recording: "Help me, Obi-Wan Kenobi. You're my only hope."†

It's a recurring theme in the *Star Wars* saga: hope.

Recently, in *Rogue One*, we hear that theme repeated by Jyn

---

* Alan Dean Foster, *The Force Awakens* (Del Rey, 2015). A novelization.

† Both *A New Hope* and *The Force Awakens* share the same beats; they are essentially the same movie, which allowed director J. J. Abrams to reboot the franchise with a proven formula.

Erso, who reminded the rebels at the council meeting on the fourth moon of Yavin that "Rebellions are built on hope."

After all these years, things have come full circle for Luke. The Rebel Alliance relied on Luke Skywalker's exceptional flying skills to save the day in *A New Hope*, which he did. Out of thirty ships flown by experienced fighter pilots from the rebel base on Yavin 4, it was a novice warrior who fired the well-aimed shot that caused the Death Star to self-destruct. Luke Skywalker took the shot and changed the world.

Luke Skywalker, a hermit who had thought his days of saving the galaxy were over, now has to embrace his destiny once again. As the last Jedi, he lives to fight yet another battle—the final battle. Only then will he find respite, the internal peace he seeks.

I'm at a small airport in northern California to meet a pilot who flew the B-29 Superfortress and a fighter plane during World War II. I had no idea what he looked like, but when I saw an elderly man with a military-style haircut, a leather bomber jacket, and an unmistakable air of confidence about him, I knew he was the droid, um, pilot I was looking for. Not cocky, you understand, but confident. Big difference.

It reminded me of a scene in *A New Hope*, when Han Solo and Luke Skywalker were blasting away with laser cannons at TIE fighters screeching past the *Millennium Falcon*. Luke scores his first hit of the day and is jubilant. Han gruffly tells him, "Great, kid! Don't get cocky."

As any pilot will tell you, cocky will get you killed. Overconfidence killed many a young pilot during World War II, who learned the hard way that a moment of inattention in a fighter cockpit could be just as deadly as a Japanese Zero fighter on his tail.

The war was a distant memory for the pilot whom I came to see. Back then, when he was in his twenties, he was brimming with optimism and ready to take on the Germans over the skies of Europe and the Japanese over their homeland, which he did.

He was, he said, a born pilot. He said he was always more comfortable in the air than he ever was on the ground. He was born to fly, to fly fast and hard and long, first as a fighter pilot and then as the aircraft commander (pilot) on a B-29.

The black-and-white pictures of him and his bomber aircrew show a bunch of college-age kids, eighteen to twenty-one, who otherwise would have been at a sock hop (look it up, kiddo) or behind the drugstore counter as soda jerks (again, look it up). They should have been having the time of their lives; instead, they were risking their lives, hoping not to get blown out of the sky or, even worse, to fall into the hands of the enemy, especially the Japanese, who were merciless.*

Their collective experience and memories prematurely aged those young men. Chronologically, they were in their teens and early twenties, but they came back from the war and felt older, because they had to grow up fast during the war. They had aged because of their life-and-death responsibilities.

Paul Tibbets, who flew the B-29 that dropped the atomic bomb on Hiroshima, recalled in *Duty* that when he took command of the unit tasked with dropping the bomb, "I was twenty-nine when I was given the assignment. But I was really thirty-five or forty. That's how I felt."†

He wasn't alone. A lot of young men felt that way, and said so in their memoirs, after the war. Combat will prematurely age you.

Flying over the hostile airspace of the Japanese homeland, the airmen had to fend off enemy fighters, dodge black clouds of deadly antiaircraft rounds so thick you could walk across them (as they said), and hope they didn't get a baka bomb (a one-man piloted jet bomb) slamming into their B-29 bomber.

The recruiting posters of the day showed smiling airmen with

---

* Some American pilots preferred to use their handguns to blow their brains out, instead of being tortured and then killed by the enraged Japanese who couldn't wait to get their hands on the foreign devils who were carpet-bombing their cities. Some fates are worse than death.

† Bob Greene, *Duty: A Father, His Son, and the Man Who Won the War* (William Morrow, 2001).

pristine teeth standing with arms akimbo as their fearless faces looked skyward, but the reality of flying combat missions over Japan quickly knocked the romance of flying right out of the sky.

Luke Skywalker, like his father before him, had always found himself at home in the cockpit. Luke flew a T-16 skyhopper, which was used by the Galactic Empire as a training aircraft because its controls and flight characteristics were similar to those of TIE fighters.

Whether in a snowspeeder or in a sophisticated X-wing fighter with dual flight capabilities, in the atmosphere or in deep space, Luke was a born pilot whose face always looked up toward the sky—unlike his farming uncle Owen, whose face was always turned downward to the soil. As far as Owen was concerned, it would have been best for Luke to be permanently grounded, because his head was always in the clouds and not on the farming chores, which never ended. After all, there was always another farming season to prepare for, which meant clipping Luke's wings and aspirations every year, until Luke finally gave up his foolish dreams.

Next year. From Luke's perspective, it was *always* "next year." That translated to "never." Stuck on the moisture farm until he, like his uncle, would grow old, his face worn with deep lines scarred by the wind that howled over the desert, Luke always looked up longingly at the sky and the stars. That's where he belonged, and he sensed it; he knew it in his heart. But that looked like an increasingly remote possibility. Stuck on Tatooine, Luke's prospects as a pilot seemed to be drying up.

But the best-laid plans of mice and men oft go astray.

As for the airmen on the B-29 Superfortresses over Japan, their plans of living an ordinary life, of getting a job and settling down with their sweethearts to raise a family, were rudely interrupted when the Japanese attacked Pearl Harbor, on December 7, 1941. Their world and their worldview changed forever. Those sneaky Japs! Who did they think *they* were? Why, they're messing with Americans! *We'll* show them!

Like them, Luke Skywalker's life changed when he, too, realized that life's circumstances had forced his hand. His destiny clearly was not to live out his life as a farmer. After he and Ben Kenobi rushed back to the farm, up in flames, only to find that it had been destroyed by stormtroopers. With his aunt and uncle dead, Luke realized he had to grow up prematurely and assume the burden of responsibility for his new life. His destiny was not terra firma but terra incognita—the stars.

On the Death Star, Luke had to fight off seasoned stormtroopers who want to kill him and prevent him from escaping.

On the *Millennium Falcon*, he sat at the controls of a laser cannon to defend the ship from TIE fighters moving in for the kill.

And in the cockpit of an X-wing fighter, he was in formation, flying from a rebel base, on what Han Solo considered to be a crazy mission: "What good's a reward if you ain't around to use it? Besides, attacking that battle station ain't my idea of courage. It's more like suicide."

In addition to becoming an integral part of the Rebel Alliance, Luke is also burdened with another responsibility. He has the Force and must become a full-fledged Jedi Knight, the ranks of which had thinned considerably, after Darth Vader systematically searched the galaxy to destroy them, one by one.

Circumstances forced Luke's hand. He had no choice but to leave Tatooine, just as the airmen in World War II had no choice but to go to war. Like the hobbits in *The Lord of the Rings*, who felt that no one would notice their little corner of the world, that they could ride out the War of the Ring in blissful ignorance and isolation, they had misjudged the war's long reach. When war comes on a grand scale, it touches everyone, directly and indirectly, as Luke soon discovered.

In Luke's case, this meant going from being a farm boy on Tatooine to becoming a commander in the Rebel Alliance, and also a Jedi Knight. He became a leader because he *had* to. The time and the circumstances demanded that he become an active participant.

From his perspective as a man in his early sixties, Luke no doubt looked back at his life and barely recognized the youth that he was when he first met Ben Kenobi. That brash young man, that earnest pilot, that impatient Jedi student who had much to learn in the ways of the Force . . . he's a stranger to himself. It was all so many years ago.

He once was Rey's age, but became a legend, a boy who became a man who walked into the sky. But that was a long, long time ago. . . .

▪ PART 2 ▪

WEAPONS

Some enthusiasts today talk about the probability of the horse becoming extinct and prophesy that the aeroplane, the tank, and the motor-car will supersede the horse in future wars. . . . I am sure that as time goes on you will find just as much use for the horse—the well bred horse—as you have done in the past.

—Field Marshal Lord Douglas Haig, 1925

It is the cold glitter of the attacker's eye, not the point of the questing bayonet, that breaks the line. It is the fierce determination of the driver to close with the enemy, not the mechanical perfection of the tank, that conquers the trench. It is the cataclysmic ecstasy of conflict in the flier, not the perfection of his machine gun, which drops the enemy in flaming ruin.

—General George S. Patton

From Flintlock to Blasters and Beyond: Small Arms and Assault Rifles

When I was enrolled in the U.S. Army Command and General Staff College, our first assignment was to write an essay about military weapons, explicating the idea of thesis and antithesis. For instance, if a bomber is the thesis, what is its antithesis? Obviously, antiaircraft weapons and missiles.

Why does this matter? Simply this: imagine how the Allied air war in Europe and Japan might have ended if ground-to-air or air-to-air missile technology had been perfected in time to be used against the United States and the British. It's not a pretty picture for the Allies.

In *Star Wars: A New Hope*, Obi-Wan Kenobi and Han Solo, on board the *Millennium Falcon*, discuss their viewpoints regarding their respective weapons: Kenobi prizes his lightsaber, Solo his blaster. Both Kenobi and Solo are wedded to their weapons; Kenobi's represents the past, Solo's represents the present.

A Call to Arms: From Yesterday . . .

Blasters, using plasma energy instead of bullets, are technologically superior to contemporary handguns, but both have roots that go back to the first modern firearm, the flintlock.

A flintlock is a relic. Outside of gun enthusiasts who collect and fire these weapons, the general public usually can't get their hands on a flintlock and fire it. But one place they can is in Virginia, at Colonial Williamsburg, which advertises, "Come fire 18th-century firearms at the Colonial Williamsburg Musket Range. Participants will fire two different reproduction 18th-century flintlock firearms commonly used during the Revolutionary War period, and learn some of their history. Participants will fire live rounds at a target."

The process of firing a flintlock is tedious, time consuming, and exacting. As Ed Crews explained:

> Overwhelmingly, civilian and military weapons of the period in Europe and America were flintlocks. The name refers to the ignition system, which relied on a piece of flint set in a movable cock. The cock fell when the trigger was pulled. The flint struck a piece of steel, creating sparks. The sparks fell into a gunpowder charge in an external pan. The powder ignited the main charge in the barrel by passing through a small hole in the barrel.*

Bill Thompson, a reenactor, elaborated:

> The musket was made for the military. You would literally starve to death if you tried to hunt with this thing. It's not accurate; it is not made to shoot at a specific target. It's made to shoot at mass troops, linear tactics. We get people that come out here all the time that think, how stupid; get out in an open field, stand up shoulder to shoulder, and shoot at each other! . . . In the eighteenth century, battles ended in hand-to-hand combat. So, the bayonet, as you can see, basically turns the musket into a spear. If you could imagine being stabbed with that, or your brains dashed out with the other end, it gets pretty nasty.†

To Today . . . US Army Handguns

Sidearm: The standard U.S. Army sidearm is currently the M9 Beretta pistol, which fires a 9 millimeter round with a range of fifty meters. It's going to be retired soon, and for good reason. As Matthew Cox

* Ed Crews, "The Gunsmith's Shop," history.org.
† Bill Thompson, "Firing a Musket: 18th-Century Small Arms," learnnc.org.

noted, "Soldiers who have served in Iraq and Afghanistan have complained that the 9 mm round is not powerful enough to be effective in combat."*

In January 2017, the U.S. Army finally settled on the SIG Sauer Model P320, to be designated by the military as the XM17. It will enter the service in 2018. "The 10-year agreement calls for Sig to supply the Army with full-size and compact versions of the gun. The pistols can be outfitted with silencers and accommodate standard and extended capacity magazines."†

Assault weapon: The U.S. Army and Marine Corps currently issue the M4 assault rifle to their troops. It fires a 5.56 x 45 millimeter NATO ball round with a maximum range of 3,600 meters. It takes a thirty-round magazine. It's the latest iteration of the venerable M16, which was put into the inventory in 1964, a year before the U.S. involvement in Southeast Asia. Its variants include the M16A3 (used by U.S. Navy SEALs) and the M16A4 (used by support and non-infantry Marines).

And Tomorrow . . . Blasters

In the technologically sophisticated world of *Star Wars*, the blaster pistol and the blaster rifle are standard issue. Observing stormtroopers in battle, we can conclude that they are the worst shots in the world, which speaks of inadequate training on the gun range or of the difficulty of firing while wearing a standard stormtrooper helmet, a "bucket." Just imagine wearing it and viewing the battlefield without the benefit of peripheral vision.

The advantage of a blaster is its lethality and range. Presumably, at some point it must be "reloaded" (reenergized or recharged), but despite its high-tech energy beam, it still shares a major defect that dates back to the flintlock: one must aim it using line-of-sight.

* Matthew Cox, "Army Wants a Harder-Hitting Pistol," military.com, July 3, 2014.
† Matthew Cox and Hope Hodge Seck, "Army Picks Sig Sauer's P320 Handgun to Replace M9 Service Pistol," military.com, January 19, 2017.

Though blasters are sophisticated technology, they are still "dumb" weapons with "dumb" ammunition. But at some distant point in the future, there will be "smart" weapons with "smart" munitions.

And Beyond Blasters

Smaller, lighter, and more lethal, these weapons won't necessarily be dependent on line-of-sight for firing. Instead of firing a single round, they will fire larger rounds of various configurations, depending on what is optimal for the tactical situation. Moreover, these rounds will be "smart"—able to track and home in on a target until impact.

Just as field artillery personnel match shells and fuses to optimize their effect on the target, so too will the infantry personnel of tomorrow have multiple choices.

The "smart" rifle will not fire small 5.56 millimeter rounds but larger ones, up to 40 millimeters, which is the size of the grenade-like munitions fired from an M203 grenade launcher (to be replaced by the M320).

The future soldier will have a fully integrated tactical battlesuit, with helmet, and built-in weapons, in addition to any hand-carried weapon. Moreover, the suit/helmet will enhance a soldier's situational awareness: the soldier will be able to "see" the battlefield from multiple perspectives, including live feeds from drones flying over the enemy, and audio updates and warnings as necessary.

The tactical suit's targeting system, built into the helmet, will assess enemy capabilities and determine the optimal method of engaging them. It will quickly identify the enemy's location, analyze what they're wearing and what weapons they have, analyze the terrain and the weather, and recommend whether you should use your organic weapons or you need more firepower in the form of air or artillery support.

For instance, if the enemy is in open terrain, in hasty fighting positions, with some cover and concealment, your weapons system may choose a round that explodes above them at an optimal height of burst to shower shrapnel, like a high explosive artillery round with its fuse set for an air burst.

"Smart" munitions are incoming. Imagine the enhanced effectiveness of rounds that, like small missiles, can home in on their targets. Just "fire and forget." It locks on a designated target and changes flight trajectory as necessary to hit it.

When East Meets West:
The Jedi Knight

When George Lucas constructed the fictional universe of *Star Wars*, he drew heavily on worldwide mythologies, language, and culture, significantly from the inscrutable world of the Japanese. In fact, as a student in film school, he was first exposed to the work of Japanese director Akira Kurosawa, whose film *Seven Samurai* had a big impact on him and on countless other filmmakers. Lucas cites it as "my favorite of all time."*

The lightsaber, an energy beam weapon, is first seen in *A New Hope*, when Obi-Wan Kenobi shows it to Luke Skywalker. That lightsaber, in fact, previously belonged to Luke's father. Kenobi passes it on to Luke.

Obi-Wan Kenobi, or General Ben Kenobi, who fought in the Clone Wars, bears a name that suggests its Japanese origins. An obi is a sash that goes around the two-piece uniform of one who studies the martial arts, which is associated with Asian culture. And the word "ken" is a reference to a straight, double-edged sword blade made of steel, dating back to the third through sixth centuries. Eric P. Nash ("The Names Came From Earth," *New York Times*, January 26, 1997) quoted Lucas:

> Basically, I developed the names for the characters phonetically . . . I obviously wanted to telegraph a bit of the character in the name. The names needed to sound unusual but not spacey. I wanted to stay

---

* Criterion collection, "George Lucas on Akira Kurosawa," youtube.com/watch?v=E9V2T1ONA2I.

away from the kind of science fiction names like Zenon and Zorba. They had to sound indigenous and have consistency between their names and their culture.

As for "Jedi," the *Times* article mentions Edgar Rice Burroughs's Martian world of Barsoom as an influence: a Jed, or Jeddak, is the title of a lord in that world. Moreover, the roots of "Jedi" can be found in ancient Japanese culture, and "knight" clearly is a reference to a mounted soldier in armor who, during the Middle Ages, served his lord. Thus, East meets West: a Jedi Knight is a fusion of the European knight (particularly the Knights of the Round Table, who swore fealty to King Arthur) and the Japanese samurai warrior, who swore fealty to his daimyo (great lord).

The essence of a Jedi Knight is service to a great cause—to be a guardian of "peace and justice," inspired by the samurai code of conduct called Bushido (the way of the warrior), which incorporates honor, discipline, and morality.

Obi-Wan Kenobi, then, is a "peace warrior." He and his kind have mastered the discipline needed to wield the power of the lightsaber and the Force, tempered by morality. But just as there are noble "white" knights, there are ignoble "black" knights, rogue warriors who have gone to the dark side.

In sum, the Jedi Knight is the idealized, futuristic version of the samurai warrior and a Knight of the Round Table, and he embodies the ideals, skills, and weaponry of both.

The Flower That Shatters the Stone

Lightsaber Advantages

One who wields a lightsaber is a formidable opponent. The lightsaber is a weapon that can cut through steel or flesh and blood with equal ease. Moreover, the blade's composition enables it to deflect the energy beams of individual weapons like blasters, if you have Jedi-like reflexes.

Their reputation as skilled and formidable warriors precedes them. A show of skill is not necessary, because enemies respect the power they wield with a blade and the mysterious Force that can be brought to bear in any combat situation.

In *The Phantom Menace*, when a droid on a Trade Federation battleship tells Daultay Dofine that his visitors are Jedi Knights, Dofine is understandably alarmed. Soon thereafter, on the bridge, when Rune is told that the Jedi Knights are mowing down battle droids, he is not optimistic about the probable outcome, because in close quarters a Jedi Knight, armed with a lightsaber, is a force to be reckoned with.* In fact, their mere presence is often sufficient to settle disputes, which is why they're often sent as peaceful emissaries. In short, nobody picks a fight with a Jedi Knight unless one has a death wish.

---

* Historical perspective: for very close-quarters fighting, the samurai warrior carried a short sword called a *wakisashi*. It had a four-inch handle and a twenty-inch blade. But the Jedi Knight is armed only with a lightsaber, which doubles as both a short and a long sword. (In *Star Wars IV: A New Hope*, in the cantina in Mos Eisley, Obi-Wan Kenobi uses his lightsaber to cut off the arm of a bounty hunter who obviously picked the wrong man for a fight.)

The Jedi Knight recalls the Sun Tzu's observation that "the supreme art of war is to subdue the enemy without fighting." In other words, let your reputation precede you. If you can be seen as so formidable that the enemy does not wish to engage you or, if he must, he does so with palpable fear in his heart, manifested by his uncontrollable shaking and loose bowels, then you have essentially won the battle before fighting it.

Unfortunately, the lightsaber is not an all-purpose weapon. It does have a significant limitation.

Blast It: Lightsaber Limitations

As seen in *Attack of the Clones*, lightsabers are principally for use in close quarters, like a samurai warrior's long sword.

In *Attack of the Clones*, we see Jedi Knights who have come to the rescue of Anakin Skywalker, Padmé Amidala, and Obi-Wan Kenobi. The Jedi are armed with lightsabers. Unfortunately, as Count Dooku points out to Jedi Knight Mace Windu, he's essentially brought a knife to a gunfight.* Count Dooku's words ring true. The Jedi Knights find that the lightsabers are useful as offensive weapons only when droids are within the reach of the blade. Moreover, the blade can deflect small arms fire, but not if they're overwhelmed with firepower at standoff range.

Though the Jedi Knights were obviously skilled in the martial arts, in the ways of the Force (enabling Mace Windu, for instance, to make extraordinary leaps), and especially in wielding their lightsabers, the battle droids, with their E-5 blaster rifles, have the advantage of overwhelming firepower. The Jedi couldn't even get close enough to fight them.

---

* In an early draft posted online at imsdb.com, in a line not used in the final movie, Dooku poses a question: "How well do you think one Jedi will hold up against a thousand battle droids?"

The Force

What exactly is the Force, and what does it have to do with light-sabers?

Ask one hundred different people and you'll get a hundred different answers, all variations on a theme. Most people will say that it's a "life force," because Obi-Wan Kenobi tells us so in *A New Hope*.

Kenobi's explanation is thoughtful and mystical, whereas Han Solo's perception of it is what you'd expect from a skeptic. He's dismissive, preferring his blaster.

Clearly, the Force is an energy that emanates from all living things. So a rock, for instance, has no Force—unless it's thrown. But a fragile flower possesses the Force; thus, the flower can shatter the stone.

The Lightsaber

The lightsaber is wielded like a traditional sword, its blade constructed of a plasma ray powered by a kyber crystal (the same energy source used in the Death Stars). Moreover, the lightsaber is not an off-the-shelf item; a Jedi Knight constructs his own lightsaber by hand.

So where did George Lucas get the idea for lightsabers? Because he's never given a specific answer, just as he's not been too specific about the Force, we can only speculate. A good place to start would be science fiction pulp magazines, which fueled Lucas's imagination as a young boy.

Science Fiction

Star Wars has deep roots in popular culture, specifically in comic books, television serials, movies, and pulp magazines of the thirties, forties, and fifties. The "science" in science fiction isn't what mattered to Lucas;* instead, the "fiction" is what mattered, because the

---

* "I just wanted to forget science," Lucas said. Chris Taylor, *How Star Wars Conquered the Universe* (Basic Books, 2014).

Star Wars saga is essentially romance literature with a pop culture twist.

Catering to male power fantasies, pulp science fiction was skewed heavily toward its adolescent male audience. The stories often featured a fearless, handsome male protagonist with rippling muscles and a beautiful girl draped around him, who always needed saving. She was often scantily clad, although the man was always heavily armored.* It's mental junk food for young male minds, not unlike George Lucas's steady diet of chocolate and milk shakes during high school and college.

The heroic science fiction that sparked his interest started with Buck Rogers, who first made his appearance in a science fiction pulp magazine called *Amazing Stories* (1928). Buck blasted on the scene in the wake of fantastic novelists like Jules Verne (*Twenty Thousand Leagues Under the Sea*) and H. G. Wells (*The War of the Worlds*). But the most prolific and influential of all the pulp writers was Edgar Rice Burroughs, whose many novels featured Tarzan, John Carter of Mars, and other stalwart male heroes cut from the same bolt of cloth.

Buck and his buddies came first, but after him it was Flash Gordon who captured the public imagination. Seemingly in a flash, the old was out and the new was in. Goodbye, Buck Rogers; hello, Flash Gordon (think Han Solo), along with his supporting cast: Ming the Merciless (think Darth Vader), Dale Arden (think Princess Leia), and Dr. Hans Zarkov (think Ben Kenobi).

Ironically, Lucas failed to obtain the rights to turn Flash Gordon into a movie, because the syndicate asked for more than what Lucas was willing to pay. As a result, Lucas decided to write his own space fantasy, inspired by Flash Gordon, Buck Rogers, the science fiction pulp magazines, and their visual adaptations—Saturday matinee movies and serials on television.

---

* The artist who best illustrated such romantic visions was Frank Frazetta, whose paperback book covers influenced countless fantasy illustrators. We see this trope in contemporary comic books, where men go into battle dressed in full armor while beautiful, unusually buxom women sally forth tiny bikinis bursting at the seams.

The iconic crawl with its bombastic, military-inspired music that preceded the first *Star Wars* movie, and many thereafter, came from the *Flash Gordon* Saturday matinee serials from the 1930s.[*] One of the serials was titled "Flash Gordon Conquers the Universe." Look and sound familiar?

The lightsabers wielded by the Jedi Knights? They can be found in the science fiction of Edmond Hamilton, Fritz Leiber, Isaac Asimov, Gordon R. Dickson, Larry Niven, and M. John Harrison. The best description, historically, can be found in a pulp magazine called *Magic Carpet*, which published Edmond Hamilton's novella, *Kaldar, World of Antares* (April 1933):

> The sword seemed at first glance a simple long rapier of metal. But he found that when his grip tightened on the hilt it pressed a catch which released a terrific force stored in the hilt into the blade, making it shine with light. When anything was touched by this shining blade, he found, the force of the blade annihilated it instantly. He learned that the weapon was called a lightsword.

In Lucas's *Star Wars* universe, it just wouldn't do if the good and bad guys battled it out with traditional steel swords. Instead, the swords would have to be more imaginative, and thus they morphed into lightswords or, more elegantly termed, lightsabers.[†]

In all the science fiction stories in which they appeared, the lightsword/saber is an energy weapon that uses a beam of light in lieu of a blade. Thus, we can surmise that Lucas found the inspiration for his elegant weapon in the pages of science fiction literature.

But where did he get the culture surrounding the lightsaber? He clearly wasn't inspired by Europeans. Instead, one must look to the East, not the West, far back in history to medieval Japan.

---

[*] For a comparison, see "Star Flash Gordon Wars," www.youtube.com/watch?v=qnOL8F x3Tvc.

[†] A saber is a specialized kind of sword. See "History of Sabres," Sword History, www .swordhistory.info/?p=56.

The Way of the Honorable Warrior

Imagine a warrior wearing an unmistakable helmet, with a fearsome-looking iron mask that covers the lower half of his face. He's wearing padded clothing and shielding to protect himself, and he's armed with a formidable weapon, a deadly sword capable of chopping off his opponent's head in one swift stroke.*

Doesn't Darth Vader come to mind? Well before his time, though, that description would also describe the traditional samurai warrior armed with two long, razor-sharp swords and a short sword.

The Japanese word "samurai" comes from the word "*saburau*," which means "to serve." The samurai existed to serve their emperor, just as Vader served Emperor Palpatine, whom he called "master."

The samurai's life was invested with an uncompromising code of honor called Bushido, "the way of the warrior." But when he wasn't wielding his fearsome blade, he sat on a tatami (mat) and held a brush with its tip dipped in black ink to write, in one swift stroke, a Japanese symbol in calligraphy. The goal was to get it right the first time, attesting to his control and discipline. He was a refined gentleman. But that's not what he's traditionally known for. Mostly, he was a formidable warrior, confident in himself and his abilities, invested with power by virtue of his skills. He knew his honored position in society. He stood in a class above, and apart from, the commoners. According to *Encyclopedia Britannica*,

> The precise content of the Bushido code varied historically as the samurai class came under the influence of Zen Buddhist and Confucian thought, but its one unchanging ideal was martial spirit, including athletic and military skills as well as fearlessness toward the enemy in battle. Frugal living, kindness, honesty, and personal honour were also highly regarded, as was filial piety.

* It can be done, but it takes two hands to wield the blade.

In other words, they were warriors who had a strong sense of military duty, tempered by morality, and a heightened sensitivity toward ethics. For good reason, the samurai were both respected and feared. You exchanged cross words with a samurai at your own peril, because crossed swords would inevitably follow, like your guts spilling out of your abdomen.

Superb sword masters, the samurai cherished their blades, which were handmade by craftsmen. Considered the best blades in the world, ancient Japanese samurai swords, back in the day, were not mass-produced; they were constructed individually, serving as superb examples of unrivaled craftsmanship.* Of the sword-smiths, Dr. Rick Vinci, a Stanford-trained materials scientist and engineer at Lehigh University, said, "They created an elegant device that has both a serious purpose and a serious beauty to it as well." He added,

> The samurai sword is not just a killing implement. It also embodies all sorts of concepts like honor and trustworthiness and responsibility. The people who carried these were supposed to have personal characteristics and attitudes that were perhaps different from what an ordinary soldier might have when he carried a spear or something of that nature. These people had to have an unusual set of qualities, and the sword is the representation of those.

The Katana Sword

This is the samurai's long sword. As Vinci pointed out, the sword, representationally, *is* the swordsman; they are as one.

The process of building a sword is time-consuming, painstaking, and arduous. They are as much works of art as they are weapons of war.

---

* During World War II, Japanese officers carried samurai swords, but because of the sheer numbers needed to complete their ensemble, many were mass produced. After the war, the officers were forced by Americans, the occupying force, to relinquish their swords.

A detailed discussion of how the sword is constructed is beyond the scope of my discussion.* Here's an overview:

> The traditional katana sword is fashioned only from the purest steel, which the Japanese call *tamahagane* ("jewel steel"). Over three days and three nights, smelters using ancient techniques shovel roughly 25 tons of iron-bearing river sand and charcoal into the mouth of a *tatara*, a rectangular clay furnace built specifically to produce a single batch of tamahagane. Composed of carbon, the charcoal is as much a key ingredient in steel as a source of fuel for the furnace. The tatara will reach temperatures of up to 2,500°F, reducing the iron ore to steel and yielding about two tons of tamahagane. The highest quality tamahagane can cost up to 50 times more than ordinary steel made using modern methods.

Thus the blade is made, but the samurai also must be trained, for what good is the blade without its warrior? And what is the warrior without proper training? For that, we seek answers in the Japanese discipline called kendo.

Kendo: The Way of the Sword

Just as Bushido is the way of the warrior, kendo is the way of the sword. The two go hand in hand. According to Kendo America,

> Modern Kendo bears but faint resemblance to Kenjutsu and to its feudal origins of sword wielding samurai warriors which are today depicted in movies and television. Kendo, literally translated "the way of the sword," cannot be traced to a single founder or given an exact founding date. The story of the rise of modern Kendo *begins with the samurai* and extends over the culture of several centuries (italics mine).†

---

* If you want more information, consult *Nova*'s detailed explanation of how they're made ("Making a Masterpiece," pbs.org/wgbh/nova/samurai/swor-nf.html).
† Kendo America, "About Kendo," kendo-usa.org.

We see the dual roots of the samurai code that went into making him a gentleman warrior. On one side is the warrior, whose blade cuts fast and deep; on the other, a sublime gentleness and a sensitivity to an aesthetic that belies his warlike reputation, as he wields a brush, rendering calligraphy. But the pen is not as mighty as the sword.

Jedi Knight

Obviously, in many ways, we see the incorporation of several Japanese influences in the Jedi Knights. As the samurai warrior lives and dies by a strict code of honor, so too does the Jedi, unless he goes to the dark side, as did Anakin Skywalker, who became Darth Vader. (The first six *Star Wars* movies, in fact, were conceived to tell the tragic story of Darth Vader's rise and fall.)

As Obi-Wan Kenobi told Luke Skywalker in *A New Hope*, Obi-Wan and his kind were, in essence, intergalactic peace warriors who had stood the test of time, for countless generations, until they were betrayed by Darth Vader.

We see in the Jedi a strong sense of duty rooted in obligation. They are guardians as opposed to warriors. They are defensive by nature and inclination, but offensive when necessary. As such, the Jedi Knights, like the samurai, were both respected and feared. Unlike those who went to the dark side, the Jedi Knights did not kill wantonly.

Like a person skilled in the martial arts, a Jedi's true power resides within; in this instance, his force comes from the Force. The lightsaber is an extension of it, a symbol of that power. Thus, after extensive training, the Jedi is confident when wielding his lightsaber, which is not taken lightly. He is a formidable opponent when the occasion calls for it, but otherwise a gentleman in manner, conducting himself accordingly, like a samurai warrior.

Obviously, there is very little original about the Jedi Knights. There's a good reason why the word "Jedi" sounds vaguely Japanese, for it comes from the Japanese word "*jidaigeki*" (period dramas), a Japanese genre of theater, films, television, and video games focused on the lives of the samurai and others, usually set during the Edo period (1603–1868).

As George Lucas knew, making his mythic star saga for a modern world required reshaping the original clay into new forms, as he transformed the samurai warrior into a Jedi Knight. Though the Japanese samurai are long gone, their fighting spirit and skill remain to inspire us. They also are firmly fixed in George Lucas's stellar world of *Star Wars*, where the Jedi Knights—despite their grievous attrition—are still held up as shining examples. They will always be the guardians of peace and justice in the galaxy.

For where there's a "whill," there's always a way. . . . *

---

* See "Guardians of the Whills" and its relationship to the Force, which is the basis of strength for Jedi Knights, at starwars.wikia.com/wiki/Guardians_of_the_Whills.

Size Matters Not: The AT-AT

In *The Empire Strikes Back*, the Galactic Empire attacks a remote rebel base on Hoth, an ice planet. The Empire's mission is to destroy a generator powering a shield surrounding the planet, which protects the base, and to keep rebel ships from escaping. The Empire's principal weapon is the All Terrain Armored Transport. The Empire has deployed five of them to attack the base.

How effective was the AT-AT, principally an assault vehicle, in combat against the rebels?

The answer may surprise you. But first we must consider its historical antecedent: the war elephant.*

Shock and Awe, Historically

The first major battle using war elephants occurred around 1100 BC, when Darius III used them against Alexander the Great. Understandably, because Alexander's troops had never seen elephants, their presence on the battlefield had an immediate psychological effect. As warfarehistorynetwork.com notes:

> The role of elephants went far beyond mental terrorism in war. They
> provided an excellent means of transportation and could be used to

---

* In *The Lord of the Rings: The Return of the King* (2003), war elephants are prominent in the climactic battle. It should be noted that in the film adaptation the "oliphants," as Tolkien termed them, were computer-generated images and towered above real-world elephants, which range in height from eight to eleven feet, depending on whether they are Indian or African in origin.

move heavy equipment and supplies over large distances. They were also their own form of cavalry, able to charge at tremendous speed. Their sheer size made war elephants all but unstoppable. Many armies used elephants to charge the opposition, particularly the enemy's cavalry, crushing all who got in the way. On some occasions, the elephants' tusks were mounted with spikes to inflict even more damage. This type of outfit was particularly useful in elephant-on-elephant combat. The sturdy elephants often carried howdahs, or canopied saddles, on their backs, complete with archers and javelin throwers. Larger elephants were outfitted with tower-like devices protecting occupants from ground-level attack and providing an excellent battlefield vantage point.[*]

Now consider the futuristic "war elephant," the Empire's AT-AT. First, its monstrous size gives it an overwhelming psychological effect. Think shock and awe. Imagine what it was like for the rebel forces at Hoth, when they looked out over the trenches and saw, in the distance, seventy-four-foot-high AT-ATs walking relentlessly toward them with laser cannons firing.

Second, the height of the AT-ATs allowed the crew to view the battlefield from a vantage point that made their target identification and acquisition significantly easier, as opposed to viewing from ground level.

Third, thick armor plates protected the AT-AT from ground fire. The rebel forces' small arms fire, crew-served weapons fire, and even emplaced guns (please, not "cannons") proved ineffective.[†]

The thick armor also was impervious to the rebels' landspeeders, armed principally with blasters, as Luke Skywalker discovered when he fired at an AT-AT.

Finally, the AT-AT is principally a troop carrier, holding a

---

[*] "War Elephants: From Ancient India to Vietnam," warfarehistorynetwork.com, October 11, 2016.

[†] In *Rogue One*, Baze Malbus fires a rocket launcher (a shoulder-fired missile) at an AT-AT, with no discernible effect; its thick armor is impenetrable.

platoon-size force of forty troops, who electronically fast-rope down from its sides. (The AT-AT also carries speeder bikes.)

AT-AT Drawbacks

Despite its strengths, the AT-AT also has some drawbacks.

1. *Lack of speed.* Moving at maximum speed of 37 mph, the AT-AT is not ideally suited as a troop transport. It's simply too slow to move troops to the battlefield.

2. *Fields of fire.* The AT-AT's firepower is strictly limited to the front. It lacks a topside gun and one in the rear for 360-degree protection.

3. *No antiaircraft weapons.* The AT-AT carries no missiles, making it vulnerable to air attack. If the imperial troops had had them for this mission, the missiles could have homed in on the heat signature of the attacking snowspeeders. The AT-AT weapons officer could "fire and forget," letting missiles destroy the snowspeeders, allowing the AT-AT to continue unimpeded on its course.

4. *High center of gravity.* The AT-AT's Achilles' heel is that it's top-heavy. It's vulnerable to being tripped up, as seen in the Battle of Hoth, when the snowspeeders used steel tow cables to encircle the AT-AT's legs, causing them to fall. (Note to the Rebel Alliance: instead of requiring manual detachment, the cables should be magnetically attached and thus easily disengaged.)

5. *No steel collar.* The AT-AT lacks a ring around the collar. The AT-AT has armor cladding on the sides and on top, which protects it from ground fire, but its exposed neck is a significant weakness, as was seen at the Battle of Hoth.

Given the hazards of trying to encircle an AT-AT's legs with steel cable, the preferred method would be to use snowspeeders or X-wing fighters to come in high and fast from above, at a steep angle of attack, and target its exposed, vulnerable neck.

6. In lieu of using an AT-AT for this particular mission, the preferred weapons platform would have been a Republic Gunship (or its equivalent), which is highly maneuverable, fast, deadly, and car-

ries a platoon. Its hypersonic missiles are sufficient to take out a DSS-02 shield generator.

Assessment

In the end, the AT-AT's principal virtue is its shock value, due to its size. However, its effectiveness is compromised when it must serve double duty as both a tanklike weapon and a troop carrier. It's not ideally suited for either because of its slow speed.

In a fast-moving, mobile battlefield, a large, plodding weapon like an AT-AT is principally a target of opportunity. For that reason, the Empire would have been better off using an airborne troop carrier* for this mission.†

---

* The Russian HIND helicopter, Mi-24, Mi-25, or Mi-35, comes to mind. Soviet pilots rightly called it a "flying tank." Heavily armored, it carries eight troops and flies up to 200 miles per hour. The U.S. military, alas, has nothing comparable. The Empire's low-altitude assault transport is comparable, and was first used during the Clone Wars at the First Battle of Geonosis, as seen in *Attack of the Clones*.

† The U.S. Air Force's A-10 Thunderbolt II, nicknamed the "Warthog," fires a 30 millimeter GAU-8/A seven-barrel Gatling gun, a devastating weapon that fires 3,900 rounds per minute (popularmechanics.com). On its Facebook page, one trooper praised the "Hawg":

> As a former Army ground pounder [infantryman, or grunt], I can tell you there are few better sights than some A10's streaking over, hitting some ground targets with that big gun, then banking hard . . . little dots leaving them and headed down . . . the aircraft still leaving hard and roaring . . . Wow! Right up there with the drama of overhead heavy artillery going over, then down in front of you. The shock waves go right through you.

Troop Transports

On land, the U.S. Army's Stryker infantry carrier vehicle transports up to eleven combat personnel. It's a wheeled vehicle that can go up to 62 miles per hour.

By air, the US Army's aged CH-47D Chinook can ferry up to thirty-three combat-equipped troops. (It's high time the army replaced it with a faster, better armed helicopter that can carry more personnel.)

Also, the recent-vintage Black Hawk helicopter, traveling up to 183 miles per hour, can carry eleven combat-equipped troops. (It replaced the venerable Huey, which is still used by other countries.)

The Death Star

The concept of an orbiting Death Star as an all-powerful weapon is the basis for two movies in the franchise: *A New Hope*, with Death Star I; and *The Empire Strikes Back*, with Death Star II.

What do we know about the first Death Star? According to *The Complete Star Wars Encyclopedia*, it's 160 kilometers in diameter, with an operating crew of 265,000. Additional personnel ("gunners, ground troops, and starship support crews and pilots") raises the total personnel to more than one million. Moreover, it also holds seven thousand TIE fighters and four strike cruisers, and it bristles with armament such as turbolasers and tractor beams. Its main weapon is a superlaser.

In *A New Hope*, Admiral Motti, in conversation with Darth Vader, makes it clear that the Empire holds the trump card over any planet that doesn't cave in to their demands, because of their superweapon.

In *The Empire Strikes Back*, the Death Star is back, bigger and badder, though its construction is incomplete. What's important is that the main weapon, a superlaser, is functional.

But, we ask, why a superweapon at all? Does it make any strategic or tactical sense? Or, as Grand Moff Tarkin pointed out, what good is a superweapon if you don't use it?

Today's Superweapons: Bigger Is Better

The idea of a superweapon is particularly appealing to military planners, which historically has resulted in an arms race as nations compete in a game of one-upsmanship. In our case, the air force wants to acquire faster, more maneuverable fighter planes, bombers, and unmanned vehicles (drones), all armed with increasingly lethal munitions; the navy wants bigger and faster ships and submarines; and the army wants more advanced tanks, armored vehicles, attack/transport helicopters, field artillery, and individual/crew-served weapons.

Ironically, the United States has a superweapon—plenty of them, in fact—but its use is so fraught with political repercussions that they've been used just twice during wartime, against Japan's Hiroshima and Nagasaki in 1945. The hope was that their use would immediately end the war against Japan and prevent the necessity for a protracted and bloody ground battle, which would have resulted in catastrophic casualties, both military and civilian.

But the "small" atomic bombs of yesterday were not doomsday weapons, which we now have in the inventory. We have enough of them to blow up the world's population many times over.

So, too, do the Russians. According to army-technology.com, the world's biggest atomic bomb is Russia's Tsar Bomba, a hydrogen bomb with a yield of fifty megatons. That's the equivalent of 3,800 of the atomic bombs dropped on Hiroshima. The runner-up is the American B-41, a thermonuclear bomb with a yield of merely twenty-five megatons, or the equivalent of 1,900 of the bombs dropped on Hiroshima.

Current US doctrine regarding employment of nuclear weapons, both tactical (i.e., battlefield) and strategic, is simply stated in a White House fact sheet: "The United States will only consider the use of nuclear weapons in extreme circumstances to defend the vital interests of the United States or its allies and partners."

Traditionally, the use of atomic weapons on the battlefield was limited to situations in which there was an imminent and catastrophic loss of friendly troops; strategically, their use is limited by the "first use" doctrine (that is, we respond in kind), with the fervent hope that no foreign power will ever use them in the first place. That's a very broad strategy, with too much room for human error, as we have discovered.*

For obvious reasons, the development of the atomic bomb itself was top secret. Imagine what might have resulted if Japan had knowledge of the bomb's existence and its intended use. To what lengths would Japan have gone to stop its development and subsequent employment against two metropolitan cities?

It's a superweapon that no country wants to use. It could conceivably end in World War III and the destruction of all life on the planet.

No nation *uses* the atomic bomb to project power; for that, they use a portable weapons platform that can project military power anywhere in the world: the modern aircraft carrier.

The Aircraft Carrier

If the atomic bomb can be likened to the Death Star's superlaser, then the Death Star itself can be likened to a modern aircraft carrier. It is self-contained and self-sustaining for extended periods of time. It can move freely to project power anywhere it's needed. It has sufficient personnel to man its defensive and offensive weapons systems, and its mere presence is a show of force that serves as a major deterrent; if necessary, it can go on the offensive, delivering overwhelming firepower.

---

* I recommend the movie *WarGames* (1983), as well as a documentary, *The Man Who Saved the World* (2015), which tells the late Stanislav Petrov's story: During the height of the Cold War, on September 26, 1983, while on duty, the forty-four-year-old lieutenant colonel got an alarm that an intercontinental ballistic missile had been fired by the United States and was headed to Russia. He had to determine, quickly, whether it was a false alarm. "I realized that I had to make some kind of decision, and I was only 50/50." Obviously, had he determined in error that the attack was real, the Soviet Union would have retaliated immediately, which in turn would cause the United States to fire its missiles in response. The escalating situation might well have ended in the destruction of everyone on the planet.

Because of its worth as a high-value target, a US aircraft carrier is accompanied by other ships for its defense, typically a Ticonderoga-class cruiser with Tomahawk missiles, an Arleigh Burke–class destroyer for antiair warfare, a Los Angeles–class attack submarine for antisub and antiship operations, and a Supply-class replenishment ship for logistics support (providing ammunition, oil, and miscellaneous supplies). In short, the aircraft carrier is protected from air attacks, surface attacks by other ships, and underwater attacks. It's a mobile military "city" surrounded by smaller "towns" for support and capable of sustained operations anywhere in the world. (The only limitation is a human one: there are practical limits to the length of a deployment, because personnel are tethered back home to their families and homes. A typical deployment is eight months.)

The U.S. Navy currently has ten carriers in operation, with an eleventh that in April 2017 completed its sea trials: the *Gerald R. Ford*, which is 1,092 feet long, cruises at 34.5 miles per hour or more, displaces 100,000 long tons fully loaded, is manned by a crew of 4,539 personnel, and carries seventy-five or more fighter aircraft. It is state of the art in every possible way. Computer designed using 3-D modeling, it has two newly designed nuclear reactors, 250 percent more electrical capacity than its predecessor, and an electromagnetic launch system.

Such technology doesn't come cheaply, nor is the technology yet proven in actual combat. The new carrier itself cost over $10 billion, exclusive of aircraft and service personnel costs. It's spent eleven years in dry dock for its construction.*

Obviously, an aircraft carrier battle group is the closest thing the United States has to a Death Star, with the carrier itself representing the Death Star and its group representing Star Destroyers.

---

* Former Secretary of the Navy Ray Mabus explained, "The *Ford* is a poster child for how you don't build a ship. . . . They were designing the *Ford* while they were building it—not a good way to build a ship. This is just a dumb way to build any type of ship, particularly something as big and complicated as a carrier. . . . Not only did the price go through the roof, but the schedule just became terrible because there were so many new technologies, because it was so unproven and it wasn't completely designed" (David Martin, "New Warship 'Poster Child for How You Don't Build a Ship,' says Ex-Navy Secretary," *CBS News*, March 2, 2017).

Death Star

To give an idea of its size, the first Death Star is equivalent in diameter to 180 aircraft carriers of the *Gerald R. Ford* class laid end to end. Its more than one million personnel approach the number of all U.S. active duty forces, which is 1.4 million. In other words, losing the Death Star would be a catastrophic loss in terms of material and manpower.*

Given the devastating firepower of the Death Star's superlaser, it's easy to see why its senior officers place their full confidence in it. After all, no other power in the galaxy wielded such overwhelming destructive capabilities.

But such thinking inevitably leads to complacency, which is the principal reason why Death Star I was doomed. If its senior officers considered it to be impregnable and unassailable, why spend time worrying about formulating defensive and offensive postures? Just move the Death Star into firing position and await a response to the threat—*Surrender or die*. And forget about everything else. Who'd be dumb enough to even attack it?

Obviously, the Rebel Alliance would have to assemble a formidable armada in opposition, and the staffers on the Death Star did plan for that eventuality. But they never considered all of the enemy's other options, especially the possibility that, whereas a large-scale frontal assault would likely fail, a small sneak attack would prevail. They saw the big picture but failed to see the small picture.

The Element of Surprise

In two significant instances, sneak attacks against the United States proved to be overwhelmingly effective. In both instances, the attacks were so audacious that the enemy had the upper hand because

---

* We're told the first Death Star took two decades to build. We're also told that the second Death Star took only six years to build. Maybe Darth Vader found new ways to motivate the workforce?

he used the principle of surprise. Nobody could have imagined that either mission was in the works, because both were inconceivable.

In the first instance, on December 7, 1941, the Imperial Japanese Navy struck at Pearl Harbor, significantly damaging Battleship Row, the berthing place of the Pacific Fleet. The attack was the catalyst for the United States to enter into a war against Japan that ended four years later, after the Japanese were bombed into submission through (mostly) firebombings and (two) atomic bombings. They had no choice but to surrender—or die. Resistance *was* futile.

But who would ever have thought that the Japanese would steam a battle group toward Hawaii to launch carrier-based aircraft in successive waves, bombing stationary targets on a quiet weekend morning? Nobody. The U.S. military had let its guard down.*

In the second instance, sixty years later, Islamic extremists linked to al-Qaeda hijacked four U.S. airliners. Two struck the World Trade Center's twin towers in New York City, one struck the Pentagon, and one was forced to abort its mission after the heroic passengers courageously attempted, but failed, to overpower the hijackers. That plane crashed in an open field in Pennsylvania, thus preventing it from striking its intended but unknown target, possibly the White House or the Capitol Building.

The Death Star's Fatal Flaw

Just as the element of surprise worked heavily in favor of the Japanese during World War II and of the terrorists on September 11, 2001, the Rebel Alliance knew they had a losing hand, so they played the wild card. They had correctly surmised that the Empire had planned for a large-scale assault but not a small one. Once the Death Star's vulnerability was identified, the attack plan took

---

* Even today, the debate still rages: Who at Pearl Harbor should be held accountable for not preparing for the Japanese attack, Admiral Kimmel, the commander in chief of the Pacific Fleet, or General Short, the Army commander? Who was to blame? Where did the responsibility lie? From strictly a military point of view, which is the only way to look at it, both senior officers should be held accountable, because as any commander knows, the buck stops there.

place. A fleet of X- and Y-wing rebel fighters attacked its Achilles' heel. It was a long shot, but it only takes one successful shot to destroy the Death Star, thanks to the information Jyn Erso acquired (see *Rogue One*).

The Art of War

The new student of military history should begin the study of military science with Sun Tzu's classic book *The Art of War*. A testament to the fact that although times change, human nature doesn't, the age-old tactics that Sun Tzu writes about in *The Art of War* still apply today.

As Robert Cowley and Geoffrey Parker (*The Reader's Companion to Military History*, 1996) point out:

> Sun Tzu's approach to warfare, unlike that of Western authors, does not put force at the center; indeed, the Chinese character *li* (force) occurs only nine times in the text's thirteen chapters. This reflects the conditions of warfare in China at the time (force was then in fact of limited utility) as well as Sun Tzu's conviction that victory and defeat are fundamentally psychological states. He sees war, therefore, not so much as a matter of destroying the enemy materially and physically (although that may play a role), but of unsettling the enemy psychologically; his goal is to force the enemy's leadership and society from a condition of harmony, in which they can resist effectively, toward one of chaos (*luan*), which is tantamount to defeat.

Redesigning the TIE Fighter

The principal fighter aircraft for the Galactic Empire is the twin ion engine fighter, which in my opinion is long overdue for a substantial upgrade. Designed to be a short-range fighter, it has significant shortcomings that need to be addressed.

Its principal design flaw is the lack of visibility from the pilot's point of view. Sitting in a sphere, with large panels on both sides, the pilot is visually handicapped, and severely so. In contrast, as Kyle Mizokami points out,

> The [U.S. Air Force's] F-16 Viper has excellent visibility, thanks to a bubble canopy with the pilot in the center. The F-35 Joint Strike Fighter has poor visibility, but the Distributed Aperture System helmet is expected to help the pilot "see" 360 degrees.
>
> The unfortunate TIE fighter pilot on the other hand has two large panels on both sides of him, preventing him from seeing anything more than perhaps a 50 degree cone in front of him. He would be unable [to] see other TIE fighters flying abreast of him, or even in a staggered formation—unless he too had a Distributed Aperture System helmet.*

Obviously, the short-term solution is to add a Distributed Aperture System helmet, which would give an electronic view of the combat air space. The long-term solution, though, is to redesign the

---

* Kyle Mizokami, "5 Reasons *Star Wars* Spaceships Make Absolutely No Sense," *Popular Mechanics*, December 15, 2015.

ship itself by extending the pilot's sphere well forward of the twin panels—or, better yet, repositioning the wings horizontally instead of having them in a fixed, parallel vertical position.

Its fighting capability could further be enhanced with the inclusion of a backup pilot who can double as a weapons officer, which allows the primary pilot to concentrate on flying, leaving the weapons officer to concentrate on target acquisition. The two-seat F-16B jet used by the U.S. Air Force is thus configured. The plane also can be flown from the backseat, because it has a full set of instrumentation and controls. This redundancy enhances its combat effectiveness and survivability.

As for the TIE fighter, a redesign, with more room inside the fighter itself, would allow for an integrated enhanced life-support system. Currently, the TIE pilot must wear a special suit that serves as the life-support system. It's a paramount concern: the pilot, flying in the vacuum of space, needs a one hundred percent reliable source of oxygen, with a backup system in case of primary failure. In terms of life support, the ship itself should be the first line of defense, and the pilot's suit the second line of defense.*

Also, since the TIE fighter's principal mission is to fly in space, its wings can be configured as needed. They need not be fixed in a vertical position. (Visually, as Jason Torchinsky put it, a TIE fighter looks like an eyeball sandwich.†) A variable wing design, allowing for horizontal tilt, would give the pilot much-needed 360-degree visibility.

As seen in *The Force Awakens*, the TIE fighter also can fly in atmosphere, for which the variable wing design would be especially useful in tight quarters, if they could be folded to reduce its physical

---

* The Russians have developed an onboard oxygen generation system for all their fighter jets. "Oxygen is produced from the atmosphere as the system takes it from the engine's compressors and redirects it to [the] pilot's mask. Flight time no longer depends on oxygen supply," according to Mikhail Dudnik, a chief specialist for Zvezda, a research and development enterprise ("Rarefied Air: Russian 5G Fighters Boast Cutting-Edge Life Support Systems," rt.com, July 17, 2013).

† See his article on jalopnikon.com, "How Do The New Spaceships in *Rogue One* Compare With Classic *Star Wars* Ships?," May 17, 2016. One illustration puts everything in the proper perspective: a human eyeball positioned between two pieces of white bread. Yup, design-wise, that's what a TIE fighter looks like.

signature. Case in point: in *The Force Awakens*, the TIE fighters pursue the *Millennium Falcon* inside a derelict Star Destroyer. More than anything else, the inability of its pilots to see laterally led to needless loss of life and fighter craft.

TIE Fighter Capabilities

So what do we know about the TIE fighter's limitations? Volume 3 of *The Complete Star Wars Encyclopedia* points out that the TIE fighter "carried only two days' worth of supplies and often needed to refuel after the first few hours of combat. . . . TIE fighters had no shields, secondary weapons, or drive systems, minuscule fuel supplies, and no onboard life-support system. Pilots wore fully sealed flight suits with self-contained atmospheres."

In other words, the TIE fighter was optimally designed for maneuverability at the expense of everything else; long-term sustainability and survivability were not considered as design parameters. As the *Encyclopedia* points out, "TIEs were short-range fighters without hyperdrives, to save weight and increase performance." Thus, they weren't even able to pursue X-wing fighters that had light speed capability. This limitation severely affects its effectiveness as an offensive weapon: air superiority cannot be achieved with aircraft technology that is markedly inferior to that of the enemy.*

The limitations of the TIE fighter meant that it required the constant presence of a cargo ship or a Star Destroyer for safe harbor, especially since a TIE fighter lacks landing gear.†

TIE Pilot Discomfort

Because the TIE fighter was designed as a short-range fighter and can only stay on station for two days, pilots had to put up with its

---

* Likewise, the vaunted Japanese Zero, which principally depended on its maneuverability for survival, was outmatched by the P-51 Mustang, the best piston aircraft of World War II.
† As seen in *The Force Awakens*, the TIE fighter is customarily stored in a tethered and racked configuration, floating above the flight deck.

inadequate life-support capabilities, including limited toilet functions. Moreover, the TIE pilot must rely on his self-contained flight suit for life support. If there's a breach in the hull, it's the suit itself, not the ship, that must protect him. But if the suit is sufficiently damaged during combat—a likely possibility—the pilot has just flown his last mission, because he will have no life-support system.

Today's Life-Support Systems

Today's fighter pilots face the same issues as the TIE fighter pilot. They are captives of their aircraft for an extended period and must forgo personal comfort and individual mobility for the sake of the mission, which is paramount.

Life support is critical; thus, the Russians have designed a 9g antigravity suit that allows the pilot to fly "an unprecedented 30 seconds [when] the plane is thrust into a bone-crashing missile evasion maneuver." As one of its design specialists pointed out, it's groundbreaking technology. "This system is our know-how; no one in the world has managed to develop such a system so far." *

The issue of personal pilot comfort must be addressed. During World War II, for instance, the design parameters for the B-29 bomber focused on maximizing the bomb load capability, at the cost of crew comfort: though there was a small heater, the crew brought its own food and used a chemical toilet.†

Again, the Russians have given this personal comfort issue some thought, providentially addressing a crappy situation:‡

---

* "Rarefied Air," rt.com.
† Hence the expression "I have to go to the can." As B-29 navigator Ralph Livengood explained, "The B-29 bomber was very different from a commercial passenger plane. It was a 'bare necessity' aircraft with no frills, designed and built to deliver the maximum payload of high explosives over the greatest practical distance. There were no flight attendants on board, the closest thing to a TV set was the radar screen, and a toilet as such did not exist. The only conversation was between crew members via intercom" (Livengood, "B29 Navigator," korean-waronline.com.)
‡ "Rarefied air," rt.com.

Some previous generation Soviet fighter jets were first equipped with "personal convenience" systems in the 1990s after pilots flat out refused to use diapers, arguing it was uncomfortable to operate a jet while wearing them. But only on the PAK-FA [Sukhoi T-50 PAK-FA fifth-generation fighter jet] is it fully integrated into the pilot's suit and [it] does not divert his attention from the mission.

In the U.S. Air Force, there are no "personal convenience" systems. Female pilots wear diapers (a disposable brand called Depend), and male pilots urinate in a plastic bag called a "piddle pack," with compressed sponges soaking up the urine. The bag is then tied off using plastic-coated wire ties.

Speaking from personal experience sitting in the backseat of an F-16B on a tactical mission over New Mexico . . . I always made sure I ate a very light breakfast. I figured I could eat when I got back. On one mission, I was forced to take a leak in a piddle pack, which was logistically challenging because of the three-point harness that held me in place. It was, to say the least, a very uncomfortable experience, which I'd rather not undertake again.*

The U.S. military should take a hint from the Russians and design a personal comfort system, especially for flights with long durations. For instance, one of our training missions (which was grounded due to weather) would have involved an eight-hour exercise, flying halfway across the country, dogfighting F-15s, and returning to base. Unlike us, the aircrews on the Stratotankers that provided our air refueling had access to bathrooms.

So what does all of this have to do with the TIE fighter? The TIE fighter pilot must deal with the same human limitations. Number

---

* The design of the "piddle pack" is antiquated. The plastic bag is thin and the wire ties can come loose. Besides, you have to store it on your person until you get back to the air base, so you're sloshing around a bag—or two—of urine in a leg pocket. And if the bag opens up in flight during a high-speed inverted maneuver, you're going to be pissed on—and pissed off. So why not design a flexible plastic bladder bag with a screw-on cap? That way, it'll fit in a flight suit pocket and it won't leak.

one, he's got to be able to relieve himself (not to mention number two). Personal elimination is the overriding issue, because so much hangs in the balance, including the mission. A pilot unduly distracted by his personal needs cannot fully concentrate on the mission.*

Beyond bathroom considerations, the pilot has got to eat, but he must do so in zero gravity, which is a challenge.† The TIE fighter pilot also must nap in place, instead of being able to stretch out, recline, and assume a comfortable sleeping position.

Obviously, as future generations of TIE fighter aircraft are developed, its designers should consider building intermediate or long-range fighters with hyperdrive capability, increased cockpit visibility, a two-man crew, enhanced life support (external to the flight suit), an adequate toilet option, attachable fuel tanks to allow for extended flight times, and the ability to destroy fighters on its tail by deploying scatterable magnetic mines or using air-to-air missiles. Until then, its fighter crews—frustrated by their ships's inadequate ergonomics—will continue to be fit to be tied.‡

---

* The Mercury and Apollo astronauts relieved themselves in place, and the stench when the door to the enclosed capsule door was opened was rather fragrant—or so I was told. So, too, the TIE fighter's aircraft would have an unmistakable odoriferous aroma.

† As far as U.S. astronauts are concerned, eating in space (as opposed to relieving oneself) is routine. "Eating in space has improved a lot since the days of cold paste in aluminum tubes and cube-shaped bites. Today, space foods are similar to those eaten every day on Earth. They include frozen vegetables and desserts, refrigerated food, fruit and dairy products. . . . Space food may be canned or wrapped in aluminum foil. It may be freeze-dried, low moisture, pre-cooked or dehydrated (with its water removed). If food is dehydrated, it cannot be eaten until the astronauts add hot water to it. Ovens are provided to warm foods to the proper temperature. Many drinks are also in dehydrated form" (ESA Kids, "Eating in Space," esa.int, September 21, 2017).

‡ In time, TIE fighters will be flown by droids, thus allowing for better integration with the aircraft itself to optimize combat effectiveness.

A Misfire: The Imperial Army's Howitzers

To destroy, neutralize, or suppress the enemy by cannon, rocket, and missile fire and to help integrate all lethal and nonlethal fire support assets into combined arms operations.

—Field Artillery mission, U.S. Army Field Artillery School

The holy trinity of infantry, armor, and field artillery is considered the beating heart of the U.S. Army's combat arms. Infantry is called the "queen of battle," and field artillery is termed the "king of battle," because of its lethality.*

Given its traditional role on the battlefield, I found it odd, as a former redleg, or artilleryman, to see so such little thought, imagination, and space devoted to cannoneers in *Imperial Handbook: A Commander's Guide* (2015). There's a one-page entry on self-propelled heavy artillery (SPHA), which has scant information. But after reading it, I concluded that if I were a ground commander in the Imperial Army, I'd immediately put in a transfer to the Imperial Navy. Here's why: Imperial Army heavy howitzers (cannons) use a standard platform, "a large, *slow-moving* artillery vehicle with [twelve] legs." We're also told that "the SPHA-T [the *T* means its a turbolaser cannon] *is not speedy*. If you are forced to retreat, the enemy may overrun your artillery line" (all italics mine).

The problem is that the SPHA-T is simply not survivable on the battlefield. Target acquisition radar, with its ability to determine the

---

* During World War II, cannon fire was the single greatest casualty producer.

source of the rounds, will result in immediate counterbattery fire, because field artillery assets are high-priority targets on the battlefield. This is why artillery must be able to "shoot and scoot." An immobile or slow-moving artillery piece is a fixed target. To survive in today's battlefield, the howitzer must put its rounds downrange and immediately displace to another firing location. This would be even more true in the future, because target acquisition capabilities would be significantly enhanced and more responsive.

Before we talk about the Empire's artillery assets, it helps to understand the current state of the art in U.S. Army Field Artillery.

Towed M777 Howitzer

The army's towed howitzer is the M777, which fires a 155 millimeter round. It also can fire the Excalibur GPS-guided shell. The advantage of a towed piece is that its lighter weight favors air transportability by helicopter or by an Osprey. It can also be towed by truck in terrain impassable by track vehicles.

The disadvantage is that it can't displace as quickly as a self-propelled artillery piece, because of its trails. The trails must be lifted to clear the ground, the spades stored, and then the trails brought together so the artillery piece can be hooked up to a vehicle for towing. All of that is time-consuming, especially in situations where every second counts—as when you're getting shelled by the enemy with counterbattery fire.

Self-Propelled M109A6 Paladin

The M109A6 Paladin is a self-propelled track vehicle, also firing a 155 millimeter round. Based on the time-tested M109 design that dates back to 1963, the Paladin is currently undergoing a major overhaul called the Paladin Integrated Management program. As military.com points out, "The PIM modernization effort is a significant upgrade of the M109A6 Paladin which includes buying back space, weight, and power-cooling. While the self-propelled howitzer's cannon will remain unchanged, the PIM will sport *a brand-new chassis, engine, transmission, suspension, steering system, to go along with an upgraded electric ramming system*" (italics mine).*

The next generation of 155 millimeter self-propelled howitzers will have significant improvements over the current Paladin model.† They will inevitably be lighter, air-transportable, capable of putting more steel on the target, and do so more accurately.

My thought is that, within the next decade, self-propelled artillery will be controlled by remote control technology, just like an air force Predator drone. The howitzer will then be able to go as far forward in the battle area as required, providing firepower deeper into the enemy's ranks, with no personnel risk, since it will lack a crew.

Imperial Artillery

Based on the specs given in the *Imperial Handbook*, the Imperial Army's artillery has some obvious drawbacks.‡

1. *There is no towed artillery.* The (comparatively) light weight of a towed piece means it's air-transportable. This gives the ground commander his own "hip pocket" firepower, on call as needed, instead of having to call in an air strike with bombers or a fighter plane to provide close air support, which may not be available because they're being used elsewhere.§ Because the battlefield is a target-rich environment with a multiplicity of targets, the air force must allocate its air assets accordingly. Moreover, unless they're on station, they are not as responsive as artillery. In contrast, the army's Paladin can go from a road march to a firing position quickly

---

* "M109 Paladin," military.com.

† "The widely used M109 carries a 155-mm howitzer and is the principal artillery support for U.S. Army divisions. It is a large tracked vehicle with a fully traversable turret [360 degrees] and prominent bustle" ("M109 Paladin," military.com).

‡ Without a detailed list of its specifications, we have to make some educated guesses about its weight, size, capability, firing range, and so forth.

§ Air assets are in high demand during combat, and prioritized accordingly based on the needs of the ground commander.

and put the first round downrange a minute later; afterward, it can sustain a rate of fire of one round per minute.

This is why having artillery is so useful: it can provide the ground commander with immediate, responsive, and dedicated fire support in a way no other asset, ground or air, can.

2. *Weight of self-propelled artillery.* The weight of the SPHA makes it unlikely that it can be transported by air. This means that it must be transported by platformed ground vehicles, especially since the SPHA's legs are too slow. Also, because it doesn't include repulsor lift technology, as imperial tanks do, an SPHA can only travel on flat, unobstructed terrain. Its weight and means of locomotion make it impossible to use in marshy areas, rice paddies, or heavily forested areas where its "legs" can easily get caught in the underbrush.

3. *Lack of speed.* As the *Handbook* states, "The SPHA-T is not speedy." That's an understatement. With ten to twelve legs that must work in unison, its speed of 5 to 10 miles per hour violates the cardinal rule of survivability on the battlefield: it can shoot but it can't scoot. In fact, it practically crawls.

The idea of a howitzer with centipede-like legs is tactically indefensible. Its engineers would be well advised to spend time with a field unit during a tactical field problem and learn firsthand what it's like to fight in a combat environment. Afterward, they'd likely go to a highly mobile, fast-moving platform. Imperial tanks use repulsor lift, an antigravity technology that allows them to float above the surface. Why isn't that technology used for its field artillery as well? It simply makes tactical sense.

3. *Manpower.* The Imperial Army's field artillery howitzers require a crew of thirty, which we're told includes "troopers who secure the perimeter against enemy attack during the vulnerable process of deployment and firing." Why so many crew members?

To put things in perspective: the U.S. Army's most current Paladin (howitzer, 155 millimeter, self-propelled, current generation) requires only *four* men (a driver, commander, gunner, and ammo loader). And in the future, as its weapons system is improved through automation, the crew requirement will likely get down to two men, and ultimately to no men, since it will someday be controlled remotely. In other words, by the time technology evolves to its logical point in the *Star Wars* universe, its artillery would be self-propelled using repulsor technology (which is already used for its tanks) and be unmanned and remotely controlled, or controlled by a one-man crew.

4. *High angle.* Only three of the SPHA-T's five configurations are designated as "high-angle" weapons. This makes no sense; *any* howitzer in the current army inventory can fire at high angle by simply elevating its tube accordingly. High-angle fire starts at 800 mils in elevation.* As the *Field Artillery Gunnery* (FM 6-40, Department of the Army, December 1984) states:

> *All howitzers are capable of delivering high-angle fire effectively.* High-angle fire is used for firing into or out of deep defilade such as that found in heavily wooded, mountainous, and urban areas. It is also used to fire over high terrain features near friendly troops (italics mine).

5. *Weapons.* According to the *Star Wars* reference books, this weapons system platform comes in several configurations, three that fire only at high angle and two that fire line-of-sight only. They include:

- a turbolaser, which is line-of-sight. Properly speaking, this is not an artillery weapon; it's a tank. Artillery is an *indirect fire* weapon. A tank is a *direct fire* weapon. A self-propelled howitzer may look like a tank because they both have long tubes, but they are clearly not the same thing.
- a disruptor ion beam, which also is line-of-sight. Again, this isn't an artillery piece; this is a tank.

---

* Because firing artillery shells requires as much preciseness as possible, U.S. field artillery units use a unit of measure called "mils." There are 6400 mils in a circle. (Think of a pie cut in 6400 pieces.)

- a missile firing only at high angle. This is too specialized. High angle is seldom used; mostly, it's used to reach the opposite side of a slope. Moreover, time of flight is an issue: it takes an extremely long time for the missile to go up, reach its maximum height, and descend. It's just not responsive enough for the ground commander.
- a kinetic energy projectile fired only at high angle.
- a thermobaric projectile fired only at high angle.

The problem with all of these is that none are of much use to the ground commander, because if he wants *responsive* fire, he won't want *anything* fired at a high angle, which greatly increases the time of flight.

If he wants direct fire capability, he will have the cavalry's armored assault tanks, not artillery, providing fire.

What he needs are artillery projectiles (shells) downrange in a hurry. For instance, a typical low angle mission will put a round downrange in seventeen seconds, but a typical high angle mission will put a round downrange in fifty seconds, which is not responsive enough to the maneuver commander who needs steel on the target fast.

The Bottom Line

The Imperial Army should dump the SPHA and design a new generation of howitzers that (1) use repulsor technology for rapid deployment; (2) have a crew of four or fewer personnel; (3) fire projectiles at low and high angles; and (4) fire any desired shell/fuse combination. Only then will the Imperial Army's field artillery be able to deliver timely fire to support the maneuver ground commander.

US Army Field Artillery Cannon Battalion's General Standards

The field artillery battalion must:

a. Provide continuous and timely FA [field artillery] fires to suppress, neutralize, or destroy the enemy.

b. Provide its component of the force FA communications, survey, and target acquisition systems.

c. Provide medical services for organic units to include medical care and intrabattalion evacuation.

d. Procure and distribute all classes of supplies to organic units, maintain appropriate supply and material records, and transport its prescribed basic load of ammunition.

e. Provide fire support personnel (FSS [fire support section]/FIST [Fire Support Team]) to maneuver units if appropriate.

f. Provide limited air defense against low-flying hostile aircraft.

g. Provide an effective, coordinated defense of the battalion areas.

h. Survive on the battlefield.

i. Plan and coordinate fire support and help integrate it into battle plans.

Source: *The Field Artillery Cannon Battalion*, Army Training and Evaluation Program (ARTEP 6-400), Department of the Army, 1984.

Rethinking the X-wing Starfighter

Let's get the pesky facts out of the way, since some people have misconceptions about spaceflight, mostly based on what they have seen in movies, especially *Star Wars*.

First, there is no sound in space because it's a vacuum. As geek .com points out, "In space . . . there is no atmosphere, no fluid to carry shockwaves, and as a result there is no sound. . . . The movies have rendered countless bass-y space explosions for us over the years, but it's the handicap in basic spatial awareness that film most misrepresents in space."* In other words, when you hear the distinctive screech of a TIE fighter streaking by in *Star Wars*, that's not what you would actually hear in space, because its passage would be noiseless.†

Second, ships in space cannot turn on a dime, maneuvering like fighter aircraft. The fighter plane's fins enable it to maneuver with hairpin turns because of the atmosphere. In space, directional nozzles or thrusters on a controlled burn would be necessary to change direction. It would be nothing like what you see fighter jets do at air demonstrations, as when the U.S. Navy Blue Angels or U.S. Air Force Thunderbirds take to the skies.

On gizmodo.com, Joseph Shoer (a PhD candidate in aerospace engineering) explains, "First, pending a major development in

---

* Graham Templeton, "The 10 Most Common Misconceptions About Space," geek.com, February 2, 2015.
† To simulate that sound, Lucasfilm recorded the sound of an artillery round going downrange. When an artillery round goes overhead, it sounds just like tearing silk or cloth—but *very* loud.

propulsion technology, combat spacecraft would likely get around the same way the Apollo spacecraft went to the Moon and back: with orbit change effected by discrete main-engine burns. . . . The craft would likely only have one main engine rather than, say, four equal tetrahedral engines [like Luke Skywalker's X-wing fighter]." *

As to the issue of fires in space, their duration is limited by the available oxygen. As geek.com points out:

> Fire is not an object, it's a reaction: the combustion of gasses in air. Without air to release its energy as light and heat, fire fundamentally cannot exist. In space, of course, we have a serious air shortage, and so every movie you've ever seen with exploding spaceships is wrong. Actually, a *short* fire or explosion could be realistic, fed by the air still trapped inside a pressurized ship. In an instant, though, this air would either be used up or sucked out, and the fire promptly smothered. [†]

Potential Crew Problems: Inexperienced Pilots

The X-wing starfighter is the standard Rebel Alliance fighter aircraft. We're told that it's simple to fly; in fact, we're told that a new pilot can learn how to fly it in a matter of weeks, because its controls are so intuitive. (A similar claim is made for the TIE fighter.)

In my opinion, this can lead to overconfidence among new pilots, who fail to see the big picture. Although it's certainly helpful that the ease of actually flying an X-wing can put pilots in seats sooner, that's just one part of what a military pilot must know—in fact, fighter pilots will tell you that the ability to fly is a given. Beyond flying the starfighter itself, new pilots must know how to react to in-flight problems.

Case in point: If you're a newbie flying an X-wing over Tatooine and you have an engine flameout, what are you going to do?

---

* Joseph Schoer, "The Physics of Space Battles," gizmodo.com, December 16, 2009.
† Templeton, "The 10 Most Common Misconceptions."

Real World

U.S. Air Force pilots plan for the possibility of flameouts during flight, using critical action procedures (CAPs):

> In the F-16, items like a flameout, or airborne engine restart, or a fire during engine start and emergency ground egress are all CAPs. You'd better know how to do those things without reference to a check-list! . . . CAPs are required to be memorized. . . . In my USAF experience, we filled out CAPs practice sheets (from memory of course) every month, and during initial training, young students were required to fill them out every week!*

Besides being able to react to in-flight crises, an F-16 military pilot must learn to fly in formation (among other skills), develop a finely honed sense of situational awareness, learn how to use proper radio procedures, provide close air support, adeptly handle the weapons systems while simultaneously navigating and flying the aircraft, and—most difficult of all—learn how to dogfight. In short, the plane has to become an extension of the pilot in every way; he must always be in command of the aircraft.

Now, let's consider the dual problem of having to learn how to fly not only within the atmosphere but also in space, which involves a different skill set. What, in fact, is involved in training for space as an astronaut?

Rather than discuss the program of instruction that a NASA-trained astronaut must go through, let's compare the novice X-wing pilot to today's space tourist, such as Dennis Tito, the first space tourist, who flew on a Russian Soyuz spacecraft to the International Space Station, on April 28, 2001.

Not surprisingly, NASA recommended against Tito's buying a seat on the Soyuz. As NASA pointed out in a press release (March 19, 2001), "The presence of a nonprofessional crewmember who is

---

* Nate S. Jaros, *Engine Out Survival Tactics* (BookBaby, 2017).

untrained on all critical station systems, is unable to respond and assist in any contingency situation which may arise, and who would require constant supervision, would add a significant burden to the Expedition and detract from the overall safety of the International Space Station."

Despite NASA's objections, Tito did in fact get to go to space, but only after undergoing nearly a year of extensive training at Star City, outside of Moscow. In doing so, he opened the door to space tourism, which is now wide open. (He also was not needed for any emergencies on the space station, for which I'm sure he was thankful.)

Bottom line: if you've got the money—Tito reportedly spent $20 million for his joyride—you can book a spaceflight; private companies like Richard Branson's Virgin Galactic and Elon Musk's SpaceX will sell you a seat.

But, of course, you're not in the pilot's seat, and if there's an in-flight emergency, you're going to be more a hindrance than a help. And if the pilot suddenly becomes disabled or, worse, dies, you're in a life-threatening situation.

So ask yourself: If you're in the Rebel Alliance and you've got a newbie checked out for atmospheric flight on the easy-to-fly X-wing fighter, how soon would you want him to fly in space as your wingman on a combat mission—especially if he's never had any military training whatsoever and no flight time as a combat pilot?

This gets back to what Chuck Yeager said about flying: that time in the cockpit, and a lot of it, is the overriding factor determining how good a pilot you are. There is no substitute for experience and extensive hands-on training in emergencies.

Yes, I know that Luke has put in some hours in his T-16 skyhopper, but that's not comparable to having to fly an X-wing fighter *in combat*.

My point is that Luke Skywalker—despite his gifts as a pilot and the time he's spent in a skyhopper—has much to learn in terms of spaceflight and combat flight operations before he can be considered an asset to a fighter squadron. In other words, Luke's rapid ascension from farm boy to fighter pilot in space, in a matter of a few days, would logically make him a liability, Force or no Force.

No Pain, No Gain: Torture

How effective is torture as a means of obtaining information?

In *A New Hope*, Princess Leia Organa, confined to a prison cell, is visited by Darth Vader, who wants information. He expects her to talk, and he will use torture to get the information if she doesn't volunteer it freely.

In addition to questioning the effectiveness of torture, one must also ask how accurate the information so obtained would be. If it's not militarily useful to Darth Vader, it's essentially useless. Bad information, if perceived as useful information, will lead one astray and divert resources to where they aren't needed. In other words, bad information is worse than no information.

Did Leia's latent talent—she is one with the Force—enhance her powers of resistance? Or perhaps she is simply strong-willed, unbreakable by traditional methods?

Whatever the reason, it's not easy to break Leia's will and obtain the elusive and much-needed information about the location of the rebel base, no matter what high-tech mind probe is put to the test.

Leia, of course, is not the only one who found herself facing an agonizing mind probe or mechanical interrogation. In *The Empire Strikes Back*, Han Solo was restrained and his body was forced forward against an interrogation machine. And in *The Force Awakens*, pilot Poe Dameron and Rey (who, like Leia, also has the Force) find themselves strapped into an interrogation chair with Kylo Ren's hope that it will yield informational results.

In the *Star Wars* universe, traditional forms of physical torture are dispensed with in favor of electronically enhanced devices that, presumably, can extract more information, especially after a subject is injected with a truth serum such as sodium thiopental, a barbiturate that affects the central nervous system.

A Torturous Past

Torturing prisoners for information goes back a long way in human history. The methods used may have been primitive, but they were very effective in getting people to talk—at least up to the point of death. Eschewing the subtleties of psychological torture, the devilish implements from the past were positively medieval.

If one is curious about torturers' tools of the trade, the place to visit is a three-story museum in Prague, Czech Republic. Near the Old Town Square, the Museum of Torture Instruments displays the heinous devices that were used back in the day. A detailed discussion of the dozens of torture devices on display is not needed here; however, anyone with a Hannibal Lecter–like appetite for more information will find it readily available.*

Truth Serum

Leia Organa, only seventeen years old, looks on with horror at an approaching interrogation device floating in midair. Her eyes are no doubt focused on the large needle of the mind probe sphere.

What drug is in the needle? Most likely, it's filled with a so-called truth drug, possibly scopolamine or a barbiturate (amobarbital,

---

* One such book is Erik C. Ruhling's *Infernal Device: Machinery of Torture and Execution* (Disinformation Company, 2007). This photo-illustrated book, with color photos of the devices, will convince you that there are things worse than death, and this book catalogs them. Alternatively, for a history of torture, with photos, Mark P. Donnelly and Daniel Diehl, *The Big Book of Pain: Torture & Punishment Through History* (History Press, 2008), is a veritable horror show.

thiopental, or secobarbital). But these "truth" drugs aren't infallible, and that's the truth.

The paper "'Truth' Drugs in Interrogation" (CIA Historical Review Program, September 22, 1993) discusses the "effects of narcosis and considerations relevant to its possible counterintelligence use." The operative question to ask is whether these drugs are necessarily effective. Do they work? Will you be able to get actionable intelligence? The CIA's study concludes that, at best, they produce mixed results.

> No such magic brew as the popular notion of truth serum exists. The barbiturates, by disrupting defensive patterns, may sometimes be helpful in interrogation, but even under the best conditions they will elicit an output contaminated by deception, fantasy, garbled speech, etc. A major vulnerability they produce in the subject is a tendency to believe he has revealed more than he has. It is possible, however, for both normal individuals and psychopaths to resist drug interrogation; it seems likely that any individual who can withstand ordinary intensive interrogations can hold out in narcosis. The best aid to a defense against narco-interrogation is foreknowledge of the process and its limitations. There is an acute need for controlled experimental studies of drug reaction, not only to depressants but also to stimulants and to combinations of depressants, stimulants, and ataraxics.

Psychological Means

In *A New Hope*, when it's clear that Leia Organa has proven resistant to a mind probe, Governor Tarkin—obviously an old hand at this kind of push-pull game—decides to use a different, more effective tactic: he threatens to blow up her home planet of Alderaan, against her vociferous protests.

This is an old but very effective tactic: *You, sir, may be able to resist anything we do. We know you're willing to die rather than talk. But what if we torture someone you love? I bet you'll sing a different tune!*

Faced with that ultimatum, Leia caves in, but deliberately feeds him misinformation. Tarkin, though, blows up the planet anyway. Why? Just because he's a badass.

The Atomic Bomb

During World War II, as the president pondered the decision about where to deploy the first atomic bomb, it was suggested that, instead of destroying a Japanese city, the bomb could be detonated elsewhere (possibly offshore) as a show of force, which some felt would be sufficient to show the Japanese that further resistance was futile. In the end, the powers that be decided to target cities in Japan that had not yet been subjected to firebombing. In the end, atomic bombs were dropped on Hiroshima and Nagasaki, bringing home the full horror of the atomic weaponry that the United States could unleash at will against Japan.*

The issue of whether it's best to demonstrate a superweapon off-site or directly against the enemy is no easy choice, unless one has no scruples, like Tarkin.

Torturous Information

In *Return of the Jedi*, C-3PO witnesses a fellow robot torturing a smaller robot. More recently, in *Rogue One* (2016), anti-Empire extremist Saw Gerrera harnesses the power of an octopus-like creature with mind reading capabilities to tap into the memories of a renegade Imperial pilot, but at a risk to his mental health.

As regimes with active torture programs have discovered, getting information per se is not the problem. The problem is with the information's *reliability*, because people being tortured will say anything to stop the pain. Lying, after all, is easy and far preferable to

---

* Today, seventy-two years after the bombs fell, the lingering effects of nuclear radiation on the townsfolk of Hiroshima and Nagasaki still plague its citizenry. Understandably, the Japanese people view atomic weapons from a unique perspective: They are the only ones to have been subjected to the superweapon.

enduring more torture. Thus, the victim will simply tell the interrogators what they want to hear. This brings the pain to a temporary stop, and the interrogators go away happy—until they discover that the information is false and come back to resume their torturous trade.

Political scientist Darius Rejali studied the effectiveness of torture and stated, "Torture to obtain information is a sign of institutional decay and desperation . . . and torture accelerates this process, destroying the bonds of loyalty, respect and trust that keep information flowing."[*] Beyond the moral issues, therefore, one must ask whether it's worth the time or effort.

Directly addressing that topic, a bipartisan committee published *The Committee Study of the Central Intelligence Agency's Detention and Interrogation Program*, a six-thousand-page report that took five years to compile, at a cost of $40 million. The controversial study, looking principally at CIA activities during the so-called War on Terror from 2001 to 2006, concluded that torturing prisoners did not generate actionable intelligence or gain detainees' cooperation. In addition, the program damaged the international reputation of the United States.

This, in large part, is why, when retired Marine General James Mattis was asked about waterboarding, he reportedly told President Trump, "I've never found it to be useful . . . I've always found, give me a pack of cigarettes and a couple of beers and I do better with that than I do with torture."[†]

In Leia Organa's case, the desired information proved elusive. And, ironically, Grand Moff Tarkin and his henchmen suffered for it in the end.

---

[*] Heather Whipps, "Torture Has a Long History . . . of Not Working," *LiveScience*, October 19, 2007.

[†] Richard Sisk, "Mattis to Trump: Beer, Cigarettes Work Better than Waterboarding," military.com November 23, 2016. General Mattis is the secretary of defense in the Trump administration.

The War of the Machines

Airborne Ramdoves

are weapons delivery systems in every sense of the word. . . . They are quickly adaptable to a multitude of air-to-air, air-to-ground missions. . . . In 60 seconds flat attending mechanics can convert a Ramdove bomber into a Ramdove ground strafing instrument. . . . In groups or wings or squadrons or whatever term is used, they respond with esprit de corps, precision, and above all, ruthlessness . . . not hatefulness, that implies a wide ranging emotional pattern, just a blind, unemotional devotion to doing the job.

The platform described is not U.S. Air Force drone technology; instead, it existed only in the imagination of the late cartoonist Vaughn Bodē, whose strip "The Machines" imagines anthropomorphic machines that wage wars.* "A war of machines rages across a sterile world . . . one goal uppermost in the dim minds of the metal and plastic combatants: kill, destroy, annihilate until there is nothing left!"

It's a war where the survivors, the last remnants of humankind, are hunkered down in underground bunkers, eating canned food, while the never-ending war rages on aboveground.

---

* For an overview of Vaughn Bodē's life and career, see Vaughn Bodē and George Beahm, *Vaughn Bodē Index* (1976).

"We just continue our mission . . . and our mission is to destroy the enemy and that's what we do here. . . . We mass produce ourselves by the multimillions and destroy each other with the same gusto as always, only now we do not fight the enemy state, we fight all the other machines that are different and inferior."

Lucasfilm Research Library

The Lucasfilm Research Library, located in the main house at Skywalker Ranch, in northern California, is a closed repository where Lucasfilm employees can check out the resources they need. It represents one of the largest libraries in private hands and has among its holdings the former libraries of Paramount Studios and Universal Studios.

Because Lucasfilm is best known for its popular culture movies—the *Star Wars* saga and the Indiana Jones story cycle—it necessarily has vast holdings of pop culture material, including (probably) comic books, which Lucas himself enjoyed reading as a young boy. It's conceivable that books of Vaughn Bodē's artwork can be found on its shelves. The design of the AT-ATs bears a strong resemblance to Bodē's artwork, which predated the 1977 release of *A New Hope*. (Bodē's work began publishing in mainstream media in the mid- to late sixties.)

Numerous licensed books by publisher DK collect the work of production designers, notably Doug Chiang, whose cross-sectional depictions of the countless machines in the *Star Wars* universe recalls Bodē's intricate cutaways of machinery, showing their innards in exquisite detail. As Chiang wrote in a foreword to *Star Wars: Complete Locations* (DK Publishing, 2016), "I imagined them as real, believable places, places that worked from the inside as well as the outside. . . . I wanted the sets to have a logic for why they looked the way they did."

These cross-sectional views give Lucas's fictional universe shape, form, and, most important, substance.

Droids

Nowhere is this more apparent than in the design and function of droids, which we first saw when *A New Hope* hit movie screens in the summer of 1977. The androids C-3PO and R2-D2 were the first of many droids that populated Lucas's universe.*

Like robots, droids are mechanical in construction, but unlike robots, droids have artificial intelligence (AI). Beyond utilitarian droids like the winsome duo C-3PO and R2-D2, droids can be configured for virtually any need, including as instruments of war.

In *The Phantom Menace* (1999), we see battle droids that fight wars for their human and alien masters; no biological beings need be risked in combat. The droids are inexpensive, expendable, and easily replaceable because they are mass-produced.

We first saw that in Bodē's art. In "The Machines," Bodē designed a four-foot-high Punkerpan Bi-Pod Model 1926, armed with a recoilless .30-caliber air-cooled gun, and a Hypocket Infantry Machine, which he termed "an effective, fairly fearless combatant" that plays an infantry role "as initial, inexpensive contact forces that are designed to take the brunt of enemy firepower."

From Bodē to Lucas . . . In *The Phantom Menace*, the sight of mass-produced, identical battle droids descending from a troop carrier in uniform rows strikes justifiable fear within the ranks of the Gungan Grand Army, which faces a formidable force when the Trade Federation invades the planet at the Battle of Naboo.

Of course, it may be that the artists and designers who worked

---

* The word "droid" is trademarked by Lucas Ltd., which claims it for "Wireless communications devices, including, mobile phones, cell phones, handheld devices and personal digital assistants, accessories and parts therefor, and related computer software and wireless telecommunications programs; mobile digital electronic devices for the sending and receiving of telephone calls, electronic mail, and other digital data, for use as a digital format audio player, and for use as a handheld computer, electronic organizer, electronic notepad, and digital camera; downloadable ring tones and screen savers; cameras, pagers and calling cards." All of which explains why Verizon paid big bucks for the use of the word for their smartphone called Droid.

for Lucasfilm never knew of Bodē's artwork, with depictions of war machines well ahead of their time.

Bodē, who died in 1975, would not have been surprised to see his visions realized in real life. He felt it was inevitable that machines would replace men in the military of the future, and he was right. His Airborne Ramdove preceded the USAF's Predator drone many decades ago.

US Air Force Pilot

According to the U.S. Government Accountability Office, it takes up to two years to put a U.S. Air Force pilot through basic flight training, just to earn the coveted wings, and costs taxpayers one million dollars. Beyond that, "the cost to fully train a pilot with the requisite operational experience can be more than $9 million. These costs will vary significantly, depending on the type of aircraft" (Government Accountability Office, *Military Personnel*, August 1999).*

In other words, the cost of a trained pilot and his combat plane can run into the many millions of dollars. The money, of course, is a secondary issue. When pilots are downed, the USAF goes to great lengths to recover them.†

Beyond the cost of training personnel, regardless of branch of service, there's the hidden cost of taking care of them medically after the war is over. This expense is across the board, and it's prohibitively expensive. According to *Business Insider*, it costs a lifetime average of $2 million to provide postcombat medical care for a

---

* The cost to train pilots in the more advanced planes, like the F-35, goes up significantly.
† This explains why the U.S. Air Force invests a lot of time, money, and training in its search and rescue operations. A rescue squadron immediately dispatches a rescue team in an HH-60/MH-60 Pave Hawk (a derivative of the UH-60 Black Hawk, which incorporates the USAF PAVE electronic systems program). A rescue squadron mission provides "rapidly deployable full spectrum expeditionary personnel recovery vertical lift capabilities to theater commanders worldwide. They tactically employ the HH-60G helicopter and its crew in hostile environments to recover downed aircrew and isolated personnel during day, night, or marginal weather conditions in contested airspace, employing skills such as weapons employment, shipboard operations, and aerial refueling" ("66th Rescue Squadron," Nellis Air Force Base, nellis .af.mil, July 12, 2012).

single U.S. soldier. In fact, the *Washington Times* (September 29, 2010) states, "The expense of caring for veterans of the Iraq and Afghanistan wars is an unfunded budget liability for U.S. taxpayers that in years to come will rival the cost of entitlement programs such as Social Security and Medicare," at a cost of "more than $1.3 trillion."

All of which explains why the U.S. military is looking into ways to mitigate its casualties, injuries, and related costs by investing significantly more in technology, which in the long term is less expensive. The Predator (an unmanned aerial vehicle) is expensive but, unlike pilots, expendable, and it has proven to be a highly effective weapons platform that the enemy has justifiably come to fear. Moreover, because it lacks a pilot—it's flown by remote control from a distant air base—the human risk is eliminated.*

Remote-controlled or AI-aware weapons systems, in the air, on the ground, and on top of or under the water, will be more fully integrated into the U.S. military in the years to come, all of which was imagined fifty years ago by Vaughn Bodē, who drew on his imagination to give us a glimpse of the future.

It's a future that entrepreneur Elon Musk and theoretical physicist Stephen Hawking, among others, fear might happen, with disastrous consequences for humanity, if it continues on its course of developing A.I. (Artificial Intelligence) war machines. In a letter presented at the International Joint Conference on Artificial Intelligence in Buenos Aires, the participants present pointed out the inherent dangers in an A.I. arms race: "Autonomous weapons select and engage targets without human intervention. . . . Artificial Intelligence (AI) technology has reached a point where the deployment of such systems is—practically if not legally—feasible within

---

* As one U.S. Air Force pilot, working out of a secure installation in Nevada, piloting by remote control a Predator in Iraqi air space, explained, "You're going to war for twelve hours, shooting weapons at targets, directing kills on enemy combatants. Then you get in the car and you drive home, and within twenty minutes you're sitting at the dinner table talking to your kids about their homework" (P. W. Singer, "Military Robots and the Future of War," TED Talks, ted .com, February 2009).

years, not decades, and the stakes are high: autonomous weapons have been described as the third revolution in warfare, after gunpowder and nuclear arms."*

Battle Droid

In *Star Wars Character Encyclopedia* (DK Publishing, 2016), we are told that battle droids stand six feet three inches and "are intended to win by strength of numbers rather than by individual ability. The droids are mass-produced and unable to think independently. . . . [They are] fearless, emotionless, and ready to do their masters' bidding."

In other words, they are more robotic than androids per se, which think autonomously. Lucas's battle droids recall Bodē's Hypocket Infantry Machines, which "are cheap enough that thousands can be lost in the classic frontal assault and not strain the military budget in the least." Specifically, "on a mass production basis" their total cost is nominal. They are "initial, inexpensive contact forces that are designed to take the brunt of enemy firepower."

That is exactly the combat role of the battle droids who fought at the Battle of Naboo.

Bodē saw the future, and it was *Star Wars*.

Elon Musk and Stephen Hawking, unfortunately, may be right in their prediction about A.I. threats to humanity. Only time will tell.

* Announced on July 28, 2015, at the IJCAI 2015 conference, "Autonomous Weapons: An Open Letter from AI & Robotics Researchers," https://futureoflife.org/open-letter-autonomous-weapons, accessed September 26, 2017.

▪ PART 3 ▪

TECHNOLOGY

We live in a society exquisitely dependent on science and technology, in which hardly anyone knows anything about science and technology.

—Carl Sagan

Peace through superior firepower.

—Unattributed

Battledress for Success:
Dressed to Kill

Clothes make the man (or woman).

This is true for civilians and it's even more true for military personnel, who must dress appropriately for every occasion, from the classroom to the battlefield.*

Recently, the U.S. Army phased out its green class A uniform. Its replacement is the Army Service Uniform, which took its design from its semiformal dress blue uniform:

> The new Army Service Uniform is rooted in tradition. In March 1778, a Congressional resolution directed General George Washington to prescribe a service uniform. The resolution "authorized and directed the Commander in Chief, according to circumstances of supplies of Clothing, to fix and prescribe the uniform, as well with regard to color and facings as the cut of fashion of the Clothes to be worn by the troops of the respective States and regiments."
>
> General Washington issued a general order October 1779 "prescribing blue coats with different facings for the various state troops, artillery, artillery artificers and light dragoons. The Adjutant & Inspector General's Office, March 27, 1821 established "Dark blue is the National colour. When a different one is not expressly prescribed,

---

* When it comes to dressing for success, civilians have it easy. In the business world, a man wears a suit and tie. That's the uniform he'll wear until he gets his gold watch at a retirement ceremony. But in the military, the mission dictates the uniform.

all uniform coats, whether for officers or enlisted men, will be of that colour."

The blue uniform is part of our bloodline. It links today's warriors to their heritage and connects them to warriors past.*

Dressing a Galaxy

Similarly, the Galactic Empire's military personnel must battledress for success. Their signature uniform is the standard battlewhite stormtroopers' plastoid body armor, which has a noticeable design flaw: it's the perfect camouflage in a snow-covered environment, but in any other environment—a forest, grassland, or desert—it's a dead giveaway.

Ideally, given the technology possible in our future, the plastoid body armor should have sensors that sample the surrounding scene and electronically "paint" the appropriate camouflage on the uniform to make it blend in seamlessly.†

Beyond the traditional battlewhite, we see in *Rogue One* the battleblack, worn by Death Troopers. In Pablo Hildago's *Star Wars, Rogue One: The Ultimate Visual Guide* (DK Publishing, 2016), we get the straight poop about their mission:

> The Death Troopers comprise an elite unit created to defend the most important operations and operatives within the Imperial military hierarchy. . . . Death Trooper physical requirements include height and weight standards that exceed typical trooper averages, and rigorous training in exotic environs produces stronger, faster, and more resilient soldiers than the norm. . . . ‡

---

* "U.S. Army Service Uniform," army.mil.

† In *Predator* (1987, directed by John McTiernan), the alien creature has a cloaking device that makes it nearly impossible to see him; the background merges seamlessly with his own body, producing a slight rippling effect. In other words, he's camouflaged and can't easily be spotted by his enemy.

‡ The average stormtrooper must be at least six feet tall. Death troopers must be at least six feet five inches tall. More height means they are physically more intimidating.

Lord Vader

Standing six feet eight inches tall,* Anakin Skywalker, aka Darth Vader, cuts an imposing figure in his all-black uniform, especially when wielding a lightsaber at close quarters and mowing down his enemies.

At the end of *Rogue One*, we see Vader in full force. He's relentless and unstoppable as he cuts down the hapless crew members of the rebel starship he's boarded. But even without his height and prowess with a lightsaber, Vader is an intimidating figure. I submit that his one-of-a-kind uniform adds significantly to his presence: clothes make the man—or, in this case, the übervillain.

Dressing Darth

Those responsible for dressing the galaxy of Star Wars people, creatures, and military personnel chose wisely in drawing inspiration from Japanese samurai battledress for Darth Vader's intimidating appearance.

Imagine for a moment, if you will, that you are a commoner, a foot soldier in ancient Japan, and you are engaged to do battle against samurai warriors. You are standing in an open field. You have steeled your resolve, and you scan the tree line from which they'll emerge.

Suddenly, samurai warriors on horseback charge out of the tree line in a thundering horde. Each samurai holds high his long sword with which to smite you.† He's dressed in full body armor from head to toe, and his iron mask presents a fearful visage. He's coming straight at you, and you are frozen in fear.

If you don't soon lose your head, you may die holding your own guts. He might also be armed with a *naginata*, a pole weapon with

---

* Actor Hayden Christensen, who portrays the adult Darth Vader, is in fact six feet two inches in height.

† There's a good reason why the name of one of his long swords, the *katana*, translates to "dispenser of enemies."

a long, razor-sharp, curved blade at its business end, which gives him standoff distance. The blade itself is two feet long, and the shaft is nearly eight feet long. He'll be able to kill you before you even get close enough to swing a sword.

As he gets closer, your first impulse—and understandably so—is to run like hell. But he'll cut you down long before you can reach safety. Even if he dismounts to engage you in close-quarters combat, he's a superb swordsman who will almost certainly kill you where you stand.

The warrior, his weapons, and his battledress all combine to present a formidable front, a fearsome entity, both psychologically and physically intimidating. *That* is the way of the warrior.

An article from Holy Mountain Trading Company (holymtn.com) states, "The samurai devoted most of his time to the art of combat. All his training was preparation for the battlefield. . . . The warlord, the daimyō, would give the order to execute, the samurai was dispatched to find and kill him; there was no mercy. It was the will of the daimyō."*

The samurai will go forth in full battledress, ready for anything:

A full set of *tosei* armor consists of a body protector, a helmet, and an iron mask.

The body protector consists of a breastplate, a skirt, shoulder guards, arm covers, thigh armor, and shin guards. To allow those parts covering the body to flex with the wearer's movement, many portions were made of thin strips of lacquered iron joined to each other with braided silk lacing. The cord's colors and their lacing and knotting style give the suit a distinctive character.

The armor protecting the torso is made of two large, leather-lined iron plates (front and back). . . .

The half mask consists of a lacquered iron face plate and a throat guard. . . .

* "Samurai: Cultured Warriors of Japan," Holy Mountain Trading Company, holymtn.com.

This whole suit of armor looks very bulky but it's so lightweight and functional that this man could actually run for a mile quickly and turn around and fight a battle, and he wouldn't be as tired as one would think he would be because this is not as heavy. It is all very well-made and made to be extremely flexible. . . .

The dramatic helmets and face covers project an almost superhuman image of power.

Don't you think that sounds a lot like Darth Vader?

Stormtrooper

Taking a page from history, from other cultures whose warriors painted their faces, often with a skull image, or dressed in similar fashion to show a unity of force, with faces covered to make them appear to be fearless, indomitable machines, stormtroopers are a formidable force* that use their appearance, physical presence, and military bearing to strike fear in their enemies.

Just as the samurai warrior capitalized on his armor to protect himself and present a fearsome front, so too do stormtroopers, whose battledress—white uniforms and "bucket" helmets—have a frightening visual impact even before the first shot is fired.† We see them not as men in uniform, but as anonymous killing machines.

---

* With the possible exception of the garrison located on the Yavin moon where the Ewoks dwell.
† Lucas's early film *THX 1138* (1971) showed us law enforcement officers wearing white plastic face masks. As with the stormtrooper design, it makes them look anonymous, and it lends a fearsome front: a large body of officers who look alike, as if they are one army.

Artificial Intelligence: The Droids
We're Looking For

In *Rogue One*, K-2SO, a former imperial security droid who has been reprogrammed by the Rebel Alliance, towers above everyone, standing seven feet tall. Nonetheless, he can blend in among imperial personnel because they think he's on their side. K-2SO is on the team that rescues Jyn Erso. It's her first encounter with him, and, like C-3PO, K-2SO has a distinct personality. Both could pass the Turing test.*

The *Star Wars* universe, in fact, is filled with sentient robots, from the diminutive R2-D2 to the towering K-2SO, all fulfilling their respective roles as designed by their creators.

From the benign (R2-D2) to the deadly (battle droids), droids are the stuff of fiction, but not for much longer. In the future, droids with artificial intelligence will almost certainly be an integral part of our lives, in ways we can't imagine today.

Androids, artificially intelligent and self-aware, are firmly entrenched in the *Star Wars* universe. They are so commonplace, in fact, that no one looks twice at them, because they don't stand out. They are such an integral part of everyday life that they are taken

---

* "A test proposed by British mathematician Alan Turing, and often taken as a test of whether a computer has humanlike intelligence. If a panel of human beings conversing with an unknown entity (via keyboard, for example) believes that the entity is human, and if the entity is actually a computer, then the computer is said to have passed the Turing test" (*American Heritage New Dictionary of Cultural Literacy*, third edition, Houghton Mifflin, 2005). The plot of Alex Garland's movie *Ex Machina* involves a young, talented computer programmer who receives an invitation from his boss to come to his distant home to meet an AI robot who, when clothed, is physically indistinguishable from any other young, beautiful woman. His job is to administer the Turing test. Can she pass as a human? (Short answer: yes.)

for granted, much like today's cell phones equipped with AI technology. (If you're a droid, just don't expect to get served at a certain bar at the Mos Eisley spaceport on Tatooine.)

That's all in the distant future, though we've taken the first, tentative steps.

United States Military

Though the military does not yet have AI capability in military hardware, it's been moving in that direction by fielding the Predator, flown remotely by a USAF pilot in the United States, out of an air base in the Middle East.

The remotely operated Predator is twenty-seven feet in length, weighs 1,130 pounds when empty, cruises up to 135 miles per hour, climbs up to twenty-five thousand feet, flies 770 miles, and fires two laser-guided AGM-114 Hellfire missiles. The USAF has 150 Predators in its inventory.

It's robotic, of course, and inoperable without a skilled pilot at its controls. The Predator itself costs $5 million per aircraft, but if lost due to enemy action, it's simply a lot of taxpayers' dollars that have gone down in smoke; its pilot is safe, and far, far away—halfway around the world.

If and when artificial intelligence is perfected, the U.S. military will be among the first to integrate it into military operations. They have the budget, the will, and the need. Why risk human life if it's not necessary?

In the meantime, we will eventually see more remotely controlled weapons in all the U.S. military services: in the navy, for underwater demolitions; in the army, for urban warfare, which often means infiltrating buildings or strongholds occupied by well-armed enemies; and in the air force, with autonomous AI-enhanced Predators.

We already have a taste of what to expect, because science fiction movies have given us a sobering glimpse.

In Stanley Kubrick's *2001: A Space Odyssey*, an onboard computer dubbed HAL methodically kills off astronauts because it has determined the humans are risking its mission, which HAL considers paramount. In Ridley Scott's *Blade Runner*, replicants rebel against their creators and are hunted down and killed because they are considered a threat to humanity. In James Cameron's *The Terminator*, androids travel back from the future to threaten humanity. And in Michael Crichton's TV series *Westworld*, androids called "hosts" are the main attraction of a theme park for rich, indulgent humans, enabling the humans to indulge in carnal or carnage fantasies.

In other words, the androids are created by humans in their own image—the good, the bad, and the ugly. But the great fear is that artificially intelligent androids, instead of being servants of humanity, will eventually become our masters. As theoretical physicist Stephen Hawking, in a BBC interview, remarked, "The development of full artificial intelligence could spell the end of the human race. . . . It would take off on its own, and re-design itself at an ever increasing rate. . . . Humans, who are limited by slow biological evolution, couldn't compete, and would be superseded."

In other words, the development and perfection of AI droids could be an extinction-level event. It'd mark the end of human rule over the planet and the beginning of dominance by droids, who will seek out and, methodically and ruthlessly, kill all biological entities they consider to be a threat to their existence.

Hawking is not alone in his dire assessment. Another prominent figure—technology entrepreneur Elon Musk of SpaceX—was equally blunt: AI, he said, is "our biggest existential threat."

The Sticking Point

Despite Hawking's and Musk's concerns, we are still a long way from developing androids with artificial intelligence. And, in the view of David Gelernter, a professor of computer science at Yale, it may never actually happen. He asserts:

It is hugely unlikely, though not impossible, that a conscious mind will ever be built out of software. Even if it could be, the result (I will argue) would be fairly useless in itself. But an *unconscious* simulated intelligence certainly could be built out of software—and might be useful. Unfortunately, AI, cognitive science, and philosophy of mind are nowhere near knowing how to build one. They are missing *the* most important fact about thought: the "cognitive continuum" that connects the seemingly unconnected puzzle pieces of thinking (for example analytical thought, common sense, analogical thought, free association, creativity, hallucination). . . .

Without this cognitive continuum, AI has no comprehensive view of thought: it tends to ignore some thought modes (such as free association and dreaming), is uncertain how to integrate emotion and thought, and has made strikingly little progress in understanding analogies—which seem to underlie creativity.*

Three Laws of Robotics

Formulated by the late Dr. Isaac Asimov, his Three Laws of Robotics comprise a protocol for sentient robotic behavior for more than a half century.[1] But George Lucas rejected Asimov's three laws and, instead, decided his droids would not necessarily adhere to human morality. Unlike humans, who must choose between the light and the dark side, the droids have no choice: they are programmed to act accordingly.‡

Thus, in *A New Hope*, we see an interrogation droid hovering near Princess Leia Organa, ready to inject her with a drug, preparatory

---

* David Gelernter, "Artificial Intelligence Is Lost in the Woods," *MIT Technology Review*, July 1, 2007.

† First law: "A robot may not injure a human being or, through inaction, allow a human being to come to harm." Second law: "A robot must obey the orders given it by human beings except where such orders would conflict with the First Law." Third law: "A robot must protect its own existence as long as such protection does not conflict with the First or Second Laws."

‡ K-2SO is an interesting exception. An Imperial security droid, he was reprogrammed by Captain Cassian Andor; as a result, he's his own man, so to speak. As *Star Wars: Rogue One, The Ultimate Visual Guide* points out, "[Andor's] work has eliminated most of Arakyd Industries' presets, with one notable side effect: K-2SO is bluntly honest in all his assessments, even when such stark observations are not welcome. In other words, he has a distinct human-like personality, to his team members' discomfort.

to a mind probe; in *Return of the Jedi*, we see a droid whose arms are torn off by another droid; and in *Attack of the Clones*, at the Battle of Naboo, we see battle droids in tanks, and their infantry counterparts, armed with blasters, advancing upon the outnumbered, courageous Gungans.

Techheads in Silicon Valley are confident that we'll see droids sooner rather than later. In fact, they consider droids the "fourth wave." The first wave was semiconductors, in the seventies; the second wave was personal computers, in the eighties; and the third wave was the internet, from the nineties on. The new wave that has engulfed Silicon Valley is artificial intelligence.*

As Ethan Baron pointed out in his story in the Bay area newspaper *Mercury News*, tech entrepreneurs are counting on AI technology to be the next gold rush:

> Silicon Valley needs its next big thing, a focus for the concentrated brain power and innovation infrastructure that have made this region the world leader in transformative technology. Just as the valley's mobile era is peaking, the next frontier of growth and innovation has arrived: It's Siri in an Apple iPhone, Alexa in an Amazon Echo, the software brain in Google's self-driving cars, Amazon's product recommendations and, someday, maybe a robot surgeon who saves your life.

The robot that *saves your life*? If *Star Wars* is any guide, they're coming. At the end of *The Empire Strikes Back*, we see Luke Skywalker, who lost his hand to his father in a lightsaber battle, get a fully functional prosthetic hand in a surgery performed by a robot surgeon.

If David Gelernter is wrong, and we see AI as part of our everyday world, a hospital patient in the future will wake up and see a robot surgeon nodding solicitously over him, with eyes that never blink.

---

* Ethan Baron, "AI: Silicon Valley's Next Frontier," mercurynews.com, December 14, 2016.

The United States Has Death Stars

Surprisingly, the United States possesses Death Stars, though they may not be what you are imagining. They're not moon-size orbiting space stations capable of emitting a superlaser beam that can destroy a planet.

However, we *do* have space-based weapons systems that have informally been dubbed "Death Stars." These are orbiting satellites equipped with nuclear-pumped lasers powered by plutonium-238. National Public Radio tells us that it is "far more radioactive than its cousin, plutonium-239, which is used in bombs. It's so radioactive, it stays hot to the touch for decades. It is useless for commercial nuclear power plants, but ideal to make small, long-lasting batteries for devices such as space probes and espionage equipment."

Superlasers aren't confined to space. Did you know that, on a navy warship called the USS *Ponce*, there exists an operational laser weapons system? As CNN reported:

In the Persian Gulf, an instantaneous burst of energy destroys targets—first on the surface, then in the air. It's deadly firepower moving, literally, at the speed of light. Obliterating its target, the Navy says, like a long-distance blowtorch. . . .

[It's used] to defeat incoming threats at sea but multiple countries around the world are testing lasers that can reach space. These directed energy weapons could be used from the ground or deployed on space assets to temporarily blind or permanently damage satellites.

Make no mistake: if and when a major war breaks out between the superpowers, satellites are a prime target, because they are the gateways of information essential for command and control. During wartime, the country that controls the satellites will be able to call the shots.

There actually was a space-based war, but again, it's not what you'd think. Who would have thought that George Lucas would go to war against the U.S. military? He gave a new definition to the slogan An Army of One.

The U.S. Strategic Defense Initiative was dubbed "Star Wars," sparking George Lucas's righteous indignation and a lawsuit, filed in 1985.* He charged "trademark infringement, unfair trade practices and appropriating the goodwill and reputation of Lucasfilm" but met with unforeseen, stiff resistance. The Coalition for the SDI, founded by retired Lieutenant General Daniel O. Graham, said they would not stop using the name.

Lucas lost the lawsuit. As he discovered, you can win the battle but not necessarily the war; in this case, the Star Wars.

---

* This is not surprising, considering that Lucas feels very proprietary toward the use of the words "Star Wars," especially in the case where big government uses it to further its own objectives. A pacifist who objected to the Vietnam War on principle and strongly objected to involuntary drafting into the army, Lucas goes to war when he feels his cause is just.

The Death Star on Wheels

It's bad enough to have to contemplate the possibility of a Death Star orbiting a planet, but now we're not safe on the ground, either. The *Register*, a British newspaper, reported that U.S. defense contractor Lockheed Martin is ready to "deliver its most powerful laser weapon yet to the U.S. military. This Death Star on wheels can shoot down drones, missiles, and similar stuff, we're told," wrote Iain Thomson. "The American weapons conglomerate self-funded the building of a 30kW [kilowatt] test system and then scaled the design up. The 60kW version is mounted on a heavy expanded mobility tactical truck (HEMTT), which has an onboard generator capable of producing 200kW of power."

Thomson quotes Dr. Robert Afzal, senior fellow for laser and sensor systems, who said: "The inherent scalability of this beam-combined laser system has allowed us to build the first 60kW-class fiber laser for the U.S. Army. . . . We have shown that a powerful directed energy laser is now sufficiently light-weight, low-volume and reliable enough to be deployed on tactical vehicles for defensive applications on land, on sea and in the air."

Fly the Unfriendly Skies: The Fighter Pilot's View from the Cockpit

If you're filming an antiwar movie like Francis Ford Coppola's *Apocalypse Now* (1979), you won't get any support of any kind from the Department of Defense. Coppola had to lease Huey helicopters and pilots from the Philippines government, which was using those same helicopters to fight its drug war.

But if you're filming a 110-minute celebration of naval combat fighting that doubles as a recruiting movie, the Department of Defense will solicitously ask, "What can we do to help?" That's the kind of unparalleled military support director Jerry Bruckheimer got for *Top Gun* (1986). The Department of Defense happily supplied an aircraft carrier and an F-14 Tomcat fighter squadron (members of the VF-51 Screaming Eagles, disestablished in March 1995), along with support aircraft for the film—though not for free, of course.*

It was cost-effective advertising for the navy. No doubt the men in Recruiting Command were giving one another high fives and bumping chests, as seen on the flight line in *Top Gun*. According to Olivia B. Waxman ("The Real Military History Behind *Top Gun*, *Time*, May 12, 2016):

Obviously, thousands of Americans did "feel the need—the need for speed," because military recruiters parked themselves outside

---

* Paramount paid an hourly rate for fuel and other operating costs, at a cost of $7,800 an hour per plane, and in one instance, when *Top Gun*'s director wanted to reshoot a shot on an aircraft carrier, the captain decided that turning the carrier around would cost $25,000, and the director wrote a check for that amount on the spot.

theaters and reported a surge in calls about naval aviation officer programs. The number of uniformed personnel in all branches of the military increased by 20,000 over the previous year—about 16,000 of those were just in the Navy, according to an article in the U.S. Naval Institute's magazine *Proceedings*.

Incentive Flights

If you're a civilian and feel the need for speed, and you want to fly with the navy's Blue Angels or the air force's Thunderbirds, you may be in luck—if you meet the criteria. The Department of Defense authorizes civilians to fly in the backseat of an F-16 or an F/A-18 if you're a "Key Influencer" or a member of the media (preferably TV). The regulations allow two people and two alternates per air show.

The purpose is to get as much publicity as possible out of the event itself, to serve as a recruitment tool for the military, especially to recruit pilots.* As the navy's *Blue Angels: Support Manual 2016* states, Key Influencers are:

> people who help to shape the attitudes and opinions of youth in their communities. People turn to Key Influencers for advice and information because they have credibility. They may be experts in their field, public figures, leaders of youth organizations, teachers, guidance counselors, or school administrators. . . . *Flying these deserving candidates, in cooperation with media presence, will promote the Navy and Marine Corps as professional and exciting organizations with which to serve* (italics mine).

Assuming they can meet the rigorous flight physical, on the day of the flight, the handpicked civilians show up two hours early for

---

* The Navy, Marines, and Air Force need pilots and must compete in the marketplace to get them. Not surprisingly, the airlines actively recruit pilots as well—especially ex-military pilots with years of experience—so it's an ongoing dogfight to get them.

the required briefing and outfitting of flight equipment. You can see footage of these flights on YouTube.*

Civilians are otherwise not allowed to fly in military aircraft; specifically, they are never allowed as spectators during actual training missions or combat missions.

But if there's a military need for you to fly in a fighter jet, the military will put you through a two-week orientation course at the nearest air base before you head off to provide support to the military in your specialty field and to fly on training missions.

If you ever go to an air show at a naval base and bump into a fighter pilot, ask him what he thinks about *Top Gun*'s realism, and he'll probably laugh. He'll tell you it's how Hollywood likes to depict the fighter pilot community.

So what is it like to be on an air force base with an active duty fighter wing? In other words, what is the world of fighter jocks *really* like?

You may be surprised. Mostly, it's quiet professionalism.

Forget *Top Gun*. There's no one-upsmanship in the locker room, no teeth bared, no challenges made among men in their twenties exhibiting macho behavior. There's no fist-bumping and chest-thumping on the flight line. There's no high-fiving as you return from your jet after a successful mission. (Yes, pilots can party hardy, but not on the job.)†

To understand how to direct close air support assets, I had to see what the battlefield looked like from the cockpit. I spent two weeks with a fighter wing teaching close air support tactics and army doctrine to pilots, and flew in the backseat of an F-16B to understand how the pilot saw the targets on the battlefield for a close air support mission. (I was also working with a U.S. Air Force Tactical Air Control Party, out of Hawaii.)

---

* See CNN reporter Alex Quade flying in an F-16B with Major Nicole Malachowski, at www.youtube.com/watch?v=mn7vyhoZmfo.
† I can only speak of my own experience with an F-16 fighter wing in the southwestern United States. Your mileage may vary.

A typical tactical mission looks like this: On one of the days that I was flying, I ate a very light breakfast, because I didn't want to toss my "cookies" in flight. I'd be pulling up to 8G's, and the plane controls air bladders that inflate selectively over the body, to keep me from blacking out, which means it's going to be pushing on my stomach. So forget a heavy breakfast, unless you want to have it come up unexpectedly. I usually stuck to coffee and a little something to nibble on. I knew I could always eat when I got back on firm ground.

The flight briefing is conducted early in the morning. My recollection is that it was held at about the time most civilians are just getting up, getting ready to go to work. But we were already hard at work.

The flight briefing is structured and methodical. There's a standard checklist to cover every point, in order, from administrative to tactical matters to emergencies. It's detailed. It's not just about discussing the target, as in *A New Hope* and *Return of the Jedi*.

By now, the maintenance crew's already at work, and the ops building is bustling with activity, because that's where the missions are fine-tuned, planning for last-minute considerations.

Then I suit up and head out to the flight line, hunched over because the suit straps have to be pulled tight.

I pass at least a dozen F-16s, their powerful engines revving up. Their canopies are up, ladders attached to the sides. I reach my plane, climb up the ladder, get in the backseat, and secure my three-point harness. It's called "strapping on a jet" because that's exactly what it feels like. A sergeant checks me out to make sure I have strapped myself in correctly, for obvious reasons.

As the plane is fueled, I prepare myself for the flight. The 360-degree-view Plexiglas canopy comes down. I make a fist and adjust my seat so that the distance between the canopy and the top of my helmet is exactly one fist high.*

---

* A U.S. Navy pilot's perspective on the F-16: "The ejection seat's fixed, 20-degree recline angle is great for all phases of flight except air-combat maneuvering (ACM). During a fight, the pilot

We're in a "two-ship" configuration, with an F-16B and an F-16. Ours, the one in front, is in command of the mission; the other F-16 is behind us and to the right. We taxi down the runway in tandem and go "wheels up" at the same time.

We climb rapidly to the designated altitude, above cloud level. The view from the cockpit is unparalleled. I can literally see for miles. It's bright, too, because there's nothing blocking the sun. My helmet is on securely, the sun visor down.

Somewhere down below, there's the target area. That's where the bombs will be dropped.

For the next half hour to an hour, the plane gets put through its paces. It's like being on the most intense roller coaster imaginable. The plane is fast and agile, and my flight suit's air bladders, on cue from the aircraft's computer, inflate and deflate automatically based on the number of G's being pulled. I can hear the pilot in the front seat. There's not much chatter on the radio to the control tower. It's all business. No yakety-yak. It's good radio discipline. I can hear his controlled, forced breathing, and I do the same, because I don't want to black out like a civilian on an incentive flight. Bombs fall.

After the mission, we do a barrel roll around the F16 to our right rear, to check for damage; in turn, the other pilot does the same for us. Any fuel leaking? Any holes? Any damage to the aircraft? Best to make sure before you land.

After I'm back on the ground and head back in to the operations center, we have a flight debrief. We go over how the mission went and discuss what went right and what needs work.

There's no set time length for the debriefing; it just depends on the discussion.

---

has to constantly lean forward to look over a shoulder or check six [the rear position of the aircraft], and at 7 or 8G [g-force], the fixed recline angle produces a sore neck and back in nothing flat. A flight surgeon once told me that 90 percent of all fighter pilots suffer from chronic neck and back pain and Viper [F-16] drivers suffer the most. The single-piece bubble canopy is one feature that I wish the Hornet had. The glass comes down to the elbows and wraps around the pilot; it provides great six o'clock and over-the-nose visibility without a canopy bow or heads-up-display (HUD) post to obstruct the view" (Lieutenant Commander John Tougas, "F-15 vs. F-18: A Navy Test Pilot's Perspective," Air Age Publishing, June 2003).

The next day? Rinse and repeat.

I came away from those two weeks with a new appreciation for USAF combat pilots. This was at a time when Saddam Hussein was rattling his saber in the Middle East, which meant that on a moment's notice these guys suit up, strap on their jets, and head on over there (with several midair refuelings) to do one of the most dangerous jobs in the world, because that was their principal area of operations.

Fortunately, they're very good at their jobs. In fact, they're the best. It's a synchronized team effort: the enlisted personnel pumping jet fuel, the ground crews performing maintenance, the personnel in the control tower handling the flights, and the pilots who fly the unfriendly skies.

I felt privileged to be a small part of that for two weeks, and I wished that all Americans could see the quiet professionalism that characterizes their daily activities. It's a far cry from *Top Gun*, which gives a skewed vision of the demanding and dangerous world of combat aviation.

Fly the Friendly Skies

If you feel the need for speed, and you've got deep pockets, you can fly a jet, though not a U.S. fighter jet. Instead, your choices include an L-39 Albatros or, if you're willing to go to Russia for a once-in-a-lifetime experience, a MiG 29, which can fly to the edge of space. Private companies offer those experiences and provide the pilot and the plane. Just show up with checkbook in hand and you can go on a hell of a ride (see flyfighterjet.com).

A forty-five-minute ride on the L-39 will cost you $2,999. A forty-five-minute ride in a MiG 29 will cost you $13,000. If you want to fly to the edge of space in the MiG, it'll cost you $18,565. And for the ultimate adventure, reservations are now being taken for suborbital flights through other vendors.*

---

* Virgin Galactic offers a spaceflight; because their spacecraft flies up to 333,000 feet, or 100 kilometers, you cross the Karman line and are technically considered an astronaut. But going

Disney

If you want a more affordable experience in the familiar *Star Wars* universe, you can go to Disneyland or Walt Disney World in the United States and board a flight simulator, the Starspeeder 1000, that takes you to "the underwater realms on Naboo, the bustling city-planet of Coruscant, and the dreaded Death Star," with C-3PO as your pilot and guide.

In 2019, when the *Star Wars* land is operational at the Disney theme parks, you can blast off as the pilot of the *Millennium Falcon*, the fastest hunk of junk in the galaxy. There's even AT-ATs on the premises, which prompted one fan to speculate, "Since the *Star Wars*–themed land is immersive, the AT-ATs aren't there just because they look cool. They'll have a storytelling purpose. I'm guessing they're part of an attraction, specifically the adventure one that puts guests in a battle between the Resistance and the First Order." *

The fan's speculation was right. In *The Last Jedi* (2017), AT-ATs show up in force, with TIE fighters for close air support, to attack the remnants of the Resistance holed up in a large cave protectd by a massive blast door.

---

those extra miles will set you back $200,000. You're one of six passengers, but your seat is not a cockpit view. So if you've got the bucks, you can play at being Buck Rogers.

* Amy Ratcliffe, "Everything We Know About Disney Parks' *Star Wars*–Themed Land," nerdist .com, February 6, 2017.

Luke's a Skywalker: From Fighter Pilot to Astronaut

In *A New Hope*, it's not one of the more experienced pilots who literally saves the day; it's a farm boy with stardust in his eyes, Luke Skywalker.

So how, you ask, do you go from being a farm boy to becoming an intergalactic hero and hotshot pilot getting a medal for bravery from a beautiful princess?

More to the point, based on what today's fighter pilots must go through, was Luke's rapid ascension realistic or simply a flight of fantasy? For that, we must go back to Luke's roots on his home planet of Tatooine, a desert planet in the Outer Rim, where he lives on a moisture farm with his aunt Beru Lars and uncle Owen.

T-16 Skyhopper

As a family farmhand, Luke Skywalker was not wealthy, especially since he was orphaned (along with his sister, Leia Organa). Luke obviously didn't inherit any wealth; any money he had was earned by himself.

Nonetheless, he was able to acquire a T-16 skyhopper. A new one costs 14,500 imperial credits, and a used one is 6,500 credits. We can assume he purchased a used one and did the repair work himself, because he's handy with a wrench.

So when Han Solo offered to ferry Luke's "hot" cargo off the planet for 10,000 imperial credits, Luke protests the high cost, saying, "We could almost buy our own ship for that!" Han Solo counters with a question, "Who's going to fly it, kid?" Luke protests again, saying he could fly it himself.

The key issue, though, is not whether Luke can fly it (he can) but whether Luke could have gotten past the imperial blockade of Star Destroyers in orbit around Tatooine—a problematic proposition.

More to the point, Luke has had no experience in using the sky-hopper's cannon against, say, a TIE fighter. He's used the cannon to kill womp rats, but that's about it.

Luke, then, can be considered skilled in flying a high-performance aircraft. After all, he can even thread the needle, as it were, by flying his T-16 through a narrow spindle of rock in Beggar's Canyon.* But he has had no combat experience.

Fortunately, the flight controls on the T-16 are very similar to those of the T-65 X-wing starfighter he will soon fly in combat for the first time, as part of the Rebel Alliance's fleet of X- and Y-wing starfighters. Making the transition from the T-16 to the T-65 would not have been too difficult.†

But the other issue is that learning *how* to fly is only part of dealing with in-flight emergencies, which run the gamut from annoying to catastrophic.‡

---

* The T-16 flies at roughly half the speed of sound, at 745 miles per hour, which is half the maximum speed of a USAF F-16 Fighting Falcon (nicknamed "Viper" by its pilots).

† "These airspeeders were often used as training vehicles by the Rebel Alliance (RA), due to the fact that their flight controls were similar to those of X-wings," notes the Wookieepedia entry for the T-16 skyhopper. It should be further noted that the rebels couldn't risk losing invaluable and irreplaceable T-65 X-wing fighters in training, so using the T-16 for training purposes minimized the risk. (Similarly, before U.S. Air Force pilots get to fly the $19 million F-16, they train for two years on smaller, less powerful, aircraft.)

‡ "'Murphy's Law' is constantly in the back of my mind with our new F-16 pilots . . . if it can happen, it will probably happen at the worst possible time. A pilot's preparation for the unexpected is the only thing that will help them deal with these unplanned and potentially catastrophic events. This preparation began in late August when our students started the academic portion of their training in the 54 OSS [Operational Support Squadron]. Our instructors (military and civilian) have provided them with weeks of aircraft system academics and simulator sorties to expose them to how the aircraft flies and what to do with an aircraft malfunction. There is significant joy in having the ability to operate a high performance aircraft by yourself, and there is even more satisfaction in knowing that you can deal with the unexpected issues that inevitably arise in the flying business" (Lieutenant Colonel Scott Fredrick, "White Sands 'Vipers'—Training F-16 Fighter Pilots at Holloman AFB," holloman.af.mil, November 24, 2014).

The sticking point, as any fighter pilot will tell you, is that flying the aircraft itself is a given; that is, the pilot's ability to fly must be second nature. What isn't second nature, and can only be taught through time spent in the cockpit, is the art of combat flying and fighting. As Chuck Yeager wrote in his autobiography, "I have flown in just about everything, with all kinds of pilots in all parts of the world—British, French, Pakistani, Iranian, Japanese, Chinese—and there wasn't a dime's worth of difference between any of them except for one unchanging, certain fact: *the best, most skillful pilot has the most experience*" (italics mine).*

We can take retired USAF Brigadier General Yeager at his word. As a former test pilot who was the first to break the sound barrier, at a time when the experts were dubious that it could *ever* be broken, Yeager's long hours spent in the cockpit honed his flying skills to a sharp edge.

Insofar as Luke Skywalker is concerned, my thinking is that, in terms of *combat* flight, Luke could have benefited from more time in the cockpit *before* the Battle of Yavin. He had no time to practice firing the sophisticated weapons systems on board the T-65 (two laser cannons and proton torpedoes), nor did he have any experience in aerial combat, in dogfighting with highly maneuverable TIE fighters flown by experienced combat pilots.

That is why, in the original movie in 1977, a fellow pilot comes up to him and asks, "You sure you can handle this ship?" (In O.S.P. Publishing's movie script, a fighter pilot named Red Leader asks Luke, "Are you . . . Luke Skywalker? Have you been checked out on the Incom T-sixty-five?") So, obviously, Luke's lack of formal training on a Starfighter and lack of combat experience is a cause for concern.

Time in the cockpit, training as you will fight, is what makes the essential difference between life and death, as the statistics of downed Japanese pilots during World War II reminds us:

---

* General Chuck Yeager and Leo Janos, *Yeager: An Autobiography* (Bantam, 1986).

Naturally, once the war began, the Imperial Navy started losing pilots faster than they could be replaced. For example, the 29 pilots lost at Pearl Harbor represented more than a quarter of the annual crop. The battles of the next year led to the loss of hundreds of superb pilots. This finally forced the Japanese to reform their pilot training programs. Time to train a pilot, and hours in the air, spiraled downward. By 1945 men were being certified fit for combat duty with less than four months' training. In contrast, the U.S. Navy was actually increasing its flight time, while keeping pilot training programs to about 18 months. . . . In 1944, the U.S. [flight] hours went up to 525, while Japan cut it to 275 hours. In 1945, a shortage of fuel had Japanese trainee pilots flying on 90 hours before entering combat. In the air, this produced lopsided American victories, with ten or more Japanese aircraft being lost for each U.S. one.*

Luke Skywalker was at a significant disadvantage going into battle, because he had *no* training time in the T-65 in air combat maneuvers. Fortunately, he did have the Force on his side, which he needed.

The other issue is life support, and like a TIE fighter pilot, Luke's got the bare minimum necessary to keep him alive in the cockpit.

Today's Pilots

For comparison purposes, it's important to note that the standard uniform for the X-wing pilot is almost identical to that of a standard USAF fighter pilot, who wears forty pounds of clothing and gear to protect himself, in flight or if he has to "punch out" (eject from his aircraft) and survive in enemy territory until a combat search and rescue team can locate and retrieve him, on land or in the water.

As PBS's *Nova* notes (pbs.org, NOVA, "Outfitting a Fighter Pilot, Lexi Krock, November 1, 2007), even the mission-essential

---

* "Support: Pilot Training Is Out of Gas," strategypage.com.

clothing and gear for a fighter pilot fills a lengthy list. Look up the details on its website, but here's an overview: The pilot wears a g-suit to protect him against g-forces in flight, a helmet, night vision goggles, a mask, an exposure suit (in cold weather), gloves, a liner suit, and boots. A harness secures the pilot to his ejection seat. The pilot also carries survival gear: waterproof maps, a life preserver with inflatable raft (in the ejection seat), a survival vest, a radio and beacon, signal flares, finger lights, camouflage paint, a GPS unit with two sets of batteries, matches, a tourniquet, a manual compass, magnesium fire starter, infrared tape to help the combat search and rescue team identify her with a thermal radiation sensor, a strobe light, a relief bag, and a whistle.

So what does Luke Skywalker wear? In *Star Wars: The Complete Visual Dictionary* (DK Publishing, 2012), we see his full flight ensemble, suitable for atmospheric flight: a pressurized g-suit (orange colored), a flak vest (air force and navy pilots don't wear these, because of bulk), a life-support unit (i.e., an oxygen source), an insulated helmet, bulky flight gloves, a flight harness, and boots.

Interestingly, according to the cross section of the T-65 X-wing in *Star Wars: Complete Vehicles* (DK Publishing, 2013), the fighter aircraft lacks an ejection seat and therefore lacks much of what's needed in the event the pilot must survive in case of ejection. No matter where he lands, in or out of the water, on friendly or on enemy terrain, an ejection seat itself incorporates essential survival gear, including a flotation raft.

In other words, Luke has the bare essentials needed to fly a fighter aircraft. But because the T-65 is also a *spacecraft*, the issue of life support takes on a new significance. On this count, Luke is woefully unprepared for what might happen in combat; his life support is inadequate for spaceflight.

Rocket Man

The T-65's life-support systems should be designed for pilot survivability in outer space, but it's not, so far as I can see. While flying in a planet's atmosphere, the oxygen mask and pressurized g-suit are sufficient. But once Luke leaves the planetary atmosphere (with breathable air or with thin air at high altitude) and makes the transition into space, the life-support system becomes necessarily more complicated and critical. In other words, the orange-colored, pressurized g-suit that is sufficient for in-planet flight won't cut it; extraterrestrial flight requires complete encapsulation, because in space anything can happen. In fact, Murphy's Law works overtime in outer space.*

For instance, on the space shuttle, during ascent and descent (reentry into Earth's atmosphere), everyone on board wears the internationally orange-colored Advanced Crew Escape Suit. The presumption is that, in the rare event the shuttle suffers a breach in structural integrity, all personnel are protected, even to the point where they have a survival backpack that includes a personal life raft. (There is no ejection seat, however, as there is in a contemporary fighter jet.)

In other words, during reentry, a NASA astronaut is better equipped than Luke Skywalker is when he's piloting an X-wing fighter. Luke is adequately equipped, albeit minimally, for space-flight while seated *inside* the starfighter, but a breach of the aircraft's structural integrity means certain death: in the event of an emergency, he's not sufficiently equipped for survival in space.

Consider this scenario: Luke's in outer space, in his T-65 X-wing starfighter, and headed to the Death Star. A TIE fighter shoots and destroys Luke's canopy. He's now exposed to the harsh elements of space, and will die quickly. As space.com points out:

---

* "Earth's atmosphere is 20 percent oxygen and 90 percent nitrogen from sea level to about 75 miles up, where space begins. At 18,000 feet, the atmosphere is half as dense as it is on the ground, and at altitudes above 40,000 feet, air is so thin and the amount of oxygen so small that pressure oxygen masks no longer do the job. Above the 63,000-foot threshold, humans must wear spacesuits that supply oxygen for breathing and that maintain a pressure around the body to keep body fluids in the liquid state. At this altitude the total air pressure is no longer sufficient to keep body fluids from boiling" (NASA, "Space Educator's Handbook: The Spacesuit," er.jsc.nasa.gov/seh/suitnasa.html).

Most of the gas in space is too thin to warm anything up. Essentially, there are not enough gas particles to "bump" into and transfer heat to an object. So if you were in space, but shielded from the sun, you would radiate away nearly all your heat pretty quickly and cool to the cosmic background temperature. Step (or float) into the sun, and you'd be warmed. Either way you'd need lots of protection!*

In other words, given what we see he wears when he's flying the X-wing starfighter, Luke doesn't have the necessary protective clothing or encapsulation to protect himself in outer space; he could survive in such an unforgiving environment only with a self-sustaining suit—and then hope the Rebel Alliance's search and rescue team will find and recover him before he floats away in space. According to NASA:

> A *fully equipped spacesuit is really a one-person spacecraft.* . . . The spacesuit protects the astronaut from the dangers of being outside in space. . . .
>
> Spacewalking astronauts face a wide variety of temperatures. In Earth orbit, conditions can be as cold as minus 250 degrees Fahrenheit. In the sunlight, they can be as hot as 250 degrees. A spacesuit protects astronauts from those extreme temperatures.
>
> Spacesuits also supply astronauts with oxygen to breathe while they are in the vacuum of space. They contain water to drink during spacewalks. They protect astronauts from being injured from impacts of small bits of space dust. Space dust may not sound very dangerous, but when even a tiny object is moving many times faster than a bullet, it can cause injury. Spacesuits also protect astronauts from radiation in space. The suits even have visors to protect astronauts' eyes from the bright sunlight.[†]

In this discussion, let's overlook the fact that there's no sound in space—the whizzing of TIE fighters roaring by, the *pew-pew* of laser

---

* "What's the Temperature of Outer Space?," space.com, February 29, 2012.
† NASA, "What Is a Spacesuit?," nasa.gov, February 12, 2014.

cannons blasting away from the X-wing starfighters, and the thundering explosions—and that starfighters cannot maneuver in space with the agility they possess during atmospheric flight.*

Let's overlook the scientific inaccuracies and cut to the chase: if Luke is going to fight and survive in space, he needs to wear a *space suit*, not a flight suit. It's that simple.

Of course, today's suits are bulky and cumbersome, but in the future, with advance technology available, engineers presumably should be able to design a dual-purpose fighter/spacecraft with appropriate life-support systems. Only then will Luke have a fighting chance against TIE fighter pilots and also outer space's unforgiving environment.

* By using vectored thrusters, a spacecraft can change direction in space, but not with the responsiveness and rapidity a fighter aircraft exhibits when flying in atmosphere.

Picture This: Holograms and Virtual Reality on the Battlefield

Imagine you're an ISIS fighter holed up in a stronghold in a residential area in Syria. You turn the corner and see a heavily armed, six-foot-five-inch U.S. infantryman react to your presence and aim his rifle at you. You fire away, but, to your astonishment, the soldier is still standing. How can that be?

Congratulations! You've just been punk'd. You've shot a life-size hologram. And now you're surrounded by flesh-and-blood infantrymen with weapons pointed at you. Game over.

As David Hambling (defensetech.org, "Fighting Shadows: Military Holograms"), explains:

> One of [the] suggested applications [for holograms] is "deception in an urban environment." Take a shop window and replace it with a hologram of a window display, and you have an apparently innocuous space where troops can be stationed without any hint of their presence. . . .
>
> There is the possibility of using holograms to create virtual forces or virtual obstacles, but the problems are all too apparent. The situation is much better indoors where the optical environment can be controlled. . . . Installations could have virtual doors, walls and windows as ways of confusing or misleading intruders.

Welcome to the future world of holograms. As Hambling noted, it's coming fast: the Non-lethal Technology Innovations Center is working on developing them to the point where they can be deployed on the battlefield.

In the interim, the military is already making good use of holograms. As *Wired* points out, Zebra Imaging "has been selling 2-by-3-foot plastic holographic maps to the Pentagon—its 'main customer'—for $1,000 to $3,000 a pop. The military 'sends data in computer files to the company. Zebra then renders holographic displays of, for example, battlefields in Iraq and Afghanistan.'"

Wired also notes that the technology has other useful applications, "such as post-blast IED [improvised explosive device] forensics." As it explains, "Analysts trying to understand the nature and construction of an explosive device . . . are able to understand the scene in 3-D far better than the classic 2-D 'bird's-eye view.'"*

The technology has also proven useful in training scenarios for a generation that has grown up in a virtual world. The Institute for Creative Technologies has "created several programs to train soldiers in situational awareness and for urban combat and counterimprovised explosive device missions." Moreover, what the U.S. Army calls Tactical Digital Hologram technology "has 'shown promise' with the US Army Special Forces in Afghanistan and Iraq. Special operators use the technology to create 3-D maps of villages or specific buildings."†

We've Come a Long Way

During peacetime, the army necessarily spends its time training, to keep its fighting edge sharp. But back in 1975, when I was on extended active duty at Fort Riley, Kansas, the training technology was primitive: a carousel projector using 35 millimeter color film slides was a standard training tool.‡

* David Axe, "Military One Step Closer to Battlefield Holograms," *Wired*, December 6, 2010.
† George I. Seffers, "Holograms Coming to a Military Theater Near You," afcea.org, December 2, 2015.
‡ The state of the personal computer back then was a computer in kit form, notably the MITS Altair 8800 and IMSAI 8080. It wasn't until 1976 that Steve Wozniak invented the Apple I, which was essentially a motherboard, to which the user had to add an enclosure, power supply,

I recall an installation-wide firing competition. Each infantry, armor, and field artillery battalion was tasked to send two enlisted men to fire the M-72 light antiarmor weapon (LAW) as part of the competition. (The LAW is a collapsible tube that fires a 66 millimeter rocket-propelled round up to two hundred meters against a tank.)*

My first thought was to go to Service Battery, which was responsible for requisitioning ammunition and distributing it within the battalion, and requisition some live LAWs for test-firing. After all, how can you realistically train without them?

But I was told we couldn't requisition live LAWs for test-firing purposes; instead, we had to use inert LAWs and training aids. It made no sense, but that's the way it was, so I obtained two dummy LAWs and set up the then-state-of-the-art training aid: a slide projector with a built-in screen that showed, step by step, with pictures and running text, how to set up and fire a LAW. It was a self-paced tutorial, a training aid.

My men handled the inert LAW I provided them. They could open and close it and practice aiming techniques. But when they went out on the firing range, it was the first time they felt the shock of the weapon discharge when fired on their shoulders.

The men did well enough in the competition, but I felt strongly that the training constraints degraded the learning curve; it wasn't realistic training.† The golden rule is "train as you fight."‡ In other

---

and keyboard. The Apple II, the first consumer-friendly computer, wasn't available until June 1977.

* The US Army now fields the FGM-148 Javelin, with an effective range of 4,750 meters.

† Later, when I became the executive officer of Service Battery, I made sure that if our battalion was tasked with providing personnel for live firing competitions, we trained with live equipment. It was realistic training, and it's what we would be using in combat.

‡ As globalsecurity.org notes, "The future battlefield will be characterized by high volumes of fire and lack of a distinct FEBA [forward edge of the battle area] or FLOT [forward line of troops] trace; in many cases, small-units and task forces may find themselves either bypassed or encircled. Units will frequently be cross attached in order to react to the flow of the battle or to reconstitute units. The key to winning in that battlefield environment will be the understanding of 'how we fight' at every level and the demonstrated confidence, competence, and initiative of our soldiers and leaders. Training is the means to achieve the tactical and technical proficiency that soldiers, leaders, and units must have to enable them to accomplish their missions" ("Training Challenges," globalsecurity.org).

words, you should make your training as realistic as possible under the circumstances. In our case, since we were an active duty, front-line infantry division, you'd think the training would necessarily be as realistic as possible, especially because, at the time, half the division was stationed in Germany to keep the Russians from crossing the Fulda Gap into western Europe. (In 1991, the 1st Infantry Division finally returned home permanently.)

Fortunately, we've come a long way with training tools for the army. I'm sure everyone was happy when the primitive self-paced training devices were junked and replaced with computers, more live-fire exercises, and the activation of the army's National Training Center in 1981, which provides "tough, realistic joint and combined arms training" that "focus at the battalion task force and brigade levels."*

Holograms in *Star Wars*

Though holograms have long been a staple in narrative science fiction—in short stories, novellas, and novels—their use in *A New Hope*, in 1977, was groundbreaking. There were more holograms in that movie than you could shake Luke's lightsaber at. On the light side, there was an animated chess-like game called Dejarik that Chewbacca and R2-D2 played on board the *Falcon*, where we saw alien creatures move animatedly, engaging one another. But that was just fun and games.

On the serious side, we see Princess Leia Organa kneeling down in front of R2-D2 as she feeds the diminutive droid data about the Death Star. Later, we see that stored data projected in the air, at a briefing attended by the rebel pilots prior to their assault on the Death Star.

George Lucas went on to make good use of the holographic technology in later films, including *The Empire Strikes Back*, with

* "NTC Mission," irwin.army.mil.

a 3-D visual representation of the second Death Star; in *The Phantom Menace*, with the Jedi High Council communicating with Jedi Knights on other planets; and in *The Force Awakens*, with two large star maps joined together to reveal the location of the elusive Luke Skywalker, who has sought refuge on a distant planet.[*]

Just as holograms in *Star Wars* approximate how we see the world, the technology is currently being integrated into the training process in the U.S. military, as the CEO of Hologram USA points out. "We've recently licensed a patented technology that projects the image into the audience or into the space, so you can actually put your hands through the light when you project the image. It's actually a bona fide hologram."[†]

So, What's a Hologram?

Robert Workman explains how a hologram works:

> A laser beam is split into two identical beams and redirected by the use of mirrors. One of the split beams, the illumination beam or object beam, is directed at the object. Some of the light is reflected off the object onto the recording medium.
>
> The second beam, known as the reference beam, is directed onto the recording medium. . . .
>
> The two beams intersect and interfere with each other. The interference pattern is what is imprinted on the recording medium to re-create a virtual image for our eyes to see.[‡]

---

[*] The technology is tailor-made for advertising purposes as well. To promote five differently designed *Star Wars* soft drink cups, Golden Screen Cinemas set up an acrylic, pyramid-like display that showed multiple holographic images from *Star Wars* history to engage the moviegoer. We see an imperial shuttle head toward Death Star II, the *Millennium Falcon* firing at a target, Jyn Erso making an appearance, dueling lightsabers, R2-D2, two X-wing fighters in battle against a TIE fighter, security droid K-2SO, two Imperial Walkers, a stormtrooper, and other personnel from *Rogue One*.

[†] Seffers, "Holograms."

[‡] Robert Workman, "What Is a Hologram?," livescience.com, May 23, 2013.

Holographic technology promises to revolutionize how soldiers envision the battlefield. No longer restricted to 2-D color maps, the 3-D holographic technology puts the soldiers front and center:

> Imagine going from looking at the outside of a building, to seeing the internal workings of its electrical system simply by walking around a display case. The sophistication of 3-D holographic technology allows just that. . . .
>
> It's called Tactical Digital Hologram technology, and more than 10,000 units, which at first glance look like flat plastic maps, have already been fielded to Special Forces in Iraq and Afghanistan.*

This technology is a significant improvement over the traditional, two-dimensional, printed military maps.† As a report from the Army Research Laboratory's Simulation and Training Technology Center explains:

> A visual scene of a 3-D world is a more intuitive and natural representation than a 2-D display, and a single integrated object reduces the need for mental integration of two or three separation representations. . . .
>
> "A whole unit can stand around the image to quickly plan ingress/ egress routes for a cordon and search mission, determine where their vehicles will be positioned, casualty collection points, indirect fire support, etc. You can also write on it safely with either a grease pencil or dry eraser marker," said [H. Michelle] Kalphat.‡

It's relatively new to the U.S. Army, but haven't we seen it before? In fact, we first saw it in 1977, when the use of holograms in *Star*

---

* T'Jae Gibson, "Into the Deep: 3-D Holographic Technology Provides Detailed Human Intelligence," army.mil, July 22, 2011.
† These are prepared by the Defense Mapping Agency Hydrographic/Topographic Center at a scale of 1:50,000. One grid square on the map measures 1,000 by 1,000 meters.
‡ Gibson, "Into the Deep."

Wars enlightened us about their infinite possibilities. We are, in short, going back to the future.

Augmented Reality

The army is also advancing the state of the art in augmented reality (AR). "This shows a lot of promise and adds a lot of the 'richness' of the virtual environment," [Lieutenant Colonel Jason] Caldwell remarked. Trainees in an AR scenario see people, buildings, and other virtual entities in a live environment. The Army M&S [modeling and simulation] authority noted one application for AR could permit a unit training at its home station to use a mock-up of a village at a nearby training area. "Using a set of AR goggles allows you to transform that training area into something that looks much more complex, like the current operational environment. You could see thousands of people, buildings, or both friendly and enemy vehicles, that aren't actually there," he pointed out. With AR, the training audience is also able to complete missions that otherwise could not be completed in live or virtual environments. . . . "Other training is a bit artificial because of the safety zones that prohibit soldiers from being injured in training," Caldwell emphasized.

Source: Marty Kauchak, "Holograms: A Work in Progress," *Military Simulation & Training Magazine*, August 25, 2015.

· PART 4 ·

TACTICS AND STRATEGY

In peace we concentrate so much on tactics that we are apt to forget that it is merely the handmaiden of strategy.

While the horizon of strategy is bounded by war, grand strategy looks beyond the war to the subsequent peace.

—B. H. Liddell Hart

Following Orders: Luke Skywalker, His Targeting Computer, and the Force

The situation: You are the commanding officer of an X-wing fighter squadron and one of your senior officers is giving the mission briefing. The mission plan is to use torpedoes to attack the target, using an onboard computer to calculate the complicated ballistics involved. The stakes are high. If the bomb run fails, then your air base will be destroyed by the enemy, which is using a new kind of bomb that will destroy your planet.

At the end of the briefing, one of the new pilots raises his hand and poses a question: "Instead of using a targeting computer, can I use whatever I think would be better instead?"

What would be *your* response?

Think about it before answering. Then think about the climactic scene in *A New Hope*, in which the following scenario is unfolding: The battle seems to be all but lost. A new pilot, Luke Skywalker, is the only pilot left who can fire his torpedo. The mission's success or failure hinges wholly on him.

In hot pursuit are three enemy aircraft, behind him at his "six o'clock," the ideal firing position.

After hearing on his radio that another pilot's torpedo run was unsuccessful, Luke decides to switch off his targeting computer; instead, he decides to use the Force, after hearing his late mentor, Obi-Wan Kenobi, urging him to do so.

Should he or shouldn't he? *That* is the question. Let's look at some key factors.

The Mission

As General Jan Dodonna makes clear during his briefing of Luke Skywalker and his fellow pilots in the Rebel Alliance, the Death Star has only one known vulnerability: a small "thermal exhaust port." *
A direct hit on that will set off a chain reaction initiated by the explosion of the Death Star's main reactor system.

It's not an easy shot, and the pilots know it. But the starfighters' targeting computer is the time-tested means by which to accurately guide the torpedo.

The Military Dilemma

As ADRP 6-0 points out:

> Commanders and subordinates are obligated to follow lawful orders. Commanders deviate from orders only when they are unlawful, risk the lives of soldiers, or when orders no longer fit the situation. Subordinates inform their superiors as soon as possible when they have deviated from orders. Adhering to applicable laws and regulations when exercising disciplined initiative builds credibility and legitimacy. Straying beyond legal boundaries undermines trust and *jeopardizes tactical, operational, and strategic success*; this must be avoided (italics mine).†

To summarize: Luke Skywalker has a lawful order to fire his proton torpedoes into a port on the Death Star. He will use the onboard targeting computer to calculate the necessary ballistics. So, should he have deviated from the battle plan, especially considering the fact that he willfully made an independent, tactical decision on his own, *without* benefit of counsel from the operations headquarters at the rebel base?

---

* The question of *why* the Death Star's vulnerability even exists is logically answered in *Rogue One*.

† ADRP 6-0: *Mission Command*, Department of the Army, May 2012, section 2-19.

Pros and Cons

Luke is under tremendous pressure. Although the Death Star obviously had no defensive plans to counter an air attack from a squadron of small enemy fighters, the Empire still managed to hold the upper hand for most of the battle.

Luke is not a veteran combat pilot. Granted, he's a gifted pilot, but he's had no combat flying experience. Moreover, because of combat attrition, he's the only one with proton torpedoes left, and so the burden of the mission is his alone to shoulder. Failure means the destruction of the moon on which the rebel base is located.

Luke wrestles with a pivotal question: Just how reliable *is* that targeting computer? He likely doesn't feel as confident with it as he should, perhaps because he's never used it; he's never had the luxury of practicing bomb runs to build his confidence in its use. Moreover, Luke *knows* that if he tells General Dodonna that he's going to turn it off and instead rely on a mystical Force, the general may assume that Luke is physiologically impaired.* After all, Luke's fighter aircraft is pressurized, so if the unthinkable happens—he loses partial pressurization and he's getting insufficient oxygen— he may be suffering from hypoxia and therefore hallucinating. He may be hearing voices. He may honestly *think* Obi-Wan Kenobi is telling him to use the Force. In short, Luke is mentally impaired. He's not himself and is in no position to make such a game-changing decision.

That's how it'd look to the commander on the rebel base in charge of the mission.

Think about it: Under the circumstances, what commander *wouldn't* order Luke to turn the targeting computer back on?

* Fighter pilots may suffer from hypoxia, a lack of oxygen in the body tissues. As the Federal Aviation Administration points out, symptoms of hypoxia include "increased breathing rate, headache, light-headedness, dizziness, tingling or warm sensations, sweating, poor coordination, impaired judgment, tunnel vision, and euphoria. Unless detected early and dealt with, hypoxia can be a real killer" ("Hypoxia: The Higher You Fly . . . The Less Air in the Sky," www .faa.gov).

Deviating from Orders

Make no mistake, deviating from orders is a serious matter, especially in this situation. Luke should assume that the targeting computer will work as it's supposed to. Besides, what assurances does he have that the Force will be more accurate?

The only reassurance he has is the voice of Obi-Wan Kenobi, which he hears at a pivotal moment, saying, "Luke, trust me."

Does he trust in that voice? Does he trust in himself? Does he trust the targeting computer?

The pressure Luke feels is enormous, with the entire galaxy at stake. If he's wrong and he uses the Force and misses, he'll be destroyed by Darth Vader, who is on his tail. So what is he to do?

The Decision

Oddly, neither General Dodonna nor anyone else on the rebel base questions Luke's decision to turn off the targeting computer. They simply accept his assertion that, as he said, "nothing" is wrong. "I'm all right," he tells the general. Of course, if Luke is wrong, he won't live long enough to regret it—and neither will anyone at the rebel base, since the Death Star is preparing to destroy the moon on which the base is located.

This is a classic military dilemma. One can imagine the palpable concern felt among those at rebel base headquarters when they heard Luke say he was turning off his targeting computer. They were wondering, and rightly so, what was going on.*

Fortunately for Luke, the Force was with him.

---

* From a military point of view, this climactic scene could have been tweaked to improve its suspense and story logic. Let's say Darth Vader, in the lead TIE fighter (Advanced X1), fires and hits Luke's X-wing fighter, damaging his targeting computer. Luke is then left to his own devices, with no other way to ensure that his proton torpedo is accurately aimed into the exhaust port. Back at the rebel base, the operations center is aware that his targeting computer is damaged beyond repair, and Luke is forced to rely on his own instincts to decide when to fire the torpedo. But then Luke hears Obi-Wan Kenobi's voice—"Luke, trust me"—and, without any other option, he does so. He then fires his two proton torpedoes, with his heart in his mouth.

Only One Dead Ewok

There's no question that the Battle of Endor was the turning point in the war between the Rebel Alliance and the Galactic Empire. Unfortunately, the land battle was simply not realistic; in fact, it's a cartoon for kids.

The battle of the Ewoks and General Han Solo against the local garrison of stormtroopers, which Emperor Palpatine called his "best troops," was so absurd that an adult cannot watch it with a straight face.

In terms of technology, the Ewoks fought with Stone Age weapons and the stormtroopers fought with high-tech blaster rifles, speeder bikes, AT-STs (a two-man minitank), and AT-ATs just outside the garrison's perimeter. But, in the end, the Ewoks won, suffering only *one casualty*, although numerous stormtroopers were injured or killed.*

The battle is asymmetrical: the population of Ewoks in that village numbered approximately two hundred and the garrison of troops was at least one hundred, and up to two hundred.†

In studying the battle sequences in *Return of the Jedi*, taking note of the various ways the courageous and inventive Ewoks managed to ambush, ensnare, pummel, and otherwise attrite the stormtroopers, I shook my head in disbelief. It just shouldn't have

---

* It's possible that more Ewoks died, but we only witnessed one death.
† We are not told in any source book how many troops were garrisoned on the Endor moon.

happened, and in the real world it wouldn't have happened: it strained credulity.

The Ewoks live an arboreal existence, close together in a tree village. Being close means better security. It also means that, when targeted, it wouldn't take much to destroy it with a large bomb or two. That's all it'd take to destroy the Ewok village and its inhabitants.

In Vietnam, for instance, when the U.S. Air Force wanted to clear away dense jungle foliage to create an instant landing zone for helicopters, they often dropped a massive bomb nicknamed the "Daisy Cutter." In terms of size, it's the largest bomb ever made: seventeen feet long and five feet in diameter. Carolyn Lauer explained that it carries "12,600 pounds of GX slurry [ammonium nitrate, aluminum powder, and polystyrene], and is so bulky that it cannot even be launched in a conventional method." In fact, to deploy it, it slides by parachute out of the back of a C-130 transport aircraft, and gravity does the rest.

As Lauer further explained:

Once clear of the plane, the Daisy Cutter releases its own parachute. Attached to one end of the bomb is a three-foot-long conical probe. When this probe touches the ground the bomb is detonated. Because the bomb is detonated before the majority of it hits the ground, basically no crater results. However, the bomb still inflicts heavy damage, generating pressures in excess of 1,000 pounds per square inch near the point of impact, and the shock waves can be felt miles away.*

So what's my point? Simply this: if the Empire felt the local population was a real and credible threat, all that was necessary was to drop a Daisy Cutter, or the Empire equivalent, from whatever aerial platform they wanted to use, and the Ewoks would, in one operation, be killed en masse.†

---

* Carolyn Lauer, "The Daisy Cutter Bomb," leatherneck.com.
† We can presume that the shield generator on the planet could shield itself from any blast, unless its main power supply was destroyed—the way General Solo ultimately took it out.

The Daisy Cutter, though, would have been overkill. In its place, the Empire could have used precision-guided munitions, eliminating the possibility of collateral damage to the nearby shield generator. We know the Empire has the ability to bomb targets with Star Destroyers from space with pinpoint accuracy, and then deploy TIE bombers, which was the original plan against the rebel base on Hoth, in *The Empire Strikes Back*.

Why would George Lucas end the original trilogy on such an unrealistic note? This is the ultimate battle, the final confrontation between the rebels and the Galactic Empire. It's the "money shot." Everything in *A New Hope* and *The Empire Strikes Back* sets the stage for this battle. It's the climax of the original trilogy. We'd been waiting six years for this, ever since *A New Hope* came out.

To find the answer to this question, we must go back to the turbulent sixties, when America found itself deeply entrenched in the Vietnam War overseas and civil unrest at home, which played out on college campuses and cities around the country.

George Lucas Feels a Draft Coming

When Lucas graduated with a film degree from the University of Southern California, in 1966, he faced a grim prospect that confronted every young man of draft age: a physical examination at the local draft station to determine his fitness to serve in the U.S. Army in Vietnam. Lucas had failed in his attempt to enlist in the air force, which rejected him because of his numerous speeding tickets. When he duly went for his army physical, he was surprised to discover he was diabetic—though this was no surprise in retrospect because, as Dale Pollock points out in his book, Lucas as a college student was "subsisting on a diet of Hershey bars, chocolate-chip cookies, and Cokes from the DKA cinema fraternity snack bar."

Lucas's medical condition was a mixed blessing. It meant that he'd have health issues to address immediately, but it also excluded him from serving in the army. He'd never be a ground pounder and see the rice paddies of South Vietnam up close and personal.

Lucas, who loved his sweets, eventually changed his diet, but he never changed his views about the Vietnam War, which was shared by his filmmaking friends at USC.*

Lucas saw the war through a different lens than his hawkish contemporaries on campus, some of whom believed that the United States had a moral obligation to stop the spread of communism, starting with Vietnam. But Lucas saw the war framed as the little guy against the big guy, and the little guy didn't stand a chance. More to the point, he felt the little guy was represented by the North Vietnamese regulars, known as the Vietcong. And the big guy? Well, that was Uncle Sam. As he put it, it was "a large technological empire going after a small group of freedom fighters."†

Lucas, then, never saw the war through the gunsight of an M16 rifle; he saw it through the lens of the movies he and his filmmaking friends produced: Francis Ford Coppola's *Apocalypse Now*, his own *American Graffiti* and its sequel *More American Graffiti*, and *A New Hope*, in 1977.‡

With war on his mind, it's no wonder that, when he decided to use that as a theme for a movie, it wouldn't just be a localized war but an interplanetary war: a star war, but essentially a romantic vision unlike, say, Tolkien's *The Lord of the Rings*, which drew on his combat experiences in the trenches during World War I, or George R. R. Martin's *A Song of Ice and Fire*, where death is a signature motif.

Ewoks

Hard-core *Star Wars* fans hate the Ewoks almost as much as they hate Jar Jar Binks, because some felt that Lucas was abandoning his

---

* "I was angry at the time, getting involved in all the causes. . . . The draft was hanging over all of us, and we were bearded, freako prehippies" (Lucas, quoted in Dale Pollock, *Skywalking: The Life and Films of George Lucas* [Da Capo, 1990]).

† Rosa Prince, "Star Wars Secrets Revealed," *The Telegraph*, September 21, 2014.

‡ If you want a taste of what the Vietnam War was like, read Michael Herr's nonfiction book *Dispatches* (Avon, 1978). It's an acid trip, man.

adult audience to cater to kids in order to sell more licensed product.* But, in fact, Lucas was principally interested in framing the principals in the Vietnam war in their respective roles, from his viewpoint: the Ewoks were the underdogs, the little guys, and they were up against a large, well-equipped, and technologically superior force, representing the U.S. military. Therefore, in his eyes, the little guys should win against the big guys for once.

It's no surprise, then, that we see the Ewoks using guerilla tactics in their fight against the Galactic Empire. We see booby traps aplenty, ranging from small to large in size, improvised using local resources, taking a physical and mental toll on the troops.

Insofar as strategy was concerned, the U.S. military had everything it could possibly want to conduct a winnable war, but the bad guys didn't play to win; they were simply buying time for a stalemate, prolonging the war until the Americans back home, who were increasingly impatient for the unpopular war to end, cried "Enough!"

Part of the North Vietnam's strategy was to take maximum advantage of the local terrain, which they knew intimately. They made the "imperialist running dogs" pay for every step they took, booby-trapping rice paddies, jungles, and roads, using low-tech, inexpensive devices that proved very effective.

They also built vast networks of underground tunnels to survive the relentless pounding from B-29s. It was a proven tactic that they had learned from the Japanese strategy on Iwo Jima during World War II.†

Like the North Vietnamese Army, the Japanese, and the insurgents

---

* Annemarie Moody writes about the *Star Wars* bobblehead toys given out to children with their Happy Meals, which included, among others, Wicket the Ewok. "Adding to the fun, McDonald's invites its youngest customers to continue their *Star Wars* experience online with a Jedi quest at the new Happy Meal Virtual World" (Moody, "*Star Wars*, McDonald's Join Forces," awn.com, August 14, 2008).

† Today's troops in the Middle East deal with insurgents' deadly improvised explosive devices (IEDs). "Somewhere between more than half to two-thirds of Americans killed or wounded in combat in Iraq and Afghanistan wars have been victims of IEDs planted in the ground, in vehicles or buildings, or worn as suicide vests or loaded into suicide vehicles, according to data from the Pentagon's Joint IED Defeat Organization or JIEDDO" (George Zoroya, "How the IED Changed the US Military," *USA Today*, December 19, 2013).

in the Middle East, the Ewoks fought an asymmetrical war on home turf against a technologically superior force. But in the Ewoks' case, they couldn't lose, because military realism was not the objective: the stormtroopers didn't stand a chance. They were simply expendable pawns on a chessboard, positioned and played by George Lucas.

I suspect this is one reason why hard-core *Star Wars* fans found the Ewoks so offensive and aggravating: the hard-core fans wanted true grit in the battle scenes, but what they got was sand thrown in their eyes. The trilogy should have ended triumphantly for the good guys, but at some cost in blood.

I am reminded of how J. R. R. Tolkien ended *The Lord of the Rings*, with a chapter titled "The Scouring of the Shire." In it, the triumphant hobbits—Frodo, Samwise, Pippin, and Merry—return home, satisfied that they have saved the world from certain doom. They look forward to returning to their idyllic life. They expect to see things just as they left them: their beloved Shire, far from the field of battle, untouched and pristine.

But that's not what Tolkien had in mind. He realized that winning a war comes at a price. When the hobbits got a good look at how their homeland had been scoured, it was shocking:

> It was one of the saddest hours in their lives. The great chimney rose up before them; and as they drew near the old village across the Water, through rows of new mean houses along each side of the road, they saw the new mill in all its frowning and dirty ugliness: a great brick building straddling the stream, which it fouled with a steaming and stinking overflow. All along the Bywater Road every tree had been felled.
>
> As they crossed the bridge and looked up the Hill they gasped. Even Sam's vision in the Mirror had not prepared him for what they saw. The Old Grange on the west side had been knocked down, and its place taken by rows of tarred sheds. All the chestnuts were gone. The banks and hedgerows were broken. Great waggons were standing in disorder in a field beaten bare of grass. Bagshot Row was a

yawning sand and gravel quarry. Bag End up beyond could not be seen for a clutter of large huts.

War always exacts a cost, on the battlefield and back at home. No one is exempt—nor should they be. But in the climactic battle between the Rebel Alliance and the Galactic Empire, we see, instead, a sanitized war, a bloodless battle with only one dead Ewok, in a scene that was milked for maximum effect.* In the original version of *Return of the Jedi*, we see Ewoks dancing and singing the "Yub Nub" victory song, and much merriment in the Ewok village.

Instead, we should have seen a somber scene in which the bodies of numerous Ewoks were buried or burned on a funeral pyre. But all we got were cartoony deaths on both sides—the stormtroopers and the Ewoks—and we didn't feel a thing for anyone. Nothing.

Instead, we should feel the pain and the loss, and our hearts should be breaking as tears stream down our faces. We should be reminded that freedom isn't free, that a price in blood must be paid, because all gave some . . . and some gave all.

---

* It's worth noting, too, that I can't recall seeing anyone on Han Solo's strike team get killed. I could be wrong here, but even if there had been a death, or two, or three, they didn't stand out.

The Final Solution: Kill Them All

tar Wars: The Force Awakens opens with the First Order sending stormtroopers on a mission to the planet Jakku to recover from a Jedi Knight a star map that shows the location of Luke Skywalker.

There are eighty well-armed troops against a small village of a few dozen civilians, including women and children, who are hopelessly outgunned. It's no contest. The civilians surrender, but to no avail; they're rounded up and killed.

In the novelization of the movie, author Alan Dean Foster writes, "It wasn't a massacre. In the lexicon of the First Order it was nothing more than a prescribed chastisement."

The question arises: In terms of a military strategy, in the end, was it militarily worthwhile to kill all the villagers?

Killing off the locals for retribution or for harboring the enemy is a recurring strategy in military history. In Lithuania, in what was then known as Vilnius, in the village of Ponary, from 1941 to 1944, German troops machine-gunned an estimated ninety thousand people. There had been "rows of men and women machine-gunned down at close range. Mothers pleading for the lives of their children. Deep earthen pits piled high with corpses."*

Of course, the Germans, wanting to hide their heinous massacre of unarmed civilians, made it clear that "there must not be any trace" of what had just happened.

---

* Matthew Shaer, "The Holocaust's Great Escape," *Smithsonian*, March 2017.

More than seventy years have passed, but time's passage will never erase that haunting episode from the memory of the Lithuanians. The war is long over, but as long as they exist, they will always remember Nazi Germany's atrocities.

Not to be outdone, during the same time, the Japanese Imperial Army raised the bar. Civilian Chinese sympathizers' rescue of downed airmen who executed the Doolittle Raid* "would trigger a horrific retaliation by the Japanese that claimed an estimated quarter-million lives and would prompt comparisons to the 1937–38 Rape of Nanking."†

In recent memory, on March 16, 1968, during the Vietnam War:

> a platoon of American soldiers brutally slaughter[ed] . . . unarmed civilians at My Lai, one of a cluster of small villages located near the northern coast of South Vietnam. . . .
>
> [Led by Lieutenant William L. Calley,] the platoon entered one of the village's four hamlets, My Lai 4, on a search-and-destroy mission on the morning of March 16. Instead of guerrilla fighters, they found unarmed villagers, most of them women, children and old men.‡

In a famous cover for *National Lampoon* by science fiction artist Frank Kelly Freas, showing a fatuously grinning, baby-faced Lieutenant Calley asking, "What, My Lai?," the point is made: his heinous act was a monstrous war crime, for which Calley was given a life sentence. But he was paroled only four years later. He walks freely among us, unlike the 504 civilians he and his men murdered.§

---

* Sixteen B-25B Mitchell medium bombers, led by then–Lieutenant Colonel Doolittle, were launched from an aircraft carrier to strike targets in Japan. Though militarily ineffective, doing little damage, the psychological effect was considerable: it showed that Japan was vulnerable.
† James M. Scott, "The Untold Story of the Vengeful Japanese Attack After the Doolittle Raid," smithsonian.com, April 15, 2015.
‡ "This Day in History: March 16, 1968," history.com.
§ At a public talk at a Kiwanis Club in Columbus, Ohio, on August 19, 2009, Calley said, "There is not a day that goes by that I do not feel remorse for what happened that day in My Lai. I feel remorse for the Vietnamese who were killed, for their families, for the American soldiers involved and their families. I am very sorry. . . . If you are asking why I did not stand up to them when I was given the orders, I will have to say that I was a 2nd lieutenant getting

The problem with such military actions is that, in the end, they are counterproductive. Initially, such actions fuel the flames of resistance; subsequently, when the tables are turned, the suppressed populace will rise up and attack their former enemies with a vengeance. Case in point: during World War II, after Japan surrendered unconditionally, the long-oppressed Chinese in northern Manchuria, who had suffered terribly under Japanese rule, exacted their revenge:

> Japanese residents were surrounded by resentful populations that had long hated their exploiters. . . . Of 333,000 Japanese in the area, confirmed deaths totaled approximately 80,000. The agricultural settlers were only 14 percent of the Japanese in Manchuria; they suffered 50 percent of the casualties. [The youth volunteers] were slaughtered by the local Chinese and the Red Army. In addition, approximately 32,000 Japanese died in northern Korea.*

When Kylo Ren and Captain Phasma wiped out a small village on Jakku, it generated enormous sympathy for the Rebellion. Reprisals always come at a high cost. With *The Force Awakens*, we see the first picture of the war against the First Order. Obviously, we have no idea how long this war is going to last, but in the end the First Order, like the Galactic Empire, will suffer an inevitable defeat.

---

orders from my commander and I followed them—foolishly, I guess" (Dusty Nix, "Long-Silent Calley Speaks," *Ledger-Enquirer*, August 21, 2009).

In response, read what Duc Tran Van, who, at the age of seven, was there and survived, has to say: "During the gunfire my mother protected me, and my little sister in her fall, by lying beneath us. When the gunfire ended, and the Americans were away, my mother told me to run away immediately. . . . Only in 1975, I find out that my mother, shortly after I ran away with my sister, was killed by headshot, through the press photograph" (comment by Duc Tran Van, on Dick McMichael's *Dick's World* blog, dicksworld.wordpress.com, February 9, 2010).

For an authoritative examination of this tragedy, see Howard Jones, *My Lai: Vietnam, 1968, and the Descent Into Darkness* (Oxford University Press, 2017).

* Saburō Ienaga, *The Pacific War, 1931–1945* (Pantheon Books, 1978).

Death Star II

I would have loved to be in the war room when Emperor Palpatine, Darth Vader, and the senior-level command staff met to discuss building a second superweapon, Death Star II.

How could anyone in the military *not* want a weapon that could destroy an entire planet or target massive spaceships with such precision that it could destroy them with one shot?

Ironically, the same flaw that doomed the original Death Star also doomed Death Star II, except instead of the former's small exhaust port, the second Death Star had a very large entry port that allowed the *Millennium Falcon* and starfighters, with TIE fighters in hot pursuit, to fly into its nucleus and destroy it from within.

How large, you ask, was the passageway that General Calrissian flew through? Big enough in which to fly the *Millennium Falcon*. (The *Falcon* is eighty-four feet wide, or approximately half the width of a football field, notes Wookieepedia.)

Now, let's be honest. If you were designing a second Death Star, knowing how the first one was destroyed, wouldn't you make *sure* that this iteration *wouldn't* have an entry port so large that you could fly a starship of any size through it?

In light of what happened to the first Death Star, how could that be overlooked? Didn't the command staff conduct an after action review to identify weaknesses and glean lessons learned, so that history wouldn't repeat itself?

Instead, they were hopelessly enamoured by the "bigger is better" design philosophy; thus, the answer was simply to build a bigger Death Star with a more powerful superlaser. Blinded by the attractiveness of the second Death Star's offensive capabilities, they once again failed to see, and plan for, its defensive vulnerabilities.

It's what doomed the second Death Star.

HIJMS *Yamato*

Such thinking also doomed the HIJMS *Yamato*, the largest battleship in the world at the time, constructed by the Japanese during World War II.

During World War II, the prevailing naval wisdom was that you couldn't have too many battleships—and, while you're at it, the bigger, the better. Thus, the Japanese constructed the *Yamato*, which history.net describes as follows:

> Its name was *Yamato*, the mightiest warship yet constructed.* Displacing 71,659 tons and capable of 27 knots, the *Yamato* possessed the greatest firepower ever mounted on a vessel—more than 150 guns, including nine 18.1-inchers that could hurl 3,200-pound armor-piercing shells on a trajectory of 22.5 miles. Its massive armor was the heaviest ever installed on a dreadnought-class battleship, making it virtually impregnable to the guns of any ship in the world. The very name *Yamato* was a poetic and spiritual term for Japan itself. In its gray, armored magnificence, the great ship symbolized Japan's dreams of conquest.

On April 7, 1945, the *Yamato* steamed out of safe harbor in Japan to Okinawa on what would be its last mission. Set upon by SB2C Helldivers, TBF Avengers, F4U Corsairs, and F6F Hellcats, the *Yamato* threw up a hellish barrage of firepower, firing twenty-four antiaircraft guns and 120 machine guns, but to no avail. The mightiest battleship in the world sank. As Robert Gandt explains,

---

* She had a sister ship, the *Musashi*, of similar size.

In Japan, news of the *Yamato* disaster was withheld from the public. It fell to Navy Minister Mitsumasa Yonai to inform the emperor. With downcast eyes, Yonai stood before Hirohito and reported that Operation Ten-Go had failed.

The emperor seemed not to understand. He peered at Yonai through his spectacles. What about the navy? he asked. What was the status of the fleet? The minister spoke the truth. There was no fleet, he told the emperor. The Imperial Japanese Navy had ceased to exist.[*]

The Second Death Star

Just as the first Death Star was a symbol of imperial might, the second was an even bigger symbol. According to Wookieepedia:[†]

> Upon completion, the Death Star II would have been an immense battle station 200 kilometers in diameter that featured 560 internal levels which could house 2,471,647 passengers and crew. . . . The Death Star II had extensive point-defense capabilities, featuring 15,000 heavy and standard turbolaser batteries along with 7,500 laser cannons and 5,000 ion cannons spread across its outer surface. With the battle station housing 637,835 naval and army personnel, the installation boasted a large complement of TIE/ln space superiority starfighters and their variants, stored for space-based encounters, and a plethora of All Terrain Armored Transports and All Terrain Scout Transports for surface operations.

In short, even without its main weapon, a superlaser, Death Star II was well equipped to defend herself against all enemies with massive firepower and starfighters aplenty. But all of their armament proved ineffective because of two major flaws: poor strategic planning at the highest levels, and a hole big enough for enemy aircraft—even a large ship like the *Millennium Falcon*—to enter.

---

[*] Robert Gandt, "Killing the Yamato," historynet.com, August 4, 2011.
[†] Accessed September 23, 2017.

Leadership Failures

There were a number of leadership failures that contributed to the demise of Death Star II.

1. The leadership didn't realize that the Rebel Alliance, an asymmetrical force, would once again leverage its military assets by taking advantage of the inherent design flaws of Death Star II.
2. They suffered from a failure of imagination. Once again they were so smitten with the idea of a superweapon that they consolidated irreplaceable manpower (military and support personnel) to support it, regardless of cost or any other real-world constraints.
3. They failed to recognize that, regardless of what they did to protect the field generator protecting the Death Star, the rebels would obviously target and attempt to attack it.
4. They failed to adequately employ in-depth defensive measures against the rebel fleet, which was allowed to get close enough to the Death Star to inflict significant damage.
5. The admirals and generals were not allowed to question Emperor Palpatine's plan. Consequently, the Death Star's known vulnerabilities were once again exploited.
6. There was a tainted command atmosphere. Such was the command climate that fear poisoned the command staff, which was unable or unwilling to disagree for fear of being Force-choked by Lord Vader. No contrary views were tolerated by Palpatine or Vader.
7. There was a failure to come up with an alternative plan, such as using the existing fleet of Star Destroyers to systematically invade and conquer individual planets.
8. Because the Empire's fleet was stretched thin throughout the galaxy, they should have spent the time, money, and resources to add more Star Destroyers to the fleet rather than building yet another superweapon. Dispersing the

combat strength of the Empire instead of consolidating it would have made it more difficult for the rebels to attack the Empire.

9. They should have built smaller Death Stars, positioned throughout the star systems, each capable of defending itself from large- and small-scale attacks, with Star Destroyers on station for in-depth defense. For instance, instead of consolidating 2.5 million personnel on the second Death Star, which makes it a very high-value military target, the construction of ten smaller Death Stars, each with a manning strength of 250,000, would enable the Empire to adequately project its power in a show of force while also dispersing its prime assets to reduce overall vulnerability.

10. The Emperor was overconfident in his battle plan. As Palpatine arrogantly and erroneously told Luke Skywalker on the bridge of his Super Star Destroyer, he presumed that the battle had already been won, because it was inconceivable that the rebels could win.

The Vietnam War

In looking at how the Empire planted the seeds of its own destruction, we are reminded of how the United States did the same in the Vietnam War, which was lost, as H. R. McMaster[*] pointed out, because senior military leaders did not vigorously contest the views of their leaders, Defense Secretary Robert McNamara and President Johnson.

It was an unwinnable war with repercussions that are still being felt today.[†] As McMaster points out in his preface to *Dereliction of Duty* (Harper Perennial, 1998):

---

[*] He wrote *Dereliction of Duty* when he was a major, eventually rising to the rank of three-star general. On February 20, 2017, he became President Donald Trump's national security advisor, after retired lieutenant colonel Michael Flynn resigned at the request of his commander in chief.
[†] When the United States chose to withdraw from the battlefield, the war was then lost; the North Vietnamese Army overran South Vietnam and the country was united under communist rule.

The war continues to capture the public interest in part because, looking back, its cost seems exorbitant—and would seem so even if the United States had "won." The war took the lives of fifty-eight thousand Americans and well over one million Vietnamese. It left Vietnam in ruins and consumed billions of American dollars, nearly wrecking the American economy. Vietnam divided American society and inflicted on the United States one of the greatest political traumas since the Civil War. . . . Thirty years later, after the end of the Cold War, the shadow of the American experience in Vietnam still hangs heavy over American foreign and military policy, and over American society.

In retrospect, it's axiomatic that consolidating military power in a single superweapon carries its own potential seeds of destruction. Either others will acquire the knowledge and technology to duplicate, nullify, or equalize it, or they will find a way to destroy it, because they have no other option—its very existence tips the balance of power. That is why both Death Stars were doomed.

As Sun Tzu (544–496 BCE) wrote in *The Art of War*, "The art of war teaches us to rely not on the likelihood of the enemy's not coming, but on our own readiness to receive him; not on the chance of his not attacking, but rather on the fact that we have made our position unassailable."

In the instances of both Death Stars and of Starkiller Base, the rebels found those positions assailable and then attacked, emerging triumphant.

The Importance of Standard Operating Procedures

I knew the equipment was pretty new. In fact, the guy who was on the scope, who first detected the planes, it was the first time he'd ever sat at the scope. So I figured they were pretty green and not had any opportunity to view a flight of B-17s coming in. Common sense said, Well, these are the B-17s. So I told them, "Don't worry about it."

—Lieutenant Kermit Tyler, officer on duty at Pearl Harbor

Imagine you are on a search and seizure team to intercept an enemy vessel. As soon as you board, a fast boat speeds away from the ship you've just boarded. Do you let it go, do you fire warning shots, or do you destroy it? You've got to make a decision *right now*. As the senior officer present, what are your orders?

For Want of a Nail

In *Star Wars: A New Hope*, the *Devastator*, an imperial Star Destroyer captures a rebel ship and commences to board it.

The stormtroopers storm through a door, blasting away, engage in a close-quarters firefight, and soon have the crew of *Tantive IV* in full rout. They are quickly rounded up as prisoners.

On board the Star Destroyer, on a main view screen, we see an escape pod speeding away to the nearby planet, Tatooine. A chief pilot observes it and tells his captain, "There goes another one."

"Hold your fire," the captain says. "There are no life-forms. *It must have short-circuited*" (italics mine).

Given the chain of events, the officer in charge has only two logical choices:

1. Blow the escape pod to smithereens to prevent it from reaching Tatooine.
2. *Immediately* dispatch a ship in hot pursuit to follow it to Tatooine, recover the escape pod, and recapture its occupants *before* they can leave the pod.

So why didn't the officer do so?

He decided that because scans showed there were no *human* life-forms, there must have been a mechanical malfunction, that the pod had been jettisoned by mistake.

He chose . . . poorly. As a result, the droids, with a little pluck and a lot of luck, eventually managed to get indispensable information into the hands of the Rebel Alliance, which enabled them to formulate a battle plan to attack, which in turn allowed them to destroy the Death Star.

As Benjamin Franklin (among others) observed, "For the want of a nail the shoe was lost, for the want of a shoe the horse was lost, for the want of a horse the rider was lost, for the want of a rider the battle was lost, for the want of a battle the kingdom was lost, and all for the want of a horseshoe-nail."

And so it was in this situation. By not firing at the escape pod, and by allowing it to continue on its path, a seemingly small incident morphed into catastrophic loss for the Empire.

But if there had been a written standard operating procedure on hand, things might have turned out quite differently for all parties involved. The Empire would have prevailed and there would have been no need to build a second Death Star.

SOP: Standard Operating Procedure

ATP 3–90.90 (*Army Tactical Standard Operating Procedures*, November 2011) explains:

> A standard operational procedure is a set of instructions covering those features of operations which lend themselves to a definitive or standardized procedure without loss of effectiveness. . . . A SOP is both standing and standard: it instructs how to perform a prescribed and accepted process established for completing a task. Features of operations that lend themselves to standardization are common and usually detailed processes performed often and requiring minimal variation each time. Well-written and properly used unit tactical SOPs enhance effective execution of tasks; the benefits of SOPs are numerous. They reduce training time, the loss of unwritten information, *the commission of errors*, the omission of essential steps or processes, and the time required for completion of tasks (italics mine).

The question arises: Does the Empire use SOPs at all? If so, the SOP for boarding party procedures should have spelled out:

1. No vessels are allowed to leave the captured ship.
2. All signals, and on all frequencies, from any escaping vessel must be jammed to prevent all transmission of data.
3. All vessels must be destroyed immediately.
4. In the event a vessel reaches safety, its timely recovery is essential. A recovery team, on standby alert, will immediately pursue the vessel, recover it, and return it to the ship to determine what sensitive information or materials, if any, it contained.
5. In the event recovery is not possible, after its computer banks are scanned, the data is downloaded, and all sensitive documents are secured, the vessel must be destroyed in place, using any available means.

In this instance, a recovery effort did ensue, but it was too little and too late. With the passage of time, the escape pod lived up to its namesake; it had already landed on Tatooine while Darth Vader was otherwise occupied on board *Tantive IV*, allowing both droids to go on their merry way.

If Empire staff officers had drafted a tactical SOP, the landing party on board the *Devastator* would have known exactly what to do. They would have secured the ship: nobody else gets on, and nobody gets off. There would be no escape for the princess at this or any other time—nor for anyone else, including the droids you were supposed to be looking for.

"Standing Orders, Rogers' Rangers," by Major Robert Rogers (1759)

These orders, adopted by army Rangers, appears at the end of *Ranger Handbook* (July 1992) with a prefatory note: "Even though they are over 200 years old, they apply just as well to Ranger operations conducted on today's battlefield as they did to the operations conducted by Rogers and his men."

Based on Rogers's twenty-eight "Rules of Ranging" formulated in July 1767, a truncated, colloquial version was published in 1937 by Kenneth Roberts in his novel *Northwest Passage.*

1. Don't forget nothing.
2. Have your musket clean as a whistle, hatchet scoured, sixty rounds powder and ball, and be ready to march at a minute's warning.
3. When you're on the march, act the way you would if you was sneaking up on a deer. See the enemy first.
4. Tell the truth about what you see and what you do. There is an army depending on us for correct information. You can lie all you please when you tell other folks about the Rangers, but don't never lie to a Ranger or officer.
5. Don't never take a chance you don't have to.
6. When we're on the march we march single file, far enough apart so no one shot can go through two men.
7. If we strike swamps, or soft ground, we spread out abreast, so it's hard to track us.
8. When we march, we keep moving till dark, so as to give the enemy the least possible chance at us.
9. When we camp, half the party stays awake while the other half sleeps.

10. If we take prisoners, we keep 'em separate til we have had time to examine them, so they can't cook up a story between 'em.

11. Don't ever march home the same way. Take a different route so you won't be ambushed.

12. No matter whether we travel in big parties or little ones, each party has to keep a scout 20 yards ahead, 20 yards on each flank, and 20 yards in the rear so the main body can't be surprised and wiped out.

13. Every night you'll be told where to meet if surrounded by a superior force.

14. Don't sit down to eat without posting sentries.

15. Don't sleep beyond dawn. Dawn's when the French and Indians attack.

16. Don't cross a river by a regular ford.

17. If somebody's trailing you, make a circle, come back onto your own tracks, and ambush the folks that aim to ambush you.

18. Don't stand up when the enemy's coming against you. Kneel down. Hide behind a tree.

19. Let the enemy come till he's almost close enough to touch. Then let him have it and jump out and finish him up with your hatchet.

Ed note: *This may be the first instance of an SOP in the U.S. military.*

· PART 5 ·

LESSONS LEARNED FROM KEY BATTLES

Human-nature will not change. In any future great national trial, compared with the men of this, we shall have as weak, and as strong; as silly and as wise; as bad and good. Let us, therefore, study the incidents of this, as philosophy to learn wisdom from, and none of them as wrongs to be revenged.

—Abraham Lincoln on the 1864 Election

The operational arts—"the use of military forces to achieve strategic goals through the design, organization, integration, and conduct of strategies, campaigns, major operations, and battles"—takes a long time to master. As anyone in the military will tell you, the learning never stops.

At every rank I held—from an ROTC cadet in high school, then ROTC in college, and then from second lieutenant to major—the more I learned, the more I realized how much *more* there was to learn.

As a student at Command and General Staff College, I was reminded of that when I was studying battle analysis. The school gives its students a template that is used to write a detailed analysis, which includes tactical, strategic, and operational considerations. The purpose of the analysis is not merely to summarize what happened but, as the school tells us, to "assess the significance of the action: This is the most important step of the battle analysis process. With this step, you are turning 'combat information' in the form of the historical facts of the battle into finished analysis rendered as 'lessons learned.'"

That's the bottom line: what can be gleaned is to be shared with future leaders so that the same mistakes aren't repeated and we become better in the operational arts.

All the major battles that we've seen on screen in the *Star Wars* universe provide considerable food for thought for their fans, for students of military history, and for military professionals.

My focus is to discuss what has largely not been discussed in the official books—lessons learned from military engagements—which is best written from the viewpoint of someone in the combat arms who knows the territory. For that reason, I am leaving the summaries and detailed information about equipment and personnel to those writing the officially licensed books. Because those pop culture writers are civilians, their perspective is understandably different from mine.

With that in mind, I'll briefly cover the ground battle of Naboo (*The Phantom Menace*), the Battle of Yavin (*A New Hope*), the ground battle of Hoth (*The Empire Strikes Back*), the Battle of Endor (*Return of the Jedi*), and a skirmish on Jedha (*Rogue One*).

At the end of this section, I've reprinted the text of the Command and General Staff College student handout, its study guide for battle analysis. As you'll see, the study guide is comprehensive, specific, and is suggested as a template for "any military professional seeking insight from historical battles and campaigns to help deepen his/her understanding of warfare and the profession of arms."

Although the template is most useful for military professionals—those who have served, especially in leadership positions—it is an excellent tool for nonmilitary personnel to clarify and focus their military thinking.

If nothing else, the discussions that follow should provide ample food for thought. Because there is no one right answer for every situation, because the nature of combat is in a state of constant flux, there's plenty of room for discussion.

The Ground Battle of Naboo
Reference: *Star Wars I: The Phantom Menace*

As Roman general Publius Renatus wrote in *Epitoma rei militaris*, "If you want peace, prepare for war." Put differently, the best defense is a strong offense.

When I think about the wisdom of those words, it recalls the ground battle at Naboo in *Star Wars II: Attack of the Clones*. In that force-on-force battle, the Gungan Army could only have "won" by default, because they had never prepared—that is, trained—for war.

In official *Star Wars* reference books, we glean two critical facts: the Gungan Army is wholly composed of citizen soldiers, and their equipment is inadequate against a technologically superior force.

We have to admire the Gungans for their courage, but when facing a well-equipped, better trained fighting force, the Gungans have little recourse but to put up the best fight they can and then retreat, while hoping to minimize casualties.

The Gungans' fighting spirit recalls that of the Imperial Japanese Army, which marched into battle buoyed by its celebrated fighting spirit. This is admirable, as far as that goes, but not militarily effective, as Japanese historian Saburō Ienaga (*The Pacific War*) pointed out: "A striking feature of the doctrine is its excessive emphasis on 'spirit.' The literature is full of phrases about 'the attack spirit,' 'confidence in certain victory,' and 'sacrifice one's life to the country, absolute obedience to superiors.' . . . Even brave NCOs highly motivated by "spiritual training" saw that the Imperial Army's strategic doctrine was outdated and stupid."

There is no question that fighting spirit is important in combat, but that kind of magical thinking isn't enough to win battles. What *does* win battles: a combined arms operation in which overwhelming, decisive firepower is brought to bear against the enemy.

This is why the Imperial Japanese Army found itself at a significant disadvantage against the Americans, especially in the last year of the war, when munitions were in short supply, their logistics tail was cut off, and flagging morale took a toll. They could see their inevitable fate—catastrophic losses of men and material in combat, with inevitable and unconditional surrender.

In addition to being inadequately trained in the operational arts of fire and maneuver, the Gungan Army went into battle with inadequate resources: only one defensive weapon and one offensive weapon. In other words, the Gungans up against a droid army were like the Native American population armed with bows and arrows against the American military armed with rifles.

From all appearances, the Gungans didn't properly plan a retrograde operation, though that was their only option. It was a tactical decision that nearly cost them the loss of their entire fighting force.

The U.S. Army's Field Manual 7-20, *The Infantry Battalion*, states the purpose of a retrograde operation:

A retrograde operation can be used to avoid decisive combat under unfavorable conditions, to maintain freedom of maneuver, or to save forces for decisive action elsewhere. The underlying reason for conducting a retrograde operation is to improve a tactical situation or to prevent a worse one from occurring. A battalion conducts a retrograde as part of a larger force—

- To harass, exhaust, resist, and delay the enemy.
- To gain time.
- To reposition or preserve forces.
- To use a force elsewhere.
- To draw the enemy into an unfavorable position.
- To shorten lines of communication and supply.

- To clear zones for friendly use of chemical or nuclear weapons.
- To conform to the movement of other friendly forces.

In short, it's a defensive operation. The goal is not to try to engage and destroy the enemy but, instead, to disengage *tactically*, to preserve your troop strength, to minimize casualties, by buying time.

The tactical blunder on the part of the Gungans, though, is that they relied too heavily on a single piece of defensive equipment to protect them, and when that weapon became inoperative, the Gungans had no contingency plan.

The issue of combat strength and firepower is critical in this discussion, because the Gungan Army was simply undermanned, whereas the Empire's droids were numerous.

Likewise, firepower: the Gungans' weapons—individual, crew-served, and (very loosely defined) artillery—were effective only when direct hits were possible, but the Empire's superior weapons, when appearing on the battlefield, were enough to cause the shocked Gungans to stare in disbelief and palpable fear: the droids had high-powered blasters, backed up by rolling battle droids, and tanks.

In essence, Gungans showed up with knives to a gunfight.

Lessons Learned: Gungan Defense

The Gungans had the home field advantage but completely failed to use it. If I had been an operations officer at battalion or brigade level on the Gungan side, here are some of my recommendations, based solely on what we see in *Attack of the Clones*.

1. Dig foxholes. This would have provided some cover against small arms fire, crew-served weapons, and tanks. Because the Empire showed up at the field of battle with direct-fire (line-of-sight) weapons, the Gungans would have benefited from reducing their physical profile by having hardened foxholes.

2. Lay a minefield on all probable avenues of approach. This has two benefits: it forces the enemy to explore other avenues of

approach, which can also be booby-trapped, or it may channel the enemy into a designated kill zone. It also denies the enemy key terrain.

3. Protect offensive capability assets. The Gungans use medieval-style catapults to launch disruptor-style energy balls, but these were employed in the open. Instead, position them as far back as possible, and properly shelter them against tank fire.

4. Well before going into the battle, plan on executing a by-the-book retrograde operation. The main battle force should buy time and fall back by echelon, protected by Gungans on the flanks. This ensures an orderly movement to the rear, as opposed to what in fact happened—an unprotected, full rout as panic set in.

5. Make better use of defensive shields by studying the tactics of the Roman legions, who employed them in varying formations to minimize attrition of their ranks. This would have protected the Gungans against the individual weapons fire from the droids and perhaps from the twin-armed droidekas (rolling droids).

6. Recruit and train a standing army ready for immediate deployment.

7. Acquire technologically sophisticated individual and crew-served weapons, borrowing them from the Naboo if necessary, which would give them a fighting chance. Armed only with hand-thrown or catapult-launched disruptive energy balls, Gungans aren't equipped to fight on a modern battlefield.

8. Train combat engineers for mining, breaching, and other operations.

9. Use electronic radio communications instead of vocal commands and hand signals.

10. Take advantage of the natural terrain for cover and concealment.

11. Design a handheld weapon for close-in fighting, because many force-on-force battles end up in close-quarters fighting.

12. Keep at least a third of the forces in reserve. Don't commit all your forces at once, because some will be needed for covering fire when retreating tactically.

13. Establish a proper military liaison with the Naboo to share weapons technology and battlefield information, and train in peacetime with live-fire exercises in war games to gauge combat skills.

Lessons Learned: Galactic Empire

Without question, the Empire's biggest blunder is that the leadership failed to recognize the need for redundant power systems that would have prevented their standing army from literally collapsing on the field of battle. But, in terms of military strategy, their battle plan also was seriously flawed.

Where were the air assets? The use of close air support in this battle should have been a no-brainer, especially since the Gungans would have been defenseless.

Where was the artillery? The Gungans had no counterbattery fire assets, so the Empire was free to shell the Gungans at will.

Knowing the Gungans's defensive shield could easily be penetrated by simply walking through it, backed up by rolling droids (Droidekas), why didn't they do that first? That way, the Gungan shield would have come down a lot sooner, and then the droid army could lay down a withering fire with direct fire and indirect fire supplemented with close air support.

We can chalk up these and other battlefield considerations to the Empire's overconfidence. It may be why the commander's operations staff never drew up an order of battle to identify the Gungans' strengths and weaknesses. The Empire simply felt it was bigger, better, and couldn't lose against the militarily primitive Gungans, so why bother *studying* the military situation?

Because, as the droid army discovered, in combat you cannot take anything for granted.

The Battle of Yavin

Reference: *Star Wars IV: A New Hope*

The tactical situation, as seen from the Empire's point of view: its superweapon is under attack by a small rebel force.

Death Star I

With a franchise as large as *Star Wars*, which spans forty years, the issue of continuity is critical. Researching information about the first Death Star's specifics—its size, defensive and offensive capabilities, and manning—reveals numerous inconsistencies among various official sources. So I'll dispense with a detailed examination of the offensive and defensive capabilities of the weapons system itself and instead focus on the big picture—the tactical considerations—in a very general way.

When we first see the Death Star on the big screen, we feel a sense of awe, and then increasing dread, just as the good guys do when they get their first look at it. Even at a distance, it looks to be the size of a small moon. We can infer that its manning—the combat troops and infrastructure to support them and the Death Star itself—is commensurate.

To give a sense of scale, U.S. Army units are thus configured, from smallest to largest: section, squad, platoon (or troop), company, battalion, regiment, brigade, division, corps, and army (approximately 100,000 personnel). As noted earlier, *The Complete Star Wars Encyclopedia* notes that the first Death Star has an "operational crew" of 265,000 and additional personnel that brings the total manning to over one million.* In other words, the Death Star represents a significant portion of the Empire's military manpower, which is not easily replaced. The number of skilled personnel to run, service, and operate such a weapons platform represents a significant investment of time necessary to train all the military personnel. Their collective loss would take years to reconstitute, across the board.

The cost to construct the Death Star and the time necessary to build it are, for purposes of my discussion, secondary concerns. My primary concern is the military strategy employed by the Empire against its nemesis, the rebel air force.

A Superweapon

By definition, the Death Star is a superweapon, a weapon specifically designed to be a game changer. In other words, it's an irresistible force whose mere presence creates an immediate threat and, logically, would result in the immediate capitulation of the enemy.

The Death Star recalls Sun Tzu's observation in *The Art of War* that "supreme excellence consists in breaking the enemy's resistance without fighting."

To put things in perspective, imagine you are a planetary ruler in charge of defense and the enemy has created a weapon so devastating that you're told resistance is futile. Are you willing to take the enemy's word at face value and assume that the weapon is as powerful as it's made out to be? Or are you going to wait for a demonstration, at the cost of many lives and massive destruction of property? Or will you simply discount it altogether as a bluff or hyperbole?

The Japanese emperor, the members of his court, and the Imperial

---

* Perhaps because of the sprawling nature of the *Star Wars* universe, it's difficult to ensure uniformity in the printed and online media. According to the fan-based Wookiepeedia, accessed September 23, 2017, the first Death Star had "342,953 members of the Imperial Army and Navy, 25,984 stormtroopers, and nearly 2 million personnel of varying combat eligibility."

Army and Navy had to ponder that very question in 1945, when faced with the prospect of a new and most terrible weapon—the atomic bomb.

The Manhattan Project

On July 16, 1945, in Alamogordo, New Mexico, the world's first atomic bomb was successfully detonated. It ushered in the atomic age, casting a long shadow.*

Faced with the prospect of ending the war with Japan through invasion, planners hoped that the development of a superweapon, an atomic bomb, could bring a quick and decisive end to the war, minimizing loss of life on both sides. The alternative would be an invasion, which would take an even greater human toll.

In the end, President Truman made a decision to employ the newly developed nuclear weapon against Japan. The first was dropped on Hiroshima (August 6, 1945); the second, on Nagasaki (August 9). Six days later, the Japanese Empire surrendered. Emperor Hirohito, in a countrywide radio broadcast, told his subjects that "the enemy has begun to employ a new and most cruel bomb, the power of which to do damage is, indeed, incalculable, taking the toll of many innocent lives. Should we continue to fight, not only would it result in an ultimate collapse and obliteration of the Japanese nation, but also it would lead to the total extinction of human civilization."

In other words, the deployment of a what he termed a "most cruel bomb" put a quick end to a long and bloody war that had dragged on for four long years. Given time, the American firebombing campaign using B-29 bombers would likely have accomplished the goal, but time was of the essence.

The United States did consider a show of atomic force by detonating a bomb offshore and allowing the Japanese to witness its

---

* Seventy-two years later, it continues to resonate as we contemplate the implications of a nuclear-capable North Korea, a rogue nation that claims to have developed a hydrogen bomb.

destructive power, but the powers that be ultimately decided to employ it directly against the enemy nation. It'd show that the Allies were serious.

The first bomb got Japan's attention; the second was the knock-out punch that prompted Japan to accept the terms of the Potsdam Agreement formulated by three major world powers—the United States, Great Britain, and Russia.

The Death Star as a Superweapon

In *A New Hope*, Grand Moff Tarkin, commanding the Death Star, opts to destroy a planet populated with billions of people. For purposes of such a demonstration, an uninhabitable planet would have been plenty of proof, but annihilating a populated planet in one attack sends a clear message to everyone else in the galaxy: surrender or die. With such a superweapon at its disposal, the Empire's leadership could dictate to all the worlds the unconditional terms of surrender. In such a case, a bad choice is preferable to no choice at all.

All of this speaks to why the ragtag rebel force was forced to go up against the Death Star. It was a David and Goliath encounter—and the only hope for free people throughout the galaxy. The Empire had the force, but the Force was ultimately with the Rebel Alliance.

As the leadership on the Death Star well knew, their orbiting weapon would, sooner or later, come under attack, because it was a highly prized military asset. So its designers planned for it. Defensively, the Death Star bristled with turbolasers and tractor beams; offensively, it could deploy several cruisers and many thousands of TIE fighters.

Given the devastating power of the main turbolaser, supplemented with a full array of defensive and offensive weapons, how was the seemingly impossible accomplished? (At this very late date, four decades after *A New Hope*, no spoiler alert is necessary. Everyone knows that the first Death Star was destroyed by the rebel forces. In fact, it's the germinal plot of *Rogue One: A Star Wars Story* (2016).

But in the wake of the Death Star's complete destruction, we must put ourselves in the situation of the Empire's leadership and military planners and look back at what happened, with the hope of preventing it from recurring—especially since a second Death Star was either under consideration or scheduled for construction.

The principal consideration is that a weapons platform like the Death Star is too valuable to lose; therefore, it must be protected *at all costs*. With that firmly in mind, there's much that the ranking officers—especially the admiral in command of the Death Star—might have done to prevent its destruction.

1. Assess vulnerabilities. Before the Death Star was fielded, the command staff should have studied the weapons platform in detail to determine any flaws. (See *A New Hope*, in which that vulnerability is exploited.) Infantrymen know that, when occupying terrain, they must study the terrain and provide interlocking fields of fire for individual and crew-served weapons. The lack of this on the Death Star allowed the enemy to traverse airspace that otherwise would have been denied.

2. Determine enemy capabilities. To properly plan for defensive and offensive operations, it is critical to know the enemy's capabilities. In this case, what military assets did the Rebel Alliance have? How many fighter aircraft, of what kind, and armed with what kind of munitions? Order of battle intelligence is a crucial component of the Empire's war planning.

During the course of the battle itself, the operations staff on board the Death Star correctly determined the fighter aircrafts' target and inferred the method of engagement—but by that time it was too late.

In Field Manual 30-19 (Department of the Army, June 1959), *Order of Battle Intelligence*, we learn that it refers to

the manner in which military forces are organized, disposed, maneuvered, and supplied.

Order of battle intelligence consists of accepted data regarding the composition, disposition, strength, training, tactics, logistics, combat efficiency, and miscellaneous data applicable to an enemy military force....

Order of battle intelligence is mandatory for commanders and staffs at all echelons in the preparation of accurate estimates of the situation and effective plans of action. It is an integral part of combat intelligence. It must be considered, together with other intelligence pertaining to the enemy, to the terrain, and to the weather; in determining enemy capabilities and probable courses of action [italics mine].

In the Battle of Yavin, nothing suggests that the Empire had conducted such a study, because the Empire did not implement a battle plan in a proactive manner, either defensively or offensively.

3. Take out command and control. Because fighter aircraft leave from and return to a home base—whether a mobile platform like an aircraft carrier or a geographically fixed location such as an air base—its destruction is paramount. The Empire failed to target the remote Rebel Alliance base prior to the Alliance deployment of a fighter wing (fighters and bombers). Had it done so, it would have destroyed C & C and significantly handicapped the rebel fighters long before the air battle was engaged.

We see the advantage of preemptive strikes. When the Japanese attacked Pearl Harbor, in 1941, they wisely planned on bombing and strafing U.S. fighter planes on the ground, to prevent them from engaging in the air battle. Even though a few US planes took to the air, most of them, conveniently colocated, were methodically destroyed in place.

Destroying the remote weapons platform or air base and its assets accomplishes several objectives. First, air combat, which is obviously a chaotic environment, becomes even more so when the ground-based headquarters cannot monitor the battle and provide guidance or further assistance. In essence, the pilots are on their own. Second, it denies the pilots a safe home port after the battle. And finally, it denies air reinforcements and degrades the ability of the fighting force to reconstitute and initiate a subsequent (second-wave) attack.

Deploy as a Battle Group

By far, the Empire's biggest mistake was to deploy the Death Star, a major weapons system, by itself. Instead, it should have gone into battle as the nucleus of a battle group, like a modern U.S. nuclear-powered aircraft carrier. By looking at the construction, cost, manning, and operational life of an aircraft carrier enables us to understand why the loss of a Death Star is, in every way, catastrophic.

The U.S. Navy's newest aircraft carrier is the *USS Gerald R. Ford*, built by Newport News Shipbuilding in Newport News, Virginia. (This is, in fact, our sole source for "flattops.") Disregarding the research and development cost, the unit cost of the aircraft carrier itself is approximately $13 billion. It takes ten years to build a modern carrier, which is a floating city populated by 2,600 military personnel. With scheduled upgrades in the future, the carrier is expected to have an operational life of ninety years. In other words, it's expensive and it's a long-term investment.

Used for power projection, a carrier's presence anywhere in the world reassures allies and strikes fear in our enemies. The aircraft carrier can launch forty fighter aircraft, supplemented by support aircraft. It has Aegis missiles capable of intercepting and knocking out the enemy's short-range ballistic missiles. The carrier is capable of defending itself, but it is further protected by a ring of complementary warships and a nuclear-powered submarine.

The U.S. Navy currently has ten flattops, each representing a significant investment of time, money, and, most valuable of all, manpower. As retired Navy captain Jerry Hendrix told *Newsweek* (February 16, 2016):

> The loss of an aircraft carrier, with images of a thousand American dead, or just having it disabled, with all its airplanes and radars knocked out and huge gaping holes in it, is such a heavy political

blow that we probably wouldn't risk it unless it was for the actual defense of the continental United States. . . . So we've created an asset that we cannot afford to lose because it's such an iconic symbol of American power that to have that symbol damaged or destroyed would undermine the legitimacy of America's role in the world. . . . [It's] the calculus that no one in uniform will talk to you about.

It's certainly too awful to contemplate, which is why the aircraft carrier does not steam into battle by itself. To do so would make it unnecessarily vulnerable, even with its sophisticated defensive array of radar and weaponry.

Of course, defending it becomes complicated because it must be defensible against attack by all comers, whether by air, land, or sea (both on and below the waterline). Moreover, its defense must be projected as far out as possible, to keep the enemy at bay. You don't want the enemy to get close to the aircraft carrier under any circumstances. As Loren B. Thompson pointed out in *National Interest* (August 11, 2016): "Putting 5,000 sailors and six dozen high-performance aircraft on a $10 billion warship creates what military experts refer to as a very 'lucrative' target. Taking one out would be a big achievement for America's enemies, and a big setback for America's military."

The U.S. Navy, therefore, sends out its carriers well protected, cocooned by an accompanying battle group, configured as necessary for the mission. The group may include, among other things, a missile cruiser, two guided missile destroyers, an attack submarine, and a supply ship.

Just as the U.S. Navy's aircraft carriers sally forth into combat with plenty of protection, the first Death Star should have been similarly protected, but it was not. The equivalent of a U.S. Navy destroyer in the *Star Wars* universe is a wedge-shaped Star Destroyer. When the Death Star was deployed, it should have been accompanied by a fleet of Star Destroyers positioned to give it 360-degree protection from enemy vessels. Supplemented by the turbolasers on the Death Star, the Star Destroyers would prevent any large-scale attack. Moreover, the short-range TIE fighters, when deployed, could dogfight small enemy aircraft, notably the X-wing and Y-wing starfighters.

But because those assets weren't deployed in full force, the Death Star was essentially unprotected during the Battle of Yavin. In fact, had it not been for Darth Vader deciding to lead a three-ship formation of TIE fighters to dogfight the rebels' Starfighters, there would have been *no* Empire fighter aircraft deployed during the battle to attack the rebel fighters and bombers making their trench runs. Instead of taking the battle to the starfighters, engaging them offensively, the Empire chose to fight a defensive battle.

Defense in Depth

The Death Star should have been protected with concentric rings of defense to keep the enemy from getting close. It should enjoy air superiority in any battle and be able to attrite enemy aircraft, beginning at the farthest point of engagement, so that even if the rebels get within striking range, their numbers are reduced to a handful.

The outermost ring (number four) should be defensive in nature, an early warning system to identify the number and composition of enemy aircraft and alert the command. This will determine the Empire's method of engagement: Star Destroyers, TIE fighters, or a combination of both?

The next ring (number three), inside number four, should be Star Destroyers.

The next ring (number two) should be turbolasers, though these should be better designed for firing upon small and large enemy ships alike.

The final ring (number one) should be TIE fighters, for dogfighting.

Such an arrangement would have maximized the Death Star's chances of survival in any engagement. After all, no price can be too high to protect the Death Star. Even if a large number of its air assets were destroyed in the process, it would be justified in the end by the survival of the battle station, the loss of which would be equivalent to the loss of not just one U.S. Navy aircraft carrier but, in fact, the loss of the entire U.S. fleet of ten carriers—an unimaginable and, over time, an unsustainable loss.

In short, there's no way the Empire should lose an air battle, given its deployable assets.

War-Gaming

Short of combat itself, the best way to train for war is to war-game. The working philosophy is simply stated: train as you fight. The idea is to play war as realistically as possible, in a field environment, with calibrated safety constraints. War-gaming is the training tool that keeps the edge of the blade sharp. All the military services engage in war-gaming at every level. It's a learning experience, and its benefits are that it will enhance combat efficiency and effectiveness, and ultimately reduce casualties in combat.

When I was a newly minted second lieutenant stationed at Fort Riley, Kansas, the home of the 1st Infantry Division, we often had division-wide exercises that brought into play all of our combat assets. The combined arms exercise, which included air support from air force bases, gave us a taste of what to expect when the bullets began to fly.

We all learned a lot about what worked and what didn't in terms of field operations, and we were reminded how easy it is for things to go wrong in the fog of war. We had to keep our combat edge sharp because half of our unit was then permanently stationed in Germany, in case the Russian bear decided to lumber across the Fulda Gap—a real concern during the Cold War.

Today, the US Army trains brigade-size units at Fort Irwin, at its National Training Center, set in desert terrain. The resident "bad guys" have home field advantage and know every nook and cranny of the terrain. Visiting units, of course, have no such advantage. But the resultant force-on-force engagement will teach commanders on both sides and at every level a lot about what went right, what went wrong, and what lessons learned can be applied to future operations—the takeaway.

Similarly, when I was a ground liaison officer attached to an air force fighter wing of F-16s, one planned mission included flying the entire wing halfway across the country, refueling with air tankers, and dogfighting F-15s over Washington state. The actual time in the cockpit would have been eight hours, but how else can pilots hone their combat flying skills?

As any pilot will tell you, time spent in the cockpit is time well spent, and they can never get enough of it. During World War II, for instance, when fuel was at a premium, the Imperial Japanese Navy cut flight time for new pilots to a bare minimum, because they were hoarding fuel for the expected U.S. land invasion. As a result, U.S. pilots, with better training and more time in the cockpit, easily shot down the novice pilots.

All of which brings us to the Empire and the Death Star. We don't know what, if any, war-gaming the Empire scheduled for those deployed on the Death Star itself, but the lack of training, in combination with poor leadership at the highest levels, doomed the terror weapon.

War-gaming is the time to test battle plans, to play out different scenarios, to see what works best, what's not working, and what to correct for future operations. Lessons learned can then be incorporated into future battle strategies.

The starfighters' attack on the Death Star recalls the Japanese attack on Pearl Harbor, which was a scenario Americans had never envisioned. As a result, the United States was caught completely by surprise, with extensive damage to the berthed Pacific Fleet and significant loss of life.

The root cause of the destruction of the Death Star was not the flight skills of the X-wing fighters, or their fighting spirit, but the lack of planning at the highest levels. The Death Star's operations staff had failed to properly study the enemy capabilities and therefore underestimated its opponent. Moreover, the staff failed to anticipate possible enemy actions. The cumulative end result was that the Death Star ironically lived up to its name.

The Ground Battle of Hoth

Reference: *Star Wars V: The Empire Strikes Back*

What is the mission? In any military engagement, that is the key question. In the ground battle of Hoth, there were two missions for the Empire. The Imperial Army was tasked with destroying two critical pieces of equipment: a force field generator and an ion cannon, while the Imperial Navy was tasked with preventing rebel spaceships from escaping the planet.

The former was successfully completed, albeit in an inefficient manner; the latter was an unmitigated disaster.

After studying the battle, though, what struck me most was the poor use of combined arms, which bears discussion. As defined by the U.S. Army,

> Combined Arms are the appropriate combinations of infantry, mobile protected firepower, offensive and defensive fires, engineers, Army aviation, and joint capabilities. It is the application of these combinations in unified action that allows us to defeat enemy ground forces; to seize, occupy, and defend land areas; and to achieve physical, temporal, and psychological advantages over the enemy. By synchronizing combined arms and applying them simultaneously, commanders can achieve a greater effect than if each element was used separately or sequentially.*

---

* "Maneuver Self Study Program: Combined Arms Operations," benning.army.mil.

Frankly, the Empire's missions were textbook, and not difficult. Let's look at them separately.

The Rebel Alliance's ground troops were positioned in trenches supplemented by dismounted infantry and supported by low-level aircraft. Heavy weapons supplemented their small arms fire capability. The goal was to fight a delaying action, to buy time for an evacuation of personnel and fighter aircraft.

The Empire, in its ground attack, relied on slow-moving, large All Terrain Armored Transports.

On the face of it, because the Empire successfully overwhelmed the Rebel Alliance ground troops, it would seem that they won the battle and thus any further discussion is moot. However effective, the plan was not efficient, resulting in the needless loss of equipment and troops.

In my opinion, the operations staff on the Death Star erred by planning a ground assault when, in fact, they knew the Rebel Alliance could only fight a delaying action. In terms of accomplishing the mission—knocking out a power generator and a cannon—the Empire's optimum tactic would have been to bypass the ground troops completely and destroy the fixed targets with organic air assets (TIE fighters), while simultaneously landing a large force to take control of the rebel base.

Instead of an air attack, the Empire deployed slow-moving, ponderous AT-ATs and dismounted troops to engage the rebel ground forces, which was not necessary to the Empire's accomplishment of the ground mission. That error was compounded by not providing close air support. The AT-ATs were deployed unprotected, when they needed TIE fighters for air cover, with the result that two of five AT-ATs were destroyed by rebel aircraft.

Ultimately, the Empire's mission took too long to execute and suffered needless casualties and the loss of major weapons systems; as a result, the Imperial Army handicapped the Imperial Navy's mission, because it was unable to stop rebel ships from escaping the planet to safety.

Like the Imperial Army, the Imperial Navy was also at fault.

It had a simple task: to implement a standard blockade to prevent rebel ships from leaving the planet. But the Imperial Navy failed to use its Star Destroyers and TIE fighters in an effective manner. The Destroyers did not contain the fleeing ships, nor were they channeled into a kill zone; moreover, there were an insufficient number of TIE fighters deployed to engage the Rebel Alliance starfighters. Consequently, the Rebel Alliance was able to reconstitute after the battle for a subsequent battle—the air attack on the second Death Star: the battles at Yavin and at Hoth were instrumental in allowing the Rebel Alliance to muster all of its airpower for a subsequent battle that decisively put an effective end to the Galactic Empire.

To win the war, one must first win its battles. The small Rebel Alliance was vastly outnumbered and outgunned by the Empire, but in the end size mattered not. The Alliance prevailed militarily because the Empire failed to plan, and thus planned to fail.

Note: In *Star Wars: The Last Jedi* (2017), TIE fighters were gainfully employed as close air support, attriting the Resistance in their aged fighters.

The Battle of Endor

Reference: *Star Wars VI: Return of the Jedi*

Bigger is better.

At least that was the thinking behind the second Death Star, with construction that began soon after the first one was destroyed. Bigger in every way—more weapons and more fighter aircraft—the operational but partially built second Death Star was a calculated risk. Though the Empire quickly recovered from the destruction of the first Death Star, the second iteration of the battle station required significantly more investments of time, money, and effort.

In my opinion, the building of a second Death Star was a strategic mistake that doomed the Empire. Let's look at the reasons why.

1. Even after the first Death Star was destroyed, the Empire decided to go all in and build a second one. Though it's an even more powerful superweapon than its predecessor, the second Death Star suffered from the same fatal flaw as the first one, because it was needlessly vulnerable.

2. The time, money, and energy spent in constructing, manning, and outfitting the second Death Star would have been better spent in dispersing the Empire's assets throughout the galaxy, on various planets, to minimize their vulnerability. Effective command and control would have linked all the remote bases in a single unbreakable chain.

3. Colocating the top leadership of the Galactic Empire—the emperor and his second-in-command, Darth Vader—in one place near the Death Star meant that once they died, the Empire was lead-

erless. The failure of the Emperor to establish a chain of command beyond himself and Vader was a major blunder.

4. Compounding the loss of its top leadership, the loss of men, material, and equipment was a significant blow to the Empire's resources that it couldn't afford—especially after the loss of its first Death Star.

5. Reconstitution was impossible. The loss of all hands on the second Death Star, and the loss of the Empire's key leadership, resulted in organizational chaos. The resulting confusion, complicated by infighting, allowed the Rebel Alliance to take advantage of the situation and emerge victorious, as various factions within the Empire fought, and failed, to seize control.

Summary

Had the Empire conserved its resources and dispersed its forces to become less vulnerable to attack from the Rebel Alliance, it could have methodically and systematically attacked the rebels in preemptive strikes throughout the galaxy, using a fleet of Star Destroyers, until the Alliance ceased to be a militarily viable force.

But even if the Empire had not dispersed its assets, firmly establishing a chain of command that extended below the emperor and Darth Vader would have facilitated the reconstitution of the remaining military assets, which was still large enough in manpower strength and well equipped enough with hardware to continue the war against the Alliance.

The Rebel Alliance also was not without fault in this battle, because it relied too heavily on human intelligence, which turned out to be flawed. It significantly complicated the execution of what was already a complex ground-air mission. On the ground, the goal was to destroy the force field generator protecting the second Death Star; then, in the air, the mission was to attack and destroy the Death Star.

Unfortunately, the Rebel Alliance made plans based on two faulty assumptions: that the Death Star was not operational and that it was otherwise defenseless.

As it turned out, the Rebel Alliance air assets were able to recover, once they realized the tactical situation, and they continued to press the attack. But if they had known the facts, it would have required a different attack strategy. How do you assault and destroy a well-protected, operational Death Star?

Strategic Mistakes

The problem with making strategic mistakes is that it's screwing up on a big scale, with dire consequences for the future.

The United States eventually learned that the Vietnam War was a strategic mistake—just like its invasion of Iraq. Looking back with the benefit of hindsight, James Mattis, a retired four-star Marine Corps general and the current secretary of defense, spoke at an ASIS International conference in Anaheim, California, and said, "We will probably look back on the invasion of Iraq as a mistake, a strategic mistake."

Because of that mistake, the United States is now embroiled in the longest-running war in its history, at great financial cost, with no end in sight. No one, even at the highest levels, is currently talking about an exit strategy because no one can offer a viable solution. It's Vietnam all over again. In the end, at some distant point, the United States will simply pick up and walk away, leaving the vulnerable Afghans to their doomed fate.

The Galactic Empire can be likened to the Roman Empire, which ultimately fell. Both overextended their reach.

The Roman Empire fell due to a confluence of reasons, but one of them stands out, recalling the single greatest mistake of the Galactic Empire. As Evan Andrews points out:

> At its height, the Roman Empire stretched from the Atlantic Ocean all the way to the Euphrates River in the Middle East, but its gran-

deur may have also been its downfall. With such a vast territory to govern, the Empire faced an administrative and logistical nightmare. Even with their excellent road systems, the Romans were unable to communicate quickly or effectively enough to manage their holdings.*

The Galactic Empire suffered from the same problem: as its forces were dispersed over great distances, effective command and control became paramount. Relying on an easily severed chain of command and consolidating its major military resources in a second Death Star instead of dispersing forces, the Empire had stretched its forces too thin—complicated, of course, by ineffective C & C. In short, the Galactic Empire had overreached. And, as then-Princess Leia told Grand Moff Tarkin in *A New Hope*, "The more you tighten your grip, the more star systems will slip through your fingers."

Her words ultimately proved to be prophetic.

---

* Evan Andrews, "8 Reasons Why Rome Fell," history.com, January 14, 2014.

A Skirmish on Jedha

Reference: *Rogue One: A Star Wars Story*

By way of background information relevant to this discussion, the executive officer of Service Battery in a field artillery battalion is the battalion ammunition officer. If it's a nuclear-capable unit, its battery commander is the battalion courier officer, in charge of transporting—by air or ground convoy—nuclear artillery rounds to firing batteries.*

I've had both jobs, so when I saw *Rogue One*, in which an invaluable cargo is being transported in a ground convoy, I paid close attention to how it played out, and I put myself in the driver's seat of the transport tank.

Before going into details, let me say this up front: I would not conduct a ground convoy through a city teeming with insurgents, unless I had absolutely no other choice. I'd employ an air convoy or, if going by ground, I'd bypass the city completely. But sometimes those options are not possible, and a bad route is the only path.

I am reminded of what Chinese general Sun Tzu said, in *The Art of War*, about military operations in urban terrain: "The worst policy is to attack cities." It was true in 500 BCE, when he was the commanding general, and it's true today. In-street fighting significantly handicaps fire and maneuvering capability.

In "The Battle of Fallujah: Lessons Learned on Military Operations on Urbanized Terrain (MOUT) in the 21st Century," Tao-Hung Chang writes, "The concept of fighting in cities did not receive much

---

* The Field Artillery ended its nuclear mission in 1991.

attention from the major military powers until the middle of World War II." He cites the Allies' ineffective tactics when occupying cities: "rapid movement with massed firepower in an effort to shock and defend and in the hope that the enemy would either be killed or would surrender. However, this tactic would only have worked against a disorganized enemy. Throughout World War II, only well-coordinated combined arms were able to conquer well-fortified cities like Berlin."

The tactic of shock and awe is not enough, especially against a determined, organized, and well-equipped insurgency fighting on its own turf. The opposition clearly has the home field advantage—and knows it.

In this skirmish, the insurgents ambushed the Empire's single vehicle convoy, consisting of a transport tank with dismounted infantry.

The skirmish highlights the inherent dangers of military operations in urban terrain. It recalls a similar battle, between the Chechen resistance and the Russian Army, on December 31, 1994, which the Chechens won.

Tao-Hung Chang writes:

There was no initial Chechen resistance when the Russians entered the city at noon.... The Chechens first destroyed the lead and rear vehicles to block the street with wreckage. The Russian armor column [was] trapped in the street and hopeless as the tanks could not point their guns high or low enough to fire at the Chechens, and the infantry fighting vehicles (IFVs) and the armored personnel carriers (APCs) failed to support the tanks. By the time the brigade managed to break away from the city, the Russians had lost almost 800 men, 20 out of their 26 tanks, and 102 of their 120 other armored vehicles.

A quick study of the Jedha skirmish reveals numerous tactical errors, which led to the needless loss of its cargo. Had I been the convoy commander, I would have taken the following actions:

1. Bypass the city in an air convoy or a ground convoy. Because of the risks involved in transporting valuable cargo in a city teeming with insurgents, simply bypass it. If that's not possible, delay the mission until circumstances are more favorable. If the need is immediate and no other alternative is possible, conduct a ground convoy with adequate forces while anticipating an ambush.

2. Keep all personnel buttoned up inside their armored vehicles. Do not needlessly expose personnel in the open.

3. The tank commander should be in charge of the convoy itself, and the senior ground officer or NCO present should be in command of the dismounted troops. Tasked with both jobs, the tank commander was overwhelmed.

4. The convoy should be accompanied by at least one fighting vehicle or personnel carrier, and preferably two, to suppress the insurgents.

5. The dismounted stormtroopers should have been better armed. They had conventional blaster rifles and no way to effectively nullify the snipers in the buildings. The stormtroopers should have had weapons like a shoulder-launched multipurpose assault weapon to clear out rooms at a distance and from the street.

6. Air assets should be overhead to suppress insurgency fire coming from the rooftops.

7. Employ a forward security element. As *Tactical Convoy Ops* (March 2005) states, "Its purpose is to move ahead of the convoy as a reconnaissance element providing commanding officers with route information, as well as current enemy and civilian situational awareness."

8. Have a vehicle recovery plan in place, on the assumption that the cargo-carrying vehicle might be disabled.

9. Have medevac (medical evacuation) capability to tend to the wounded.

10. Prior to the mission, rehearse using a mock-up of the route of the march, to identify potential roadblocks and ingress/egress routes.

11. Ensure that secure communications link up ground and air assets.

12. After the mission, conduct an after action review. Learn from experience and pass the lessons learned along through the chain of command.

The After Action Review

It's axiomatic that no soldier can live long enough to learn all that he would want to know about his trade, which is why the military employs a tool to pass on its collective wisdom: the after action review. For detailed information about the review, consult *A Leader's Guide to After-Action Reviews* (Training Circular 25-20, Department of the Army, September 30, 1993).

Its format is simple but flexible enough to encompass a great deal of information. It is addressed to the primary person in the chain of command, and also is distributed to interested individuals. Its format follows:

Date: [prepared/submitted]
Subject: After Action Review/Report-[Event Title]
From: [Person preparing report]
To: [Primary Person in Chain of Command]
CC: [Courtesy copy to interested individuals]

1. PURPOSE
Establish the facts.
What was the mission description?
What did we set out to do?
What were the key tasks involved?
Define acceptable standards for success.

2. EXECUTIVE SUMMARY

Continue to establish the facts.

What actually happened?

Indicate relevant times and dates.

Cause and effect: Why did it happen? Focus on the *what*, not the *who*.

3. LESSONS LEARNED

What can we do better next time?

Focus on items you can fix, and try to suggest solutions to identify problems.

If you don't have a solution, that's OK, but you should try to provide some options.

Identify successes to maintain those strengths.

4. COMMENTS

This includes good and bad performance, and questionable actions. It also may include suggested changes in policy or, really, anything that the submitter wants the chain of command to know about. However, touchy or dangerous subjects, such as potential disciplinary items, are usually handled personally and not in a report like this that has general distribution.

5. ACTION ITEMS

Develop a list of what actions to take to fix specific needs.

Outline timelines and responsibilities.

Appendix

Who participated? List agencies/individuals.

Basic Battle Analysis*

Study Guide for Battle Analysis

General

The U.S. Army Command and General Staff College developed the battle analysis methodology to help its students structure their studies of battles and campaigns. The format can be easily applied by any military professional seeking insight from historical battles and campaigns to help deepen his/her understanding of warfare and the profession of arms.

The battle analysis methodology is a process for systematic study of a battle or campaign. This process takes the form of a checklist that ensures completeness in examining the critical aspects of the chosen subject.

There are two forms of the battle analysis: basic and advanced. Both utilize the same four steps, but the advanced is more complex and detailed. Also, the advanced analyzes the strategic influences on the battle.†

Format

The checklist is divided into four steps, each of which builds on the previous one(s) to provide a logical order for the study. The four steps are:

---

* Adapted from United States Army Combined Arms Center, "Basic Battle Analysis: Kasserine Pass (Student Handout 1)," usacac.army.mil/CAC2/CSI/docs/CombatStudiesInstitute-200804010031-DOC.doc.
† Note: Because this book is for the lay reader, the original checklist has been adapted to a more readable format.

1. Define the subject/evaluate the sources.
2. Review the setting (set the stage).
3. Describe the action.
4. Assess the significance of the action.

In the first step, you decide what battle you are going to study. In the next two, you gather the information necessary for a thorough and balanced study, and organize it in a logical manner to facilitate analysis. In the last step, you analyze the information to derive "lessons learned."

Purpose

The battle analysis methodology is a guide to help ensure that important aspects of the study of a historical battle or campaign are not forgotten. It is not a rigid checklist that must be followed to the letter. You do not have to use every part of it in your study, but all of the elements of battle analysis should be considered. Do not let the flow of your study be disrupted by the format's order.

Annotated Basic Battle Analysis Methodology

Define the Subject/Evaluate the Sources

Just like a military operation, a successful study of military history requires a clear, obtainable objective. The battle analysis format begins with the definition of the study.

1. *Define the battle to be analyzed.* Where did it take place? Who were the principal adversaries? When did the battle occur? This will become your introduction.

2. *Determine the research sources.* Once you have chosen a subject, decide what sources you will need to make a systematic and balanced study. Books and articles will make up the majority of your sources, but other media—such as video, audio, and electronic ones—can also contribute to the study.

Look for a variety of sources to get a balanced account of the battle. Memoirs, biographies, operational histories, and institutional histories should all be consulted for information on your subject. Do not overlook general histories, which can help provide the strategic setting. Articles from professional military publications and historical journals can be excellent sources of information. Documentaries containing film footage of actual events or interviews with people who took part in a battle can add to your understanding of the events. Transcribed oral history interviews with battle participants may also be available. In addition, check the internet for electronic documents on more recent military operations.

3. *Evaluate the research sources.* Finding good sources to support your study is not easy, despite the large volume of published material. As you gather the research material, evaluate each in terms of its content and bias. Determine what information the source can give you. Is it relevant to your subject? Will it help you complete your study? Decide to what extent the author is subjective or objective in his/her work. Is there a clear bias? If so, what is it? Does the bias make a difference in your use of the work?

Review the Setting (Set the Stage)

This portion of the battle analysis format establishes the setting for the study. You must have a good understanding of the strategic, operational, and tactical situations before you can analyze the battle. The level of detail in this portion of the battle analysis will depend on the purpose of the study and the audience for which it is intended. If the causes of the war and the opponents are well known, there is little reason to go into great detail.

Strategic/Operational Overview

1. Identify the war this battle is fought in, to include the time frame and locations.
2. Identify the war aims of the principal adversaries.
3. Identify and briefly describe the campaign this battle was part of, if any. What were the events that led to this battle being fought at this location with these units?

Study the Area of Operations

What was the weather like in the area of operations? How did it affect the operation? Use observation and fields of fire, avenues of approach, key terrain, obstacles, and cover and concealment factors to describe the terrain in the area of operations. What advantages did it give to the attackers or to the defenders?

Compare the Principal Antagonists (Operational/Tactical)

In many ways, this is the heart of the study—analyzing the opposing forces. Describe and analyze the forces involved in the following terms:

1. *Size and composition.* What were the principal combat and supporting units involved in the operation? What were their numerical strengths in terms of troops and key weapon systems? How were they organized?
2. *Technology.* What were the battlefield technologies, such as tanks, small arms, close support aircraft, etc., of the opposing forces? Did one side have a technological advantage over the other?
3. *Logistical systems.* How did logistics affect the battle? Did one side have an advantage in available supplies or transportation?
4. *Command, control, and communications.* What kind of command, control, and communications systems did the opposing forces employ? Were these systems under centralized or decentralized control? How were the staffs organized, and how effective were they?
5. *Intelligence.* What intelligence assets were available to the opposing forces? How well were they used? What were the major sources of intelligence? Did one side have an advantage over the other in intelligence resources?
6. *Doctrine and training.* What was the tactical doctrine of the opposing forces, and how did they use it? What was the level of training in the opposing forces? Were some

troops experienced veterans, some not, and some in between?

7. *Condition and morale.* What was the morale of the troops before the fighting, and did it change after the fighting began? How long had the troops been committed, and how did weather and terrain affect them? Did specific leaders affect morale?

8. *Leadership.* Who were the leaders, and how effective had they been in past actions? How were they trained, and what was their level of experience?

State the Mission and Describe the Initial Disposition of the Opposing Forces

What were the objectives? What plans were developed to achieve the objectives? Were there other options—such as attacking, defending, or withdrawing—open to the two sides? Were those options feasible? What were the locations of the units of the opposing forces? How were the units deployed tactically?

Describe the Action

This part of battle analysis—describing the battle itself—is what most people consider to be real military history. By following the format, you will study the battle chronologically. Do not let this approach disrupt your study of the battle. If you need to skip a phase in order to examine a combat functional area—such as maneuver, logistics, etc.—because it is more important to your overall objective, then do so.

1. *Describe the opening moves of the battle.* Examine the initial actions by the opposing forces. Did one side gain an advantage over the other in the opening phase of the battle?

2. *Detail the major phases/key events.* Establish a chronology for the battle while examining the actions after the opening moves. Look for key events or decisions that turned the battle toward one side or the other.

3. *State the outcome.* Who won the battle? Did either side achieve its objectives? Did the battle provide an advantage to the winning side, and what was it? Did the battle have any long-term effects, and what were they?

Assess the Significance of the Action

This is the most important step of the battle analysis process. With this step, you are turning "combat information" in the form of the historical facts of the battle into finished analysis rendered as "lessons learned."

1. *Relate causes to effects.* In trying to distill lessons from the study of any battle, it is important to look at why something happened. To do so you will look at the outcome and what caused it. Look for those essential elements of the victory or defeat.

2. *Establish military "lessons learned."* Lessons from the past that are still relevant today are the end product of the battle analysis process. The insights, or "constants of war," gained from the study should transcend time, place, and doctrine. You can use one of the following fundamentals (or another) to focus analysis of military operations and help find these constants. These fundamentals are defined in FM 3-0, *Operations*, and include "principles of war," "threads of continuity," and "warfighting functions."

Suggested Format for Basic Battle Analysis Paper or Briefing

Define the Subject/Evaluate the Sources

Define the battle to be analyzed (where, who, when).

Review the Setting (Set the Stage)

Provide a strategic/operational overview. Study the area of operations, including weather and terrain. Compare the principal antagonists (operational/tactical), focusing on size and composition;

technology; doctrine and training; logistics systems; intelligence; condition and morale; command, control, and communications; and leadership. Finally, state the mission and describe initial disposition of the opposing forces.

Describe the Action

Describe the opening moves of the battle, detail the major phases/key events, and state the outcome.

Assess the Significance of the Action

Relate causes to effects, and establish military "lessons learned."

Coda: "We Have Hope."

After *The Phantom Menace* and *Attack of the Clones*, fans had good reasons to be concerned with the direction the *Star Wars* franchise had taken. Though cinematically beautiful, with stunning special effects, both films were financial but not critical successes—neither satisfied fans and critics. On Rotten Tomatoes (rottentomatoes.com), *The Phantom Menace* earned a Tomatometer rating of 55 percent. The critics' consensus was: "Burdened by exposition and populated with stock characters, *The Phantom Menace* gets the *Star Wars* prequels off to a bumpy—albeit visually dazzling—start."

Three years later, *Attack of the Clones* was released, and although it did better, with a Tomatometer rating of 65 percent, the critics' consensus was that the film "benefits from an increased emphasis on thrilling action, although they're once again undercut by ponderous plot points and underdeveloped characters."

Star Wars fans despaired, and the lines of demarcation were drawn: older fans preferred the original trilogy because of its emphasis on story, but younger fans preferred the newer trilogy because of its special effects and eye candy. But what both wanted was a fusion of the two, the best of both possible worlds—story and spectacle.

After *Clones*, fans had to endure a wait of thirteen long years before another *Star Wars* movie came out. Directed by J. J. Abrams, who successfully rebooted the flagging *Star Trek* franchise, *The*

Force Awakens—its title an unintentional reference to the film franchise's long hibernation—was a cause for celebration (fans loved it, giving it a 92 percent Tomatometer rating), for cerebration (there was a lot to think about in terms of the characters and the saga itself), and for "sellabration" (merchandising dominated the shelves that Christmas).

A franchise that many had thought had fizzled out suddenly was reenergized when Disney took the helm and rejuvenated it.

On Rotten Tomatoes, the critics' consensus on *The Force Awakens* was: "Packed with action and populated by both familiar faces and fresh blood, [it] successfully recalls the series' former glory while injecting it with renewed energy."

The Force was strong with this one, and as a result, Disney had planned annual releases of *Star Wars* movies on two tracks: the main narrative story and side stories (back stories) to flesh out the principal characters.

Rogue One set the tone for the stand-alone "story" films to come. It earned an 85 percent Tomatometer rating. The critics' consensus was that it "draws deep on *Star Wars* mythology while breaking new narrative and aesthetic ground . . . suggesting a bright blockbuster future for the franchise."

Disney's $4.05 billion investment proved to be a sound one. A franchise that began forty years ago, in 1977, still had strong legs, and *Rogue One* proved why. A realistic, adult-oriented film, it draws deeply from the core values that the franchise has always celebrated. At its heart, the films—even the less successful ones—are, as *Entertainment Weekly* concluded, uplifting: "The space battles may be fake, but the sense of courage, hope, and heroism that the *Star Wars* movies have always delivered is undoubtedly real."*

Giving credit where it's due, the reality of *Rogue One* can be found in its grittiness, which recalls the battered, unwashed look and feel of the *Star Wars* universe from the original film, as well as its moral complexity: bad people die, but so do good people. No

* Anthony Breznican, "The Empire Will Rise," *Entertainment Weekly*, December 2, 2016.

one is exempt, not even the heroes. (In fact, the body count in this movie rivals that of anything from George R. R. Martin's *Game of Thrones*. Well, close enough.)*

The beating heart of *Rogue One* is its protagonist, Jyn Erso, whose name—perhaps intentionally—is a historical nod to another reluctant female warrior, Joan of Arc. Jyn, at a council meeting at the Rebel Alliance headquarters on Yavin 4, passionately argues her case that *now* is the time to strike, because to delay means the Galactic Empire is closer to its goal of ruling the galaxy.

But a spark is all that's needed to start a fire, and when fanned, the fire can become a conflagration. Jyn provides that spark.

Just one of many nondescript people eking out a subsistence existence, Jyn becomes part of something bigger—much bigger—than herself, and in doing so, she finds that her life, finally, has meaning. Her father would have been proud.

Infused with a renewed hope, Jyn sets out on a mission with a slim chance of success. *Hope.* Sometimes it's all you have.

A young woman, Jyn will not see the rest of her life unfold. Instead, she sits quietly on a beach and stoically accepts her fate.

Jyn Erso and her commando team gave all; they selflessly gave their lives for a cause bigger than themselves, reminding us that, as Michel de Montaigne, a French Renaissance writer reminds us, "There are some defeats more triumphant than victories."

---

* No doubt George R. R. Martin's epic fantasy *Game of Thrones* contributed to this element of realism. In his books, no one is immune from the vicissitudes of war. Its frequent loss of life is realistic, and its use in *Rogue One* is instrumental in making it a better film.

Afterword

It All Started with a Droid:
The Film Future of *Star Wars*

> It's just a movie.
>
> —George Lucas

To *Star Wars* creator George Lucas's great surprise, his first *Star Wars* film, which made its debut in May 1977, far exceeded his every expectation: financially, critically, and in popularity. As Lucas told his close friend and fellow filmmaker Steven Spielberg, he had grossly underestimated its box office receipts. No wonder, then, that he was surprised when he saw a long line at a California theater, musing about what movie was so popular that it drew such a crowd—only to discover it was his own *Star Wars*.

That was the first sign that Lucas's operatic space fantasy would be successful, and go on to be a film phenomenon that has maintained its popularity for more than four decades.

Given the box office success of *The Force Awakens* (2015), *Rogue One* (2016), and *The Last Jedi* (2017), Disney need not worry about its investment in the *Star Wars* universe. The Force is strong with them, especially since the game plan is to release a new *Star Wars* movie annually, along with standalone films, until fans lose interest (not likely), humankind annihilates itself (possible), or the sun eventually burns out (inevitable, in five billion years)—whichever comes first.

From the beginning, it was clear that *Star Wars* was intended to be fun for the whole family, though in its early years women often complained, and rightly so, that it was overwhelmingly skewed to a male point of view. In recent years, however, that's changed; in fact, in the last two movies, it's the wondrous women who have taken center stage.* Both Rey (*The Force Awakens*) and Jyn Erso are the beating hearts of the movies, a trend that shows no signs of abating.

Clearly, the times they are a-changin'.

The other change is that, in recent years, the tone of *Star Wars* has become properly serious. I am hopeful that this means we won't see any more fart jokes involving large mammals near Jar Jar Binks, as seen in *The Phantom Menace*, or small, cutesy teddy bear–like critters who dance and sing the "Yub Nub" song after miraculously defeating a technologically superior force comprising a garrison full of "crack" stormtroopers. As Jar Jar remarked, "Icky, icky goo!"

Instead, in *The Force Awakens*, we see Rey, independent and wholly on her own, living a hardscrabble life of scavenging parts from a space relic, a Star Destroyer, which affords her a minimal living. We also see Jyn Erso, who is forcibly separated from her parents and raised by a family friend who later abandons her. Forced to live by her wits on the streets, Jyn's had too many run-ins with both the Rebel Alliance and the Empire.

Unlike the Battle of Endor, where we see one Ewok casualty and (apparently) no casualties on General Solo's strike team, *Rogue One*'s body count is numerous.

Happy endings are more appropriate for fairy tales and family films like *The Phantom Menace*, but don't necessarily expect to see any in the *Star Wars* future.† They will likely be darker, more realistic, and more satisfying, especially for adults who want more palatable cinematic fare.

---

* There's still room for improvement: the women are perennially young, beautiful, and kick-ass überwomen. What about older, normal-looking women who aren't martial arts experts? Don't they also exist?

† Longtime *Star Wars* fans remember the saccharine Christmas holiday specials centered on Ewoks and Wookies. Thankfully, those are history and we're not likely to see such unpalatable fare again.

The kiddies, though, are not out of the picture. Their new playground can be found at the Disney theme parks. Disneyland Resort is clearly for kids, including "Jedi Training: Trials of the Temple," at which "younglings [Jedi children in training] test their lightsaber-wielding skills against new and classic villains during this commanding stage show." (Afterward, they can feast on burgers and fries at the Galactic Grill, a "*Star Wars*–inspired quick-serve eatery.")*

Walt Disney World has similarly child-centered experiences to offer, but adults are always looking forward to more adult fare. At both parks, Disney is currently developing its "largest single themed land expansion ever. These new lands at Disneyland and Walt Disney World will transport guests to a whole new *Star Wars* planet, including an epic *Star Wars* adventure that puts you in the middle of a climactic battle between the First Order and the Resistance." The other theme park attraction will allow fans to "take the controls of . . . the *Millennium Falcon,* on a customized secret mission."†
(Count me in!)

As one fan commented on the Disney Parks blog, "I really enjoy that Disney is catering to a wider target market of their park goers, including the older crowd who watched the very first *Star Wars* movies, and for children of all ages."

In other words, the Disney theme parks have seen the light and, like their recent *Star Wars* movies, is embracing the darker side. *Star Wars* is no longer just for kids, and it's reflected in how Disney is handling the licensing. The Sideshow Toy (sideshowtoy.com) line is priced for adults, with a "premium format" Rey and BB-8 costing $724.98. And if you have very deep pockets, you can treat yourself to life-size action figures: R2-D2 for $7,450, Boba Fett for $8,495, a stormtrooper for $7,999.99, Yoda for $2,499, and, my favorite, Han Solo in carbonite for $7,499.

And for fans who literally want to be immersed in the *Star Wars*

* "Star Wars at Disneyland Resort," https://disneyland.disney.go.com/events-tours/disneyland/star-wars/.
† "Disney Parks Blog: *Star Wars*–Themed Lands Coming to Walt Disney World and Disneyland Resorts," disneyparks.disney.go.com.

universe, according to the official Disney Parks Blog, a *Star Wars*-inspired resort will be a "living adventure." As Bob Chapek, Chairman of Walt Disney Parks & Resorts explained, "From the second you arrive, you will become a part of a *Star Wars* story! You'll immediately become a citizen of the galaxy and experience all that entails, including dressing up in the proper attire. Once you leave Earth, you will discover a starship alive with characters, stories, and adventures that unfold all around you. It is 100% immersive. . . ."

The earlier *Star Wars* movies were obviously family fare. The first *Star Wars* movie was rated PG, which states, "Parental guidance suggested—some material may not be suitable for children," but *The Force Awakens* and *Rogue One* were both rated PG-13: "Parents strongly cautioned—some material may be inappropriate for children under 13."

When *Star Wars* serves up family fare with *Return of the Jedi*, *The Phantom Menace*, and *The Attack of the Clones*, we get a sanitized version of war, which is not likely to offend anyone. The good guys miraculously live on, suffering few (if any) casualties, whereas the bad guys suffer extensive casualties. All off screen, of course; we don't see the blood, the gore, the pain, and the aftermath of war, with broken rebel troopers and imperial stormtroopers who are seriously injured, mutilated, or suffering from post-traumatic stress disorder, to the point of committing suicide as a way of escaping their perpetual pain, as we have seen with today's young veterans returning from Iraq and Afghanistan.* As they say, war is hell.

Although *Star Wars* is by no means the equivalent of, say, HBO's *Game of Thrones*, in which nothing is left to the imagination—beheadings, wholesale killings, gore aplenty, and raw sex—the

---

* Numerous nonfiction books written by veterans have come out of both wars, many of them very good. But my favorite is the late Michael Herr's *Dispatches*, which gives you a unique glimpse into what the Vietnam war was like. Also, read an award-winning science fiction novel that I consider indispensable: *The Forever War* (St. Martins, 1974), by Joe Haldeman, who was a combat engineer during the Vietnam War.

more recent *Star Wars* movies strike the right balance between light and darkness.

Over the years, as George Lucas fielded complaints from hardcore fans whose criticisms ranged from the tedious (Who shot first: Greedo or Han Solo?) to the justified (Jar Jar Binks and the Ewoks have taken over the *Star Wars* universe), he constantly reminded us that, in the end, *Star Wars* shouldn't be taken so seriously. It ain't the Holy Bible, nor is it *Schindler's List*, *The Deer Hunter*, *Apocalypse Now*, or *Platoon*.

Disney's running the show now, though, and George Lucas has moved on, focused on his legacy and on constructing the Lucas Museum of Narrative Art, which will be built in Los Angeles's Exposition Park. We're told it will "celebrate the power of visual storytelling in a setting focused on narrative painting, illustration, photography, film, animation, and digital art."* It, too, is aimed more for adults than for the younger crowd. Taking and treating pop culture seriously, Lucas's museum will be a monument to George Lucas's Galactic Empire and Pop Culture Universe.

Walt Disney himself, commenting on his own sprawling empire, liked to remind everyone, "It all started with a mouse"—Mickey, of course. Similarly, George Lucas can say that it all started with a droid. But as Lucas has proven, the *Star Wars* universe, like the big bang, is constantly expanding, and in every direction, thanks to Disney's empire.

For *Star Wars* fans of all ages, that's all good news, and undeniable proof that the Force is not only still with us but also will be around for a very, very long time.

* lucasmuseum.org/museum.

· PART 6 ·

RESOURCES

BIBLIOGRAPHY

In writing this book, I have been inspired by, and have drawn heavily from, numerous books. As no book on *Star Wars*, official or unofficial, has provided a detailed, annotated bibliography, I am taking this opportunity to do so, because there's a galaxy of books and other material out there, and you should know where best to spend your time and money. In that spirit, I wanted to share some of my favorites, for those who want to learn more by digging deeper.

Official *Star Wars* Books

The Art of Star Wars: The Force Awakens, by Phil Szostak. Abrams, 2015. Hardback, 253 pages.
A treasure trove of unseen conceptual art, finished art, and storyboards, blueprints, etc., for the movie directed by J. J. Abrams.

The Cinema of George Lucas, by Marcus Hearn. Abrams, 2005. Hardback, 263 pages.
An excellent overview of Lucas as filmmaker, with numerous photos and artwork drawn from the Lucasfilm Archives. If you're interested in an illustrated, biographical look at Lucas's life and work, this is the place you should begin. It tells the whole story up to 2005, in an oversize format.

The Complete Star Wars Encyclopedia, by Stephen J. Sansweet, Pablo Hidalgo, Bob Vitas, and Daniel Wallace, with Chris Cassidy,

Mary Franklin, John Kushins. Del Rey, 2008. Three volumes, hardback, slipcased. For obvious reasons, not indexed.
As with any encyclopedia covering an ever-expanding field, this was outdated immediately upon publication. With photos and detailed text, this covers everything in the *Star Wars* universe through 2008. Sansweet points out:

> When the first *Star Wars Encyclopedia* was published in July 1998, it had a single name on the title page, was a hefty but reasonable 354 pages, and took me about a year of work to complete with a little help from my friends.
>
> How the galaxy has grown! And, of course, it continues to thrive with more stories, characters, vehicles, planets, battles, and phenomena being created every day. . . . Thus this totally rewritten book . . . catches up on a decade of new movies, animation, novels, comics, video games, role-playing and card games, online material, and just about anything else that is "official" and relevant to the saga.
>
> Like the first encyclopedia, the in-fantasy conceit of this one is that it has been compiled by some omniscient committee of historians and scholars taking a look back over tens of thousands of years of galactic history.

Dressing a Galaxy: The Costumes of Star Wars, by Trish Biggar. Insight Editions, 2005. Limited edition of 2,500 copies, 1,000 of which were signed by Biggar. An oversized book with gatefolds, booklets, fabric swatches, a DVD, and other collectibles. A Japanese silk sash (called an obi) wraps around the traycase.
This is the most elaborate, beautiful, and well-designed *Star Wars* book ever made. I cannot imagine there will ever be another book inspired by the film saga that matches it in imagination, execution, or physical presence. Long out of print, it's well worth your time searching for a copy. (Like *Sculpting a Galaxy*, its original retail price is $395.)

From Star Wars to Indiana Jones: The Best of the Lucasfilm Archives, by Mark Cotta Vaz and Shinji Hata. Chronicle Books, 208 pages.

At the end of *Raiders of the Lost Ark*, our hero, Indiana Jones, interrogates FBI agents who won't say what they've done with the Ark of the Covenant. As it turns out, it's crated up, stenciled for ID purposes, and put in a massive warehouse, where it will sit and gather dust, along with countless other crates.

This book gives us a behind-the-warehouse look at the models, creatures, props, costumes, matte paintings, and artwork from the Lucasfilm Archives, which rivals the size of the FBI's secret warehouse in *Raiders*.

As Deborah Fine, director of research and archives, wrote in a foreword to the book,

> The archives of Lucasfilm came into being out of practical necessity. After eight years of producing the *Star Wars* trilogy, there was an accumulation of "stuff," which had been stored wherever storage could be found—a closet here, a warehouse there, cubbyholes at England's Elstree Studios, inaccessible corners of Industrial Light & Magic (ILM). . . . No one referred to this "stuff" as artifacts, and no one thought about museums. The dilemma was storage.

George Lucas: The Creative Impulse (Lucasfilm's First Twenty-Five Years), by Charles Champlin. Abrams, 1997. Revised and updated edition. Hardback, 232 pages.
An excellent overview of Lucas's life and career, focused on the first quarter-century. (Movie-wise, it's current through 1994, when *Radioland Murders* was released.) Though it needs updating, this is a good overview and profusely illustrated with photos.

The Making of The Empire Strikes Back, by J. W. Rinzler. Del Rey, 2010. Hardback, 361 pages.
As with his previous book, *The Making of Star Wars*, this coffee table book is a granular look at every aspect of *The Empire Strikes Back*. Beautifully illustrated with photos, art, and storyboards. Anyone with an interest in the art and complexity of filmmaking will want this oversize book. An indispensable book for anyone who

wants a behind-the-scenes look at what fans feel is the best movie in the saga. (I agree.)

The Making of Return of the Jedi, by J. W. Rinzler. Del Rey, 2013. Hardback, 361 pages.
The third and final book in the series. As with the other two volumes, this is oversize and profusely illustrated. It's a detailed behind-the-scenes look at the movie that completes the first *Star Wars* film trilogy.

The Making of Star Wars, by J. W. Rinzler. Del Rey, 2007. Hardback, 361 pages. Indexed.
This is the first and last word on the movie that started it all, the expanding *Star Wars* universe. Like Rinzler's other two exhaustive books in his *Making of* series, this one belongs in your permanent library.

Rogue One: A Star Wars Story, by Alexander Freed. Penguin Random House, 2016. Special Barnes & Noble Edition. Hardback, 319 pages.
This has an eight-page color insert with stills from the film. This is a novelization of the movie, presumably based on the film script.

Sculpting a Galaxy: Inside the Star Wars Model Shop, by Lorne Peterson. Insight Editions, 2006. Hardback, 216 pages.
Limited edition retailing for $395, encased in a foldout traycase, with figurines and small pieces of sculpture from the Death Star. With additional booklets, gatefolds, foldouts, and other add-ons, this is a model maker's dream. A trade edition was subsequently issued.

Star Wars: Blueprints, by J. W. Rinzler. Epic Ink, 2011.
This is the limited edition of 5,000 copies. In hardback with a matching traycase, the book itself is 15.5 by 18.5 inches! With more than 250 blueprints, printed in large size on heavy paper stock, and more than 500 photographs and illustrations, this book is likely the *biggest* book about *Star Wars* ever published, and long out of print.

As the *New York Times* wrote in its review, "As Yoda might put it: Forceful object, this is."

In September 2017, it was reprinted by Epic Ink in a smaller format (12.5 by 14.8 inches) and at a lower retail price ($79.99), in trade hardback. This is the affordable edition of choice.

Star Wars Character Encyclopedia (updated and expanded), by Simon Beecroft and Pablo Hidalgo. DK Publishing, 2016. Hardback, 220 pages. (First edition published in 2011.)

The *Star Wars* universe is populated with thousands of characters, which would require a detailed encyclopedia. This is more general in nature, and aimed at a younger audience. From 2-1B (a surgical droid) to Zuckuss (a Gand bounty hunter), the entries are arranged alphabetically.

Star Wars: Complete Locations. DK Publishing, 2015. Hardback, 183 pages.

Comprehensive and current through *The Force Awakens*, this collects all the key locations seen in the *Star Wars* movies that make up the main narrative, as opposed to the stand-alone movies like *Rogue One*.

What makes this book so fascinating is the level of detail in the hardware, with cutaways (printed 2-D, of course) showing the innards of buildings like Superman's X-ray vision. Scenes, for instance, of Otoh Gunga (the underwater Gungan city) are made more alive by showing not only its surface appearance but also what it's like behind, and inside, the structures themselves.

Star Wars: Complete Vehicles, by Kerrie Dougherty, Curtis Saxton, David West Reynolds, and Ryder Windham; illustrated by Hans Jenssen and Richard Chasemore; additional illustrations by John Mullaney and John Hall. DK Publishing, 2013. Hardback, 207 pages.

These cutaways of vehicles found in the *Star Wars* universe are, in a word, amazing. It's not until you see the level of detail in these drawings that you realize how much care and attention has gone into designing every nut and bolt that holds the *Star Wars* universe together. Similar to the U.S. military's technical manuals, this is a visual treat. Seamlessly integrating photos and conceptual art with the 3-D cutaways, it's supplemented by detailed text that summarizes each vehicle.

This is part of a series of similar *Star Wars* books, all of which are indeed impressive.

Star Wars: The Complete Visual Dictionary, by David West Reynolds and James Luceno, with updates and new material by Ryder Windham; special fabrications by Robert E. Barnes, Don Bies, John Goodson, Nelson Hall, and Mike Verta; new photos by Alex Ivanov. DK Publishing, 2015. Hardback, 271 pages.
This compiles the four previously published visual dictionaries into one volume; hence the word "complete." Unlike *Complete Vehicles*, this book does not have dimensional cutaways; instead, it has thousands of photos and conceptual art, supplemented with detailed text.

Star Wars, Episode I: The Phantom Menace, Illustrated Screenplay, by George Lucas. The Ballantine Publishing Group, 1999. Trade paperback, 150 pages.
The complete screenplay with storyboards. The art for the boards is necessarily sketchy; the real value of the book is the screenplay itself, which provides details one may miss when watching the film.

Star Wars: The Essential Atlas, by Daniel Wallace and Jason Fry. Del Rey, 2009. Trade paperback, 243 pages.
Illustrated with concept art, photos from the movies, and maps/star maps of the *Star Wars* galaxy, it's a planetary atlas. Very useful for getting a sense of what the planets that figure prominently in *Star Wars* are like, and their importance.

Star Wars: The Essential Guide to Warfare, by Jason Fry, with Paul R. Urquhart. Del Rey, 2012. Trade paperback, 243 pages.
As the back cover copy makes clear, *Star Wars* "is rooted in a rich

history of armed conflict." This book delves deeper into the people, places, vehicles, starships, and units involved. Written for a lay audience—unlike the *Imperial Handbook*—this is principally the military history of *Star Wars*.

Star Wars: The Force Awakens, by Alan Dean Foster. Penguin Random House, 2015. Special Barnes & Noble Edition. Hardback, 260 pages.
This has two eight-page color inserts with stills from the film. This is a novelization of the movie, presumably based on the film script.

Star Wars: Frames. Abrams Noterie, 2015. One hundred postcards in a widescreen format, with self-displaying cardboard case/frame. Covering the first six *Star Wars* movies, these oblong-shaped postcards (4.25 by 9.25 inches) reprint key scenes.

The postcard set was drawn from *Star Wars: Frames*, a two book set with an imaginatively designed slipcase. Published by Abrams in 2013, one volume includes stills (single frames from the movie) from the prequels (*Star Wars I–III*), and the other volume includes stills from the original trilogy (*Star Wars IV–VI*). The frames are reproduced two-up: two frames per printed page, which measures 5.25 by 12.25 inches. There are 1,416 images in the two books.

Obviously, if you haven't seen the movies, you won't have the necessary context to enjoy the book. As J. W. Rinzler noted in the introduction to the books, "*Frames* is a meditative look at the *Star Wars* saga. It slows the story to a standstill, democratizing the time available for each moment." The selected images were culled by George Lucas, who went through more than 150,000 frames per movie (in total, more than a million frames for the saga). The time-consuming process started on September 2005 and was completed in 2008.

Note: The first edition was published in 2011, in a limited edition of 1,138 copies signed by George Lucas. The books were boxed in an art deco-inspired wooden case and cost $3,000.

Star Wars and History, edited by Nancy R. Reagin and Janice Liedl. John Wiley & Sons, 2013. Hardback, 332 pages. Indexed.
Beautifully printed on glossy stock and profusely illustrated, this anthology collects articles by teachers and historians, tying world history together with the *Star Wars* saga. Leaning more toward the academic than toward pop culture, the book necessarily strikes a balance between the real world and the imaginative world created by Lucas. A little dry textually, though, as it was written by academics.

It is especially useful for putting the *Star Wars* universe into a historical context.

Star Wars Art: Illustration, edited by Eric Klopfer. Abrams, 2012. Hardback. 175 pages.
The third book in the series, this collects art from multiple sources, handpicked by George Lucas. Short bios of each artist are in the back.

Star Wars Art: Posters, edited by Eric Klopfer. Abrams, 2014. Hardback, 179 pages.
The fifth book in the series, this collects art from multiple sources, from every nook and cranny of the *Star Wars* universe, including fan club exclusives, foreign one-sheets, and limited edition posters from Mondo. The book's foreword is by artist Drew Struzan, who is celebrated for his iconic movie poster art for the saga.

Star Wars Imperial Handbook: A Commander's Guide, by "Admiral Wullf Yularen." Chronicle Books LLC, 2015. Hardback, 159 pages. Not indexed.
This is a packaged book from becker&mayer (Bellevue, Washington). A work of pseudo history, it provides detailed insights into "the composition and organization of the Imperial Army, Navy, and Stormtrooper Corps, plus a surprising amount of detail concerning experimental technology and superweapons," as Commander Luke Skywalker, Alliance Command, writes in a memo printed in the book. With an overview of the imperial military, followed by de-

tailed chapters on its three branches of military service, the book concludes with essays on the Empire's strategic goals, on the Rebellion itself, and on superweapons, including the imperial DS-1 Orbital Battle Station—the Death Star.

This is more for the hard-core armchair general and gamers than for the lay reader. Profusely illustrated with black-and-white and color photos, bulleted lists, and sidebars aplenty, it's essentially an illustrated table of organization and equipment, with supplemental material.

The write-up on the Empire's field artillery is egregious, or as we Redlegs say, a misfire.

Note: There are annotations by various rebel officers, including all the usual suspects. Unfortunately, they are in small, "handwritten" print and difficult to read.

Star Wars, Rogue One: The Ultimate Visual Guide, by Pablo Hidalgo, with illustrations by Kemp Remillard. DK Publishing, 2016. Hardback, 192 pages. An oversize book in full color.

One of DK's oversize, exhaustively detailed, and profusely illustrated guidebooks, this one focuses on *Rogue One*, the first stand-alone movie billed as "A *Star Wars* Story."

As with all their books in this series, the writing is detailed, and exhaustively so, backed up with numerous photographs and artwork. The emphasis, as the book's title suggests, is on its visual aspects.

Star Wars: Ralph McQuarrie, by Brandon Alinger, Wade Lageose, and David Mandel, in cooperation with the Ralph McQuarrie Archives. Abrams, 2016. Hardback, two volumes (vol. 1 is 399 pages, plus index; vol. 2 is 399 pages). Slipcased.

This book belongs on the shelf of every *Star Wars* fan. A retrospective looking at the sketches, conceptual designs, and finished pieces by artist Ralph McQuarrie, who more than anyone else was responsible for the look and feel of the *Star Wars* universe, starting with the finished pieces of art that helped sell the first movie to the studio. As Lucas wrote in a foreword to McQuarrie's book, "I needed him to envision the costumes and the demeanor of Darth Vader, Luke Skywalker, Chewbacca, and C-3PO and R2-D2, among others, to create visuals to help us budget the film."

These *are* the books you are looking for. If you only buy one book in this list, this is it.

Star Wars Storyboards: The Original Trilogy, edited by J. W. Rinzler. Abrams, 2014.

A storyboard is a sequence of drawings, often including some directions and dialogue, outlining the shots planned for a movie. This book brings together the storyboards for the three original *Star Wars* movies: *Star Wars*, *The Empire Strikes Back*, and *Return of the Jedi*.

More for film fans than for the lay reader whose interest is predominantly watching the finished film, these storyboards give a sense of the flow of the movie, beginning with the dramatic opening of *A New Hope*, in which a Star Destroyer fills the movie screen, in hot pursuit of the Rebel Alliance spaceship *Tantive IV*.

Star Wars Trilogy: Star Wars, The Empire Strikes Back, Return of the Jedi. O.S.P. Publishing, 1995 (second printing). Trade paperback. Slipcased.

Part of the Movie Script Library from *Premiere*, this set is text only, reprinting the original movie scripts. These are very useful for checking the actual dialogue against the movie, if you're a hopeless geek, an obsessive *Star Wars* fan, or a student, scholar, or pop culture writer. (Interestingly, the text and the final filmed version don't necessarily agree.)

The Star Wars Vault, by Stephen J. Sansweet and Peter Vilmur. HarperCollins, packaged by becker&mayer, 2007. Hardback, 126 pages.

Sansweet, who was director of content management and head of Fan Relations at Lucasfilm, has the largest collection of *Star Wars* material in private hands. The collection is the centerpiece of his company, Rancho Obi-Wan, Inc. In other words, he's the best person to edit/compile a scrapbook reproducing *Star Wars* memorabilia. It's billed as "thirty years of treasures from the Lucasfilm Archives with removable memorabilia and two audio CDs." Great fun, this is a trip through the *Star Wars* universe (1977 to 2007), with all sorts of interesting facsimile items.

Star Wars: Visions by J. W. Rinzler. Abrams, 2010. Trade hardback, 175 pages.
This is an unusual book in that it's not a recapitulation, textually or visually, of the known *Star Wars* universe; instead, it is, as George Lucas states in the foreword, a compilation of newly commissioned artwork:

> As *Star Wars* began to take on a life of its own, it was especially gratifying to see so many new artists expand on the Saga through our licensing program and elsewhere. And that led to the thought that was really the impetus for this project: asking a select group of great contemporary artists, of many different genres and styles, to create interpretations of *Star Wars*.

Consequently, we get, for instance, a portrait of Lucas in the cantina scene at Mos Eisley, and one of Darth Vader with drawn lightsaber held upright, standing behind a blond beauty who has a stormtrooper helmet in hand, midriff exposed, and torso body armor with shapely breasts. (The late Carrie Fisher once observed that there's no sex in *Star Wars*. Well, there is now.)

Star Wars Year by Year: A Visual History (updated and expanded). DK Publishing; 2016. Hardback, 367 pages.
Looking at the entire franchise, the emphasis is on the pop culture aspects of the series, with contextual real-world material: a printed time capsule. For instance, April and July 1976 have entries about the first Apple computer ($666.66) and the Entebbe rescue by the Israel Defense Forces, along with entries showing scenes from Tatooine and a slide of Carrie Fisher as Princess Leia, shown at a presentation at a science fiction convention, Westercon, in California.

Ultimate Star Wars, by Patricia Barr, Adam Bray, Daniel Wallace, and Rhyder Windham. DK Publishing; 2015. Trade hardback, 319 pages.

A single volume collecting detailed write-ups and photos/art for characters, creatures, locations, technology, and vehicles.

Unofficial Books About George Lucas and *Star Wars*

George Lucas: A Life, by Brian Jay Jones. Little, Brown and Company, 2016. Hardback, 560 pages.

Though this book is unauthorized, with no access to Lucas, Lucasfilm, or affiliated companies, Jones serves up the most complete and up-to-date narrative of Lucas's life and times, which makes this book *the* biography of choice. This *is* the book you're looking for.

How Star Wars Conquered the Universe: The Past, Present, and Future of a Multibillion Dollar Franchise, by Chris Taylor. Basic Books, 2014. Hardback, 450 pages.

An overview of the *Star Wars* phenomenon, with particular attention paid to the early years leading up to the first film. As the author points out, "Before *Star Wars*, no one had ever made a dime out of toy merchandising associated with a movie. . . . In 1978, the company sold more than forty-two million *Star Wars* items; the majority, twenty-six million, were action figures. . . . More than $20 billion of merchandising has been sold over the lifetime of the franchise."

The Princess Diarist, by Carrie Fisher. Blue Rider Press, 2016. Hardback, 257 pages. Illustrated with candid, black-and-white photos.

From the late, great Carrie Fisher, who had a second career as a writer (and scriptwriter/script doctor), this is an unvarnished look at her time as Princess Leia, culled from Fisher's diaries of the period when she was filming the original *Star Wars* movie in 1977. (Yes, she had an affair with Harrison Ford, but did we *really* need to know that? Too much information!)

The Science of Star Wars, by Jeanne Cavelos. St. Martin's, 1999.
   Hardback, 255 pages. Not illustrated.
From the author of *The Science of the X-Files* (1998), this is a sober look at the actual science in *Star Wars*: what's possible, what's
improbable, and what's impossible. Organized thematically (planetary environments, aliens, droids, spaceships and weapons, and the
Force). Its author, an astrophysicist, does a fine job of explaining
that, although the movie is clearly a space fantasy, it's rooted in science fiction, in its extrapolation of what we have today and what
we might see in the future. (In other words, it's not fantasy and it's
not just speculation; it's extrapolation grounded in the science of
today.) Catnip for science geeks.

The Science of Star Wars, by Mark Brake and Jon Chase. Race-
   horse Publishing, 2016. Trade paperback, 261 pages. Not illustrated.
These guys have the credentials to write this book, and they do so
in entertaining fashion. It obviously duplicates some of the ground
in Cavelos's book (see previous entry), but it's still a hoot and a
half, as Dr. Sheldon Cooper from *The Big Bang Theory* would say.

Skywalking: The Life and Films of George Lucas (updated edition),
   by Dale Pollock. Da Capo, 1999. Trade paperback, 332 pages.
   Illustrated with two black-and-white photo inserts. (The original
   edition was published in 1999. This edition includes one additional chapter tacked on the end.)
Though this book was unauthorized, as the author acknowledges, he
had "the cooperation of George Lucas. Once granted, his cooperation was total, his access unlimited, and his interest unflagging. Lucas's
close associates matched his commitment to this project."
   Though it is outdated, this biography obviously benefits from the
author's access to Lucas, who gave him an unprecedented seventy
hours of interviews, in addition to interviews with one hundred
other people who were central to Lucas's life.
   As Pollock told the *Washington Post* (May 19, 2005), Lucas
"hated it because it's honest, doesn't pull any punches, and was well

researched (i.e., does not rely on only George's version of life and the universe). I think it was upsetting to him to actually read what he said about people. . . . I was surprised by the vehemence of his reaction, because to me, 21 years later, the book is a very balanced portrait."

I agree with Pollock's assessment. For *Star Wars* fans, it's valuable because of the exclusive interviews Lucas granted. Taken as a whole, the book is good and has held up well over the years.

I don't imagine Lucas will sit for an authorized book again anytime soon, unless he has complete editorial control. I also don't imagine he'll write an autobiography, because he dislikes writing.

Military Books of Interest

The *Star Wars* canon is exhaustively cataloged in numerous books, giving verisimilitude to its "expanded universe." It's entertaining, but it's pseudo history—it's fiction.

To give those books context, we must look at military history over the centuries. On the assumption that the reader of this book has not served in the military, here's my recommended list of books, mostly contemporary, that will give you a real-world look at the U.S. military.*

The 1st Infantry Division and the US Army Transformed, by Gregory Fontenot. A long time ago, a great adventure had to take place: the U.S. Army had to reinvent itself. Demoralized and broken after the Vietnam War, the "Big Red One," the 1st Infantry Division, had to transform itself in order to restore itself to its former glory. Spanning three decades (1970 to 1991), this book, written by retired Colonel Fontenot who served in the 1st ID, takes a long, studied look at how this heavy division became great again—notably, show-

---

* My library of 20,000+ books contains hundreds of books about military history, many about WW II. So my choices are not gleaned from brief writeups of books online, but from texts—many of which are out of print—that I've culled over many years.

ing its true colors during Desert Storm. High recommended, with a ground level view of the war that toppled the late Saddam Hussein from power, this book is an insider's view on how a unit can transform itself when its leaders decide to take charge, set high standards, and push their troops toward excellence.

About Face: The Odyssey of an American Warrior, by David H. Hackworth and Julie Sherman.

(I love the ironic title. He was like that.) The late Colonel Hackworth was unquestionably an Army warrior who earned his pair of eagles (the insignia of a full colonel). He later became the Army's harshest critic, distancing himself philosophically from the Pentagon's "perfumed princes" (as he termed them). On the fast track to become a general, he refused that path. An outspoken critic of the Vietnam War, he gave an interview to ABC on June 27, 1971, sharing his view that the war was unwinnable and that it was high time for the country to get the hell out of it. As the *New York Times* pointed out in his obituary (May 6, 2005), he "enraged his superiors by lambasting the war on national television."

After retiring, Hackworth made a permanent move to Australia. The autobiography is, as you'd expect, frank and brutally honest, which was his style. For those especially interested in the Vietnam War, this book is required reading.

His website is hackworth.com.

My American Journey, by Colin Powell, with Joseph E. Persico.

General Powell was commissioned through the ROTC program, and his autobiography gives a detailed account of his life and times, with the result that you get a clear idea of what it's like to spend a lifetime serving on active duty in the army, and as a result learn a lot about leadership—what works, and what doesn't.

A former secretary of state, Powell was also chairman of the Joint Chiefs of Staff overseeing the Iraq War (see entry on General H. Norman Schwarzkopf).

He has no website but he does have a Facebook page: www .facebook.com/GenPowell/

The Art of War, by Sun Tzu.

The classic book on military strategy. As relevant today as it was more than two thousand years ago, when it was written. Read it, study it, cherish it.

The Atlas of Military History: An Around-the-World Survey of Warfare Through the Ages, by Amanda Lomazoff, with Aaron Ralby.

A coffee table book (11 by 14 inches) with extensive use of historical photos and maps. Major conflicts are covered by geographic region.

Black Hawk Down: A Story of Modern War, by Mark Bowden.

This is the book that popularized the narrative nonfiction field of military books. With a "you are there" perspective on what went down, like the eponymous Black Hawk, on October 1993, in Mogadishu, Somalia, this is the harrowing, true tale of U.S. Rangers downed in a hostile city.

We can never forget the color photos taken by Canadian photographer Paul Watson, showing a U.S. Army staff sergeant, William Cleveland, being dragged naked through the streets of Mogadishu as supporters of warlord Mohamed Aidid celebrated and lustily cheered at the spectacle.

This is what war really looks like, up close and personal. It doesn't get any uglier and brutal than this.

Common Sense Training: A Working Philosophy for Leaders, by Lieutenant General Arthur S. Collins, Jr.

Over the years, I've worn out several copies of this trade paperback, with handwritten notes, underlining, and other emendations. It was my constant companion as a young lieutenant, and I carried it with me on every field exercise. When there was a free moment, I read it, and reread it.

Collins's practical guide to small unit training in the army, published in 1978, offers time-tested and timeless advice that is still pertinent today. The original edition is long out of print, but its refreshed edition (1998) has been amended by Lieutenant General Daniel P. Bolger, author of *Why We Lost* (see entry below).

As the publisher points out, this book was "reissued without change to the main text, because in the twenty years since it was first published in 1978 it has become a genuine classic, more widely read than any other book like it."

It's especially useful for battalion commanders and below, who are the principal trainers in the army. As *Army* magazine said, this is "the best book on military training from platoon to division level that has been published in any army." I agree.

Dereliction of Duty, by H. R. McMaster.
A scathing denunciation of the leadership's conduct of the Vietnam War, McMaster—a graduate of the U.S. Military Academy who rose to the rank of lieutenant general—is currently serving as the 26th national security advisor under President Donald Trump.

The title says it all. The subtitle names the perps: President Lyndon Johnson, Defense Secretary Robert McNamara, and the Joint Chiefs of Staff, who stood mute as they knowingly extended an unwinnable war, regardless of the cost in blood and money. Too cowardly to stand up, they refused to screw their courage to the sticking place, take arms against a sea of troubles, and by opposing end them. In other words, they were derelict in their duties and, as a result, the war was needlessly prolonged and too many young Americans paid the ultimate price.

Written when McMaster was a major, the book became required reading in military circles, especially the Pentagon. It should also be read by every high level official in the U.S. government.

Dispatches, by Michael Herr.
A nonfiction account of the Vietnam War as seen through the eyes of grunts, this paints a surreal and haunting picture of a war that seemed to never end. More than any other book, this captures the hallucinogenic flavor of the war written in the vernacular of the grunts who fought it. (To heighten your reading mood, read it with sixties rock and roll music playing in the background.)

A History of War in 100 Battles, by Richard Overy.
Organized thematically ("Leadership," "Innovation," "Deception," "Courage in the Face of Fire," "In the Nick of Time"), this is principally text, with some photos for illustration. It draws on three thousand years of military history, dissecting what the author considers to be the battles that define warfare.

It Doesn't Take a Hero: The Autobiography of General H. Norman Schwarzkopf, with Peter Petre.
A four-star general who graduated from West Point and went on to command the Allied Forces in the Gulf War, H. Norman Schwarzkopf reported to another four-star general, Colin Powell. The late General Schwarzkopf was tapped to be the next U.S. Army Chief of Staff but declined, choosing to retire instead of overseeing the inevitable drawdown of the U.S. Army that he so loved and to which he devoted his life.

The book covers his military career from his days at West Point to the Gulf War. "Stormin' " Norman, also nicknamed "The Bear," was gruff and tough, and an inspirational warrior whose presence projected confidence and authority. An outspoken officer who doesn't pull punches in this book—he's especially critical of incompetent officers whom he felt should never have risen to high rank—Schwarzkopf's book title is drawn from a television interview from 1991 in which he told Barbara Walters, "It doesn't take a hero to order men into combat. It takes a hero to be one of those men who goes into battle."

Military History: The Definitive Visual Guide to the Objects of War.
Chronologically arranged, this is the history of warfare as seen through the weapons of war. Profusely illustrated, which is a hallmark of DK Publishing, this book makes history come alive in a way that text-only books cannot.

No Easy Day: The Firsthand Account of the Mission that Killed Osama Bin Laden, by Mark Owen, with Kevin Maurer.
Drawing its title from a Navy SEAL motto (The Only Easy Day

Was Yesterday), this memoir, a blow-by-blow recounting of the mission to capture or kill Osama bin Laden on his home turf, is a riveting read.

In the closed community of SEAL team members, the explosion of books penned by former SEALs is controversial because of their traditional code of silence. That these books have gone on to make their authors big bucks is also offensive to the SEAL team community, because it's cashing in, when what they do is not about money—it's about duty, honor, country. Moreover, the public appetite for information by and about SEALs has resulted, some say, in too much revelation about the inner workings of the SEALs, especially its elite Seal Team Six.

No Excuse Leadership: Lessons from the U.S. Army's Elite Rangers, by Brace E. Barber.
A West Point graduate and former Airborne Ranger with eleven years in service, Barber explains why "Rangers lead the way." The chapters are organized by attributes: "Rangers are persistent. Humble. Focused. Driven. Instinctual. Honest. Selfless. Confident. Dutiful. Determined." An insider's look at the Rangers' world that is as useful for military personnel as it is for leaders in the business community.

Small Unit Leadership: A Commonsense Approach, by Colonel Dandridge M. Malone (U.S. Army, Ret.). A complementary book to *Commonsense Training*.

Why We Lost: A General's Inside Account of the Iraq and Afghanistan Wars, by Daniel P. Bolger.
A retired lieutenant general who speaks frankly and bluntly, Bolger opens the book with an author's note that begins, "I am a United States Army general, and I lost the Global War on Terrorism. . . . Well, I have a problem. So do my peers. And thanks to our problem, now all of America has a problem, to wit: two lost campaigns and a war gone awry."

Makes you wish he had been around during the Vietnam War,

because he would have stood up against the secretary of defense and the president and spoken his mind when the other generals stood mute.

A sobering read and a reminder that our leaders should go to the Vietnam Veterans Memorial Wall and look at the names of the fallen etched on the black granite memorial, and then think long and hard before sending troops to a war zone.

Tom Clancy

For an overview of the U.S. military, written in consultation with high-ranking officers, the late Tom Clancy's nonfiction books, though outdated and in need of refreshing, are entertaining and educational. Had Clancy been a military officer, he would have made an excellent intelligence officer in the army or navy. He was a lifelong student of military history, always analyzing the world of the warrior. It was his passion.

He's best known, and celebrated for, his first book, *The Hunt for Red October*, which was published by Naval Institute Press in 1984. President Reagan read it, loved it, and said it was "my kind of yarn." It's his best book, and like an ICBM, it launched his career.

Clancy's nonfiction books include *Battle Ready* (with Marine General Tony Zinni), *Shadow Warriors: Inside the Special Forces*, *Submarine: A Guided Tour Inside a Nuclear Warship*, *Carrier: A Guided Tour of an Aircraft Commander*, *Every Man a Tiger: The Gulf War Air Campaign* (with Air Force General Chuck Horner), *Airborne: A Guided Tour of an Airborne Task Force*, *Into the Storm: On the Ground in Iraq* (with Army General Frederick M. Franks, Jr.), *Marine: A Guided Tour of a Marine Expeditionary Unit*, *Fighter Wing: A Guided Tour of an Air Force Combat Wing*, and *Armored Cav: A Guided Tour of an Armored Cavalry Regiment*.

MISCELLANEOUS *STAR WARS* RESOURCES

Products

Even before George Lucas sold *Star Wars* to the Walt Disney Company, he saw the value of licensing as a means of ongoing revenue and as a promotional vehicle. The result, even back then, was a tsunami of product, with something for everyone, from children to adults. As a result, sorting through the offerings to find the primo stuff is a chore. Where do you begin?

You could literally fill a large house with all the licensed product, which is what longtime *Star Wars* historian and collector Stephen J. Sansweet has done with a former chicken ranch. His refurbished barns hold all the memorabilia he accumulated when he was director of content management and head of Fan Relations at Lucasfilm. Welcome to Rancho Obi-Wan (yes, that's the real name of his nonprofit *Star Wars* museum). To store it all takes nine thousand square feet, which will need to be expanded, now that Disney's merchandising mavens are working on how to add to the number of tie-in products.

In Chicago, the hog capital of the world, it's said that they have found a use for every part of the pig except the squeal . . . and they're working on that. Well, Chicago's got nothing on Disney. No company has figured out how to market their consumer products better than the Mouse.

If you're interested in *Star Wars*–related products, here's the creme de la creme.

1. *Star Wars: The Complete Saga*. A boxed set of *Star Wars I–VI*, with nine discs, three of which are bonus discs with supplemental

material. Running time, 805 minutes. Retail cost, $139.99, but it's often discounted. Of course, in December 2017, the set became out-dated, because it lacks *Star Wars VII: The Force Awakens* (2016) and *Star Wars VIII: The Last Jedi* (2017).

I don't expect to see the set updated until 2018, when the Blu-ray of *The Last Jedi* is released, so buy this now—or buy the previous edition, which has the same content, gorgeously packaged in a hard cardboard book with a matching slipcase. (Meesa own that one.)

2. *Star Wars VII: The Force Awakens.* There are several editions available, depending on where you buy it. Get any edition in Blu-ray and you'll be happy.

3. *Star Wars: The Ultimate Soundtrack Collection*, by John Williams. As with the film sets, this music set will need to be up-dated because of the recent and forthcoming releases. Packaged in-dividually in sleeves and, collectively, in a traycase, this collects the soundtracks to *Star Wars I–VI*. It also adds a DVD (*Star Wars: A Musical Journey*) and a bonus disc with interviews (John Williams and Harrison Ford), plus a foldout contents page and three small color prints of movie poster photos/art on flimsy stock.

4. For authentic-looking figurines, go to sideshowtoy.com. De-pending on the piece, the size starts out one-sixth scale (10.62 inches high, for the Jyn Erso figurine). The Premium Format line offers bigger figurines (19.5 inches). Prices for the one-sixth-scale pieces of Jyn Erso cost approximately $250, with the Premium For-mat costing approximately $500.

The company is also a distributor for Hot Toys Collectible Fig-ures, which issues its own line of figurines.

For the *Star Wars* fan who has very deep pockets and a house large enough to hold them, life-size figures are available at a corre-spondingly higher cost: R2-D2 ($7,450), Yoda ($2,499), Boba Fett ($8,495), a stormtrooper ($7,999.99), and my favorite, Han Solo in carbonite ($7,499), which stands ninety-one inches high (roughly seven and a half feet!).

My recommendation: get the R2-D2 Deluxe (one-sixth scale) at $149.99, or its Premium Format model ($379.99); C-3PO (one-sixth scale, $229.99; Premium Format, $399.99); or Darth Vader (one-sixth scale, $229.99; Premium Format, $499.99).

Finally, if your family is all in with *Star Wars*, book yourself a room at the *Star Wars*-inspired Themed Resort at Walt Disney World Resort, when they begin taking reservations. But make 'em early because they'll be in more demand than space heaters on the ice planet Hoth.

Websites

1. starwars.com. The single best place for information, especially for newbies.

2. Wookieepedia. The *Star Wars* wiki (starwars.wikia.com), which currently has 140,395 (and counting) pages for your edification.

3. disney.com. The one-stop shop for *Star Wars*–related, family-friendly collectibles, toys, clothing, etc.

4. disneyworld.disney.go.com (Orlando, Florida). For information about Disney's Hollywood Studios, where the *Star Wars*–themed rides and activities are located (Star Tours—The Adventures Continue). That will tide you over until 2019, when *Star Wars* Land opens.

5. disneyland.disney.go.com (Anaheim, California). For information about Star Tours—The Adventures Continue and other *Star Wars*–related activities.

6. www.starwarscelebration.com. For the *Star Wars* geek in you, this annual convention is where wookies hobnob with droids, where smugglers snuggle with Princess Leias, and you'll find the droids—and much more—that you're looking for. Bring lots of cash and plastic money, because you're going to need them.

LIST OF OPERATIONAL TERMS

(FM 101-5-1, October 1985)

The working vocabulary of the U.S. military can be found in FM 101-5-1, *Operational Terms and Symbols*. I've handpicked terms that I believe are useful to lay readers of my study on the military science of *Star Wars*. Those wishing more detail should, of course, consult the field manual.

advance guard ▪ The security element operating at the front of a moving force.

air assault ▪ Operations in which air assault forces (combat, combat support [CS], and combat service support [CSS]), using the firepower, mobility, and total integration of helicopter assets in their ground or air roles, maneuver on the battlefield under the control of the ground or air maneuver commander to engage and destroy enemy forces.

air defense ▪ All measures designed to nullify or reduce the effectiveness of an enemy attack by aircraft or guided missiles in flight.

air liaison officer (ALO) ▪ The senior Air Force officer at each tactical air control party (TACP). Advises the Army commander and staff on the capabilities, limitations, and employment of tactical air operations. He operates the Air Force request net. He coordinates close air support (CAS) missions with the fire support element (FSE), and assists in planning the simultaneous employment of air and surface fires. He supervises forward air controllers (FACs) and will assist the fire support team (FIST) in directing airstrikes in the absence of a FAC.

air movement operations ▪ Operations using airlift assets, primarily helicopters, to move combat, combat support (CS), and combat service support (CSS) forces and/or equipment whose primary purpose is *not* to engage and destroy enemy forces.

air strike ▪ An attack on specific objectives by fighter, bomber, or attack aircraft.

ambush ▪ A surprise attack by fire from concealed positions on a moving or temporarily halted enemy.

artillery preparation ▪ Artillery fire delivered before an attack to disrupt communications and disorganize the enemy's defense.

assembly area ▪ An area in which a force prepares or regroups for further action.

attack, frontal ▪ An offensive maneuver in which the main action is directed against the front of the enemy forces, and over the most direct approaches.

attack, main ▪ The principal attack or effort into which the commander places the bulk of the offensive capability at his disposal. An attack directed against the chief objective of the campaign or battle.

axis of advance ▪ A general route of advance, assigned for purposes of control, which extends toward the enemy. . . . A commander may maneuver his forces and supporting fires to either side of an axis of advance provided the unit remains oriented on the axis and the objective.

booby trap ▪ A device designed to kill or maim an unsuspecting person who disturbs an apparently harmless object or performs a normally safe act.

bypass ▪ Maneuvering around an obstacle, position, or enemy force to maintain the momentum of advance. Previously unreported obstacles are reported to higher HQ. Bypassed enemy forces are reported to higher HQ.

camouflage ▪ The use of concealment and disguise to minimize detection or identification of troops, weapons, equipment, and installations. It includes taking advantage of the immediate environment as well as using natural and artificial materials. Also:

The process of making a person or object blend with the background.

chain of command ▪ The succession of commanding officers from a superior to a subordinate through which command is exercised.

close air support ▪ Air action against hostile targets that are in close proximity to friendly forces and that require detailed integration of each air mission with the fire and movement of those forces.

collateral damage ▪ Undesirable civilian personnel injuries or material damage produced by the effects of friendly nuclear weapons. (Note: This is now used in a general sense to include all inadvertent damage using conventional munitions as well.)

combat intelligence ▪ That knowledge of the enemy, weather, and geographic features required by a commander in planning and conducting combat operations. It is derived from the analysis of information on the enemy's capabilities, intentions, vulnerabilities, and the environment.

combat maneuver forces ▪ Those forces which use fire and movement to engage the enemy with direct fire weapon systems, as distinguished from those forces which engage the enemy with indirect fires or otherwise provide combat support (CS). These elements are primarily infantry, armor, cavalry (air and armored), and aviation.

combat service support (CSS) ▪ The assistance provided to sustain combat forces, primarily in the fields of administration and logistics. It includes administrative services, chaplain services, medical services, supply, transportation, and other logistics services.

combined arms team ▪ Two or more arms mutually supporting one another. A team usually consists of tanks, infantry, cavalry, aviation, field artillery, air defense artillery, and engineers.

command and control (C2) ▪ The exercise of command that is the process through which the activities of military forces are directed, coordinated, and controlled to accomplish the mission. This process encompasses the personnel, equipment, communications, facilities, and procedures necessary to gather and analyze information, to plan for what is to be done, and to supervise the execution of operations.

commander's intent ▪ Commander's vision of the battle—how he expects to fight and what he expects to accomplish.

counterfire ▪ Fire intended to destroy, neutralize, or suppress enemy indirect fire systems.

covering fire ▪ Fire used to protect friendly troops from enemy direct fires.

dedicated battery ▪ A cannon battery whose total firepower is immediately available to suppress enemy weapons which threaten a designated company/team during a movement to contact.

defensive operations ▪ Operations conducted with the immediate purpose of causing an enemy attack to fail. Defensive operations may achieve one or more of the following: gain time; concentrate forces elsewhere; wear down enemy forces as a prelude to offensive operations; and retain tactical, strategic, or political objectives.

defilade ▪ Protection from hostile observation and fire provided by an obstacle such as a hill, ridge, or bank. To shield from enemy fire or observation by using natural or artificial obstacles.

delaying operation ▪ An operation usually conducted when the commander needs time to concentrate or withdraw forces, to establish defenses in greater depth, to economize in an area, or to complete offensive actions elsewhere. In the delay, the destruction of the enemy force is secondary to slowing his advance to gain time.

delay in sector ▪ A low-risk mission which requires a unit to slow and defeat as much of the enemy as possible without sacrificing the tactical integrity of the unit. This mission can be given to forces in the covering force area (CFA) or in the main battle area (MBA).

direct fire ▪ Fire directed at a target that is visible to the aimer or firing unit.

displace ▪ To leave one position and take another.

double envelopment ▪ A form of enveloping maneuver executed by forces that move around both flanks of an enemy position to attack the flanks or objectives in the rear of the enemy. The enemy normally is fixed in position by a supporting frontal attack or by indirect and/or aerial fires.

emplacement ▪ (1.) A prepared position for one or more weapons or pieces of equipment for protection against hostile fire or bombardment, and from which soldiers can execute their assigned tasks. (2.) The act of fixing a gun in a prepared position so that it may be fired.

engagement area ▪ An area in which the commander intends to trap and destroy an enemy force with the massed fires of all available weapons.

evasion and escape (E&E) ▪ The procedures and operations whereby military personnel and other selected individuals can emerge from an enemy-held or hostile area to areas under friendly control.

exploitation ▪ An offensive operation that usually follows a successful attack to take advantage of weakened or collapsed enemy defenses. Its purpose is to prevent reconstitution of enemy defenses, to prevent enemy withdrawal, and to secure deep objectives.

field of fire ▪ The area that a weapon or a group of weapons may effectively cover with fire from a given position.

fire support ▪ Assistance to those elements of the ground forces that close with the enemy, such as infantry and armor units, rendered by delivering artillery and mortar fire, naval gun fire, and close air support (CAS). Fire support may also be provided by tanks, air defense artillery, and Army aviation.

forward air controller ▪ A member of the tactical air control party (TACP) who, from a ground or airborne position, controls aircraft engaged in close air support (CAS) of ground forces.

forward observer ▪ An observer with forward troops trained to call for and adjust supporting fire and to pass battlefield information. (Note: This refers most often to a field artilleryman calling in indirect fire.)

fragmentary order (FRAGO) ▪ An abbreviated form of an operation order (OPORD) used to make changes in missions to units and to inform them of changes in the tactical situation.

ground tactical plan ▪ An airborne or air assault operational plan covering the conduct of operations in the objective area.

guerilla warfare ▪ Military and paramilitary operations conducted in enemy-held or hostile territory by irregular, predominantly indigenous forces. It is conducted to complement, support, or extend conventional military operations.

high-angle fire ▪ Fire delivered at angles of elevation greater than the elevation that corresponds to the maximum range of the gun and ammunition concerned. (Note: On a handheld gunner's quadrant, used in a field artillery for towed howitzers, there are two sides: low angle and high angle. Low-angle elevation, marked in mils, starts from 0 to 800; high-angle elevation starts from 800 to 1,600 mils.)

high value target (HVT) ▪ A target whose loss to the enemy can be expected to contribute to substantial degradation of an important battlefield function.

indirect fire ▪ Fire delivered on a target which cannot be seen by the firing unit.

intelligence ▪ The product resulting from the collection, evaluation, analysis, integration, and interpretation of all available information concerning an enemy force, foreign nations, or areas of operations and which is immediately or potentially significant to military planning and operations.

jamming ▪ The deliberate radiation, reradiation, or reflection of electromagnetic energy to prevent or degrade the receipt of information by a receiver.

liaison ▪ The contact or intercommunication maintained among elements of military forces to ensure mutual understanding and unity of purpose and action.

logistics ▪ The planning and carrying out of the movement and the maintenance of forces. In its most comprehensive sense, those aspects of military operations which deal with (1) design and development, acquisition, storage, movement, distribution, maintenance, evacuation, and disposition of material; (2) movement, evacuation, and hospitalization of personnel; (3) acquisition or construction, maintenance, operation, and disposition of facilities; and (4) acquisition or furnishing of services.

maneuver ▪ The movement of forces supported by fire to achieve a position of advantage from which to destroy or threaten destruction of the enemy. A *principle of war.*

METT-T ▪ Describes factors that must be considered during the planning or execution of a tactical operation: mission, enemy, terrain, troops, and time available.

Mission: The who, what, when, where, and why of what is to be accomplished.

Enemy: Current information concerning the enemy's strength, location, disposition, activity, equipment, capability, and a determination as to the enemy's probable course of action.

Terrain (includes weather): Information about vegetation, soil type, hydrology, climatic conditions, and light data is analyzed to determine the impact the environment can have on current and future operations for both enemy and friendly operations.

Troops: The quantity, level of training, and psychological state of friendly forces, to include the availability of weapons systems and critical equipment.

Time available: The time available to plan, prepare, and execute operations is considered for both enemy and friendly forces.

military operations on urbanized terrain (MOUT) ▪ All military actions planned and conducted on a topographical complex and its adjacent natural terrain where man-made construction is the dominant feature. It includes combat in cities, which is that portion of MOUT involving house-to-house and street-by-street fighting in towns and cities.

mission-oriented protective posture (MOPP) ▪ A flexible system for protection against a chemical attack, devised to maximize the unit's ability to accomplish its mission in a toxic environment.

This posture permits maximum protection from a chemical agent attack without unacceptable reduction in efficiency. (Note: There are five levels of MOPP, ranging from 0, in which the mask and hood are carried, to 4, in which the soldier is fully protected with chemical protective clothing and gear.)

objective ▪ (1.) The physical object of the action (for example, a definite terrain feature, the seizure and/or holding of which is essential to the commander's plan, or the destruction of an enemy force without regard to terrain features). (2.) The *principle of war* which states that every military operation should be directed toward clearly defined, decisive, and attainable objectives.

offense ▪ A combat operation designed primarily to destroy the enemy. Offensive operations may be undertaken to secure key or decisive terrain, to deprive the enemy of resources or decisive terrain, to deceive and/or divert the enemy, to develop intelligence, and to hold the enemy in position. Offensive operations include deliberate attack, hasty attack, movement to contact, exploitation, pursuit, and other limited-objective operations. The offensive is undertaken to seize, retain, and exploit the initiative, and, as such, is a *principle of war*.

operational control (OPCON) ▪ The authority delegated to a commander to direct forces assigned so that the commander may accomplish specific missions or tasks that are usually limited by function, time, or location; to deploy units concerned; and to retain or assign tactical control of those units. It does not of itself include administrative or logistics control.

operation order (OPORD) ▪ A directive issued by a commander to subordinate commanders for effecting the coordinated execution of an operation; includes tactical movement orders.

operation plan (OPLAN) ▪ A plan for a military operation. It covers a single operation or a series of connected operations to be carried out simultaneously or in succession. It implements operations derived from the campaign plan. When the time and/ or conditions under which the plan is to be placed in effect occur, the plan becomes an operation order (OPORD).

order ▪ A communication—written, oral, or by signal—that conveys instructions from a superior to a subordinate. In a broad sense, the terms "order" and "command" are synonymous. However, an order implies discretion as to the details of execution whereas a command does not.

order of battle ▪ Intelligence pertaining to identification, strength, command structure, and disposition of personnel, units, and equipment of any military force.

pursuit ▪ An offensive operation against a retreating enemy force. It follows a successful attack or exploitation and is ordered when the enemy cannot conduct an organized defense and attempts to disengage. Its object is to maintain relentless pressure on the enemy and completely destroy him.

rally point ▪ An easily identifiable point on the ground at which units can reassemble/reorganize if they become disbursed.

reconnaissance (recon) ▪ A mission undertaken to obtain information, by visual observation or other detection methods, about the activities and resources of an enemy or potential enemy, or about the meteorologic, hydrographic, or geographic characteristics of a particular area.

remotely piloted vehicle (RPV) ▪ A remotely piloted airborne reconnaissance, surveillance, and target-acquisition and designation device. RPVs provide timely and accurate intelligence and locate targets behind enemy lines.

reserve ▪ That portion of a force withheld from action at the beginning of an engagement so as to be available for commitment at a decisive moment.

single envelopment ▪ Maneuver made against one flank, or around one flank, against the rear of the initial dispositions of the enemy.

sortie (air) ▪ One aircraft making one takeoff and one landing. An operational flight by one aircraft.

special operations (SO) ▪ Military operations conducted by specially trained, equipped, and organized Department of Defense (DOD) forces against strategic or tactical targets in pursuit of national military, political, economic, or psychological objectives.

staging area ▪ A general locality between the mounting area and the objective of an amphibious or airborne expedition. It is the area through which a force or parts thereof pass after mounting for refueling, regrouping of ships, and/or the exercise, inspection, and redistribution of troops.

warning order ▪ A preliminary notice of an action or order that is to follow. Usually issued as a brief oral or written message, it is designed to give subordinates time to make necessary plans and preparations.

ABOUT THE AUTHOR

Former U.S. Army Reserve major George Beahm served on extended active duty at Ft. Sill and Ft. Riley, in the National Guard in Norfolk, Virginia, and in the Army Reserve. He is a graduate of the Resident Field Artillery Officer Basic Course and Resident Field Artillery Officer Advance Course, was a student at the Army's Command and General Staff College, and was inducted into the Honorable Order of Saint Barbara.

A *New York Times* bestselling author, Beahm has published more than thirty books in twenty-two languages worldwide.

He and his wife live in Virginia. His website is georgebeahm.com.

ACKNOWLEDGMENTS

Though it takes but one person to write a book, it takes a small army to bring it into print. It starts with an idea: in this case, what if we were to look at the military aspects of *Star Wars* as seen through the binoculars of someone who's been in the military?

From there, the topics suggested themselves, which I bounced off **Mary Beahm,** my wife of thirty-three years. A former English teacher, she's also my first reader of the final manuscript.

Then I write a book proposal, the "pitch" document submitted to publishers. My long-time agent, **Scott Mendel,** reads it, suggests changes, helps shape it, and makes it letter-perfect. He's simply the best there is in this crazy book business, and I'm privileged to have him by my side every step of the way.

Once again, I am enormously pleased to be working with St. Martin's Press, on the heels of *The Stephen King Companion* (third edition). For that book, and this one, they brought to bear their collective expertise in transforming a pile of loose pages (the manuscript) into a handsome book.

As every commander knows, when credit is due to the troops, they need to be recognized for their accomplishments. So, too, does a book project of this magnitude, which required a seasoned team working in unison to make it successful.

For the printed edition: the officer-in-charge and in-house editor **Brendan Deneen,** who mustered the troops and led them to successfully completing the mission; his lieutenant and editorial assistant **Christopher Morgan,** who worked behind the scenes to ensure all was well, and also kept the commo lines open; the detail-oriented production editor **Jessica Katz,** who dotted the i's and crossed the t's; the perspicacious copyeditor **Todd A. Manza,** and proofreader **Marlene Tungseth,** who systematically had my back grammatically and syntactically; the eagle-eyed production manager **Karl Gold,** who shepherded the book through production; art director **Seth Lerner,** cover designer **Daniela Medina,** and designer **Heather Saunders,** who worked in tandem to ensure the book was squared away; and the exuberant publicist **Lauren Jackson,** who shouted from the rooftops to promote this book.

For the audio edition: the talented **Robert Petkoff,** who lent his voice to bring the book to life; the meticulous **Matie Argiropoulos,** who produced and recorded it with her characteristic exactitude; the hardworking executive producer **Laura Wilson,** who kept everything rolling and on track; and the diligent **Danny Meltzer,** who wrapped everything up in post-production.

I am indebted to these talented and dedicated comrade-in-arms. It's been a privilege working with all of you in the service of this book.

I am also greatly indebted to **Ellis B. Levine,** an IP attorney who scoured the manuscript with an eagle eye: nobody does it better.

There's a truism in the army that amateurs study tactics, but professionals study logistics. In this case, Brendan's well-picked and experienced team handled all the logistics, from start to finish. Their collective expertise is evident every step of the way. Without them, the mission could not have been accomplished.

I have also consulted several former army officers who have served in its various branches, all of whom have asked to remain anonymous. Sirs, I thank you. As we say in the military: *Outstanding!*

These are the fine folks, civilian and military, whom I salute on this book project. To one and all, I extend my heartfelt thanks.

Weapons and robots from *Star Wars* are making their way into real life. . . . A Hong Kong company recently made an ultra-powerful handheld laser that looks like a lightsaber. Walking robots resembling the giant AT-ATs that Imperial Forces used to attack rebels are being developed for the military to carry equipment where conventional vehicles can't go. The U.S. Army's Future Soldier Initiative went so far as to draft plans for armor that looked much like what Imperial storm-troopers wore. . . . This means if all goes well, a future influenced by *Star Wars* could go on to save millions of lives. May the Force be with it.

—Charles Q. Choi, "How *Star Wars* Changed
the World," space.com.